The Jazz Ensemble Companion

The Jazz Ensemble Companion

A Guide to Outstanding Big Band Arrangements
Selected by Some of the Foremost Jazz Educators

Michele Caniato

Published in partnership with
MENC: The National Association for Music Education

ROWMAN & LITTLEFIELD EDUCATION
A division of
ROWMAN & LITTLEFIELD PUBLISHERS, INC.
Lanham • New York • Toronto • Plymouth, UK

Published in partnership with MENC: The National Association for Music Education

Published by Rowman & Littlefield Education
A division of Rowman & Littlefield Publishers, Inc.
A wholly owned subsidary of The Rowman & Littlefield Publishing Group, Inc.
4501 Forbes Boulevard, Suite 200, Lanham, Maryland 20706
http://www.rowmaneducation.com

Estover Road, Plymouth PL6 7PY, United Kingdom

British Library Cataloguing in Publication Information Available

Library of Congress Cataloging-in-Publication Data

Caniato, Michele, 1956–
  The jazz ensemble companion : a guide to outstanding big band arrangements selected by some of the foremost jazz educators / Michele Caniato.
      p. cm.
  "Published in partnership with MENC: The National Association for Music Education."
  Includes bibliographical references and indexes.
  ISBN 978-1-60709-277-3 (cloth : alk. paper) — ISBN 978-1-60709-278-0 (pbk. : alk. paper) — ISBN 978-1-60709-279-7 (electronic)
  1. Big band music—Bibliography. I. MENC, the National Association for Music Education (U.S.) II. Title.
  ML128.B29C36 2009
  016.7844'165—dc22
                                                                                    2009015761

Printed in the United States of America

Selections by

Kevin Blancq	Director of jazz studies, Fiorello La Guardia Performing Arts High School, New York, New York
Brian Coyle	Associate professor of music and director of jazz studies, Hope College, Hope, Michigan
Thomas Everett	Director of bands, Harvard University, Cambridge, Massachusetts
Lou Fischer	Professor of music and jazz studies coordinator, Capital University, Columbus, Ohio
Victor Goines	Artistic director of jazz studies, the Juilliard School, New York, New York
Fred Harris	Director of wind ensembles, Massachusetts Institute of Technology, Cambridge, Massachusetts
Keith Javors	Director of jazz ensembles, University of North Florida, Jacksonville, Florida
John La Porta	Professor emeritus, Berklee College of Music, Boston, Massachusetts
Richard Lawn	Professor of jazz pedagogy, College of Performing Arts at the University of the Arts, Philadelphia, Pennsylvania
Jeff Leonard	Director of bands and the jazz program, Lexington High School, Lexington, Massachusetts
Bart Marantz	Director of jazz studies, Booker T. Washington/Dallas Arts Magnet High School, Dallas, Texas
Bob Morgan	Director emeritus of jazz studies, High School for the Performing and Visual Arts, Houston, Texas
Ted Pease	Distinguished professor of jazz composition, Berklee College of Music, Boston, Massachusetts
Dave Rivello	Assistant professor of jazz studies and contemporary media, Eastman School of Music, Rochester, New York
Haig Shahverdian	Supervisor of the Department of Fine and Performing Arts and former director of bands, William H. Hall High School, West Hartford, Connecticut
Gunther Schuller	Composer, conductor, author, Newton, Massachusetts
Dee Spencer	Professor of music, San Francisco State University, San Francisco, California
Janis Stockhouse	Director of bands, Bloomington High School, Bloomington, Indiana

Contents

Preface

When I began directing jazz ensembles, I quickly discovered that finding quality arrangements to perform was a challenging enterprise since many of the great recordings I knew had no published charts, and many of the charts available from publishers had no recordings. Many charts with missing parts were out of print, and many great sets of parts had no score. In addition, a large number of wonderful arrangements belonged to the grade 5 to 6 category, making them accessible only to the most advanced ensembles. Thanks to the efforts of many devoted publishers and musicians over the past two decades, much transcription and publication work has been done, and more quality charts in the easy and medium category have been printed.

Jazz pedagogical materials on improvisation and instrumental technique clearly outnumber the ones on composing and analysis. While a number of invaluable texts[1] focus on jazz ensemble performance practice, they are not designed to comment on specific charts. Conversely, the classic studies[2] that analyze a select number of pieces in detail are not designed as resources for jazz ensemble programming. Perhaps because of an established canon and because of its longer history, classical music provides analytical writings that address a large number of existing compositions from the standpoint of both composition and performance practice. In this publication I wanted to explore and overview the techniques found in a sizable amount of well traveled, quality jazz ensemble literature.

This quest led me to survey many prominent high school, college, and professional jazz band directors and educators to obtain recommendations for arrangements they deemed of the highest quality. It came as no surprise that the jazz composers represented in the survey were well-known figures such as Duke Ellington and Billy Strayhorn, Thad Jones, the Count Basie and Stan Kenton band writers, Oliver Nelson, and Bob Mintzer among others.[3]

My survey yielded very similar results to the ones found in a survey made by Chuck Owen in 1992[4] that polled an almost entirely different panel of contributors.

Because of the commercial aspects of jazz arranging and the ongoing creation of new jazz ensemble music, the idea of a representative pool of charts constituting a canon of jazz ensemble writing may be viewed as tenuous. If a canon existed it might very well comprise several hundred or perhaps thousands of entries. What seems to draw a consensus rather is the distinguished artistry of a relatively small pool of great composers and arrangers whose music stands at the core of jazz arranging. It is my hope that this publication will help music educators, jazz ensemble directors, and arrangers in the endeavor of finding, studying, and performing their music.

The analyses here are intended as beginning points for further inquiry. While focusing on salient aspects of the music, these analyses are meant to be accessible to individuals from a broad spectrum of backgrounds. As discoveries made through one's own inquiry tend to be the ones that resonate longer, it is my hope that even the time-pressed jazz band director will set time aside for the rewarding activity of score study and critical listening of recordings. Likewise, it is hoped that the arranger will experience arranging techniques through the validation of performance, while leading or playing in an ensemble.

I chose not to focus on basic aspects of jazz performance such as rhythm section playing, individuality of sound, improvisation, and swing feel because many excellent manuals that discuss those topics are available (see Bibliography). I tried rather to focus as much as possible on aspects of the music that are unique to these specific charts rather than common to most jazz. This information is presented as needed in the Technique Highlight and Making Music sections.

I also did not include any historical, anecdotal, and biographical information. It is widely available from dictionaries, books, the Internet, oral histories, and some of the players themselves. Historical and biographical information can be assimilated by students through assignments such as papers and presentations.

At the time of publication all the arrangements included in the text are in print, unless otherwise noted. The fact that charts go out of print is a reality to be acknowledged.

Many more charts exist that need to be listed, discussed, transcribed, commissioned, printed, or reprinted. This book will always be a work in progress.

The complete list of recommended charts can be found in Appendix A. Given the number of recommendations and the limitations of space, not all of them have been discussed here. The list is meant to provide a resource for further inquiry and programming. Other than a few combo charts and P.O.P.s they are readily available and belong to the same pool of quality literature.

It has been thrilling to make new discoveries in the universe of outstanding jazz ensemble music and I sincerely hope that you will be rewarded as much as I have by the study of these works. Best wishes in preparing and rendering these scores, and making music flow from your ensemble and your pencil.

Michele Caniato

Notes

1. John La Porta pioneered the field in 1965 with his *Developing the School Jazz Ensemble* (Berklee Press, out of print). Richard Lawn's *The Jazz Ensemble Director's Handbook* (Barnhouse Company), followed in 1981 and has been reprinted ever since. Two other resources followed in 2002: *The Jazz Educator's Handbook* by Jeff Jarvis and Doug Beach (Kendor), and *Jazz Pedagogy: The Jazz Educator's Handbook and Resource Guide* by J. Richard Dunscomb and Dr. Willie L. Hill, Jr. (Warner Bros).

2. Rayburn Wright, *Inside the Score* (Kendor, 1982) and Fred Sturm's *Changes over Time: The Evolution of Jazz Arranging* (Advance Music, 1995).

3. A complete list can be found in the List of Most Represented Composers in Appendix C.

4. Chuck Owen, "Jazz Big Band Composition in the 1990s," *Jazz Educators Journal* vol. 24, no. 3, (1992): 30–33+. A comparison of the findings can be found in my article "Outstanding Charts for Jazz Ensemble: Data from a Recent Survey," *Jazz Research Proceedings Yearbook* (Manhattan, Kansas: International Association of Jazz Educators, 2005).

Acknowledgments

This book would not have been possible without Steven Lipman of the Berklee College of Music. Since my first sharing the idea of this book with him, Steve has been a continual source of support, sharing his lifelong professional insight into jazz education, his ideas, contacts, and resources. Steve also edited and made insightful suggestions to many revisions of the manuscript. I am extremely grateful to him for his generosity and guidance.

Natalie Wisenbaker, while a student at Fitchburg State College, committed her tremendous skill, ideas, and perseverance to the process of contacting the contributors. Fitchburg State College generously provided a Faculty/Creative Award to alleviate my teaching load when I began the project in the fall of 2002. I would like to thank Dr. Shirley Wagner and Dr. Jane Fiske for making that possible. My brother-in-law Giovanni Tonon, scientist and pianist extraordinaire, initiated me to the marvels of database software, a necessary component for this project.

All contributors have been generous with their time and insightful with their selections and comments. Their collective knowledge reflects hundreds of years of experience in jazz ensemble music conducting, arranging, composing, listening, and transcribing. Their selections span much of the history of the medium. I am grateful for the opportunity to correspond with them, and for them to allow their legacy to be transmitted to present and future generations of jazz band conductors, arrangers, and educators.

I wish to thank also the devoted publishers of this marvelous music, among them Sierra Music, Kendor Music, Jazz at Lincoln Center, Walrus Music, Advance Music, Second Floor Music, and Hal Leonard.

This music would not exist without the writers past and present, and the players who originally brought it into the world and those who continue to perform it. To them this book is dedicated, as they are the ones who create and recreate it.

Among the people who commented on this book at various stages of the process, I wish to thank Frank Battisti and Jeremy Yudkin. Many thanks also to Todd Krohne, Larry Monroe, Hans Gruber, Maria Schneider, Herb Pomeroy, Caris Visentin, Dave Liebman, Sherrie Maricle, Joseph Wright, James O'Dell, Larry Fine, and my Boston University and Fitchburg State College Jazz Ensemble students.

I am grateful to Pat Woofter and Sue Rarus at MENC for moving this project forward, and to Tom Koerner, Paul Cacciato, Maera Stratton, and Lynda Phung at Rowman & Littlefield Education for steering the publication to completion.

To the Director

As musical backgrounds of jazz ensemble directors are varied, it is natural that one's strength might be someone else's weakness. An accomplished jazz performer might not be an effective ensemble builder, a classical music player might be lacking a jazz background, a wind ensemble or choral conductor might have good conducting and rehearsing skills but little experience with improvisation, a musical theater player might have great sight-reading skills but few arranging ones. Capitalizing on strengths and developing areas of less knowledge and experience can help anyone learn the task at hand.

Jazz is mostly tonal music, and traditional theory can be transferred to jazz. Roman numeral analysis is similar. Instrumentation differs only in the drum set part, generally not found in orchestral and choral music but used at times in band and musical theater. Some of the differences occur in the areas of chord changes and voicings. These can be learned from a jazz piano or guitar manual, or a jazz harmony or theory book.

Ultimately, since theories are produced mostly after the compositions or performances themselves, the key to understanding many musical techniques lies in the score or recording.

Aside from administrative tasks, in jazz ensemble the areas that cannot be overlooked are score study, understanding how the rhythm section works, and basic conducting skills. I will describe each briefly and refer to further readings on the subject.

Score study is the process of learning the score. This is done most effectively without listening to a recording or playing it on the piano. This is good news, since everyone can become accomplished at this, without having to be an accomplished pianist. Score study involves many steps and requires transposition skills. These can be learned. In jazz ensemble they are quite moderate in comparison to orchestra, but fluency in the keys of B♭ and E♭, and possibly F if French horns are used, is required. Score study is a fundamental part of the director's work, as it allows assimilating the seventeen parts of the jazz ensemble score and developing a clear image of the music so it can be communicated and checked against what is played. Score study is one of the most important responsibilities of the band director, who needs to set aside time for this task well in advance of scheduled rehearsals. A book that addresses the process in depth is *A Guide to Score Study for the Wind Band Conductor* by Frank Battisti and Robert Garofalo (see Bibliography).

Because the rhythm section is unique to the jazz ensemble, this is a crucial area of learning to be addressed. One does not need to be a rhythm section player to develop a concept of what the roles of those instruments are. Developing an understanding of how basic styles are played on the drum set such as swing, ballad, Latin, jazz and jazz-rock fusion and time feels such as swing feel, even eighths, and double time helps render the basic groove for many charts. Comping on piano and/or guitar is helpful, as well as creating bass lines with the piano left hand. These skills are best developed in a combo setting, where more time can also be devoted to improvisation. Materials on comping, bass line creation, drum set playing, and improvisation abound, and much can be learned from recordings. Try building your ensemble from the rhythm section up: get the bass and drum tandem playing good time in the specific style of the chart, add piano and/or guitar comping, then the lead instruments for each section (trumpet, trombone, alto) to turn it into a sextet or septet, then the low range instruments (bass trombone and baritone sax), and then the rest of the players.

While the term "directing" is frequently used for jazz ensemble, elements associated with traditional "conducting" skills are employed, including score study, gestures, and rehearsal techniques. After all, written material in jazz ensemble wind parts outweighs improvisation. Some excellent books on jazz ensemble directing are listed in the bibliography. It might be useful to also consult traditional texts on the subject or take some conducting lessons.

Among the differences with traditional conducting is the fact that in jazz a baton is not used, and a continuous beat pattern or constant time beating is not needed when there aren't changes of tempo and the bass and drums tandem assumes the role of time keeper. Countdowns to a particular bar number (generally four bars, waving "4, 3, 2, 1" fingers in sequence and then cueing in the next section) are used frequently. The initial count off is verbal (generally four bars for fast cut time, two bars for a medium tempo, and one bar for a ballad), often in conjunction with a finger snap on beats 2 and 4, and endings with a fermata are held and sometimes feature the drummer or other brief improvisations. This information and more on ensemble set-up and stage etiquette can be found in the books mentioned above. While this book does not focus on the technique of directing, observations specific to individual pieces can be found in the Making Music sections.

To the Arranger

Scores are available from most publishers for a moderate price and so are recordings.

A list of publishers and distributors can be found in Appendix D.

User's Guide

There are three components to the book: the individual chart analyses, the indexes of musical features, and the indexes. Individual chart analyses feature an At a Glance section followed by Form and Texture; Melodic, Harmonic, Rhythmic Material; Technique Highlight; Making Music; and Self-Test Question narratives. Indexes of Musical Features list instrumentation, feature, solos, soli, style, tempo, form, key, modulation, and meter. The Indexes are organized by title, composer, arranger, grade, and date. Also, the General Index locates techniques encountered and discussed in the charts. The appendixes provide information on the contributors' selections, most represented composers, and publishers. All of these components are designed to aid the selection process and the teaching of specific topics or techniques.

The following explanation duplicates the outline used for each chart:

Title:	title of chart.
Composer:	original composer.
Date:	of the original tune or piece. The copyright date on the score is given, though when it is much later than the actual date of composition (many tunes and arrangements were registered long after they were composed), the date of first recording is given.
Arranger:	arranger of the chart.
Date:	same criteria as above, for the arrangement.
Grade:	discrepancies among grades assigned by contributors and publishers are retained in the Index by Grade and averaged here.
Duration:	timing indicated in the score when available, or timing of recording.
Instrumentation:	standard numerical listing of saxes, trumpets, trombones, rhythm section, in score order. Additional instruments, doublings, and optional parts are specified in parentheses. When "3" is marked for rhythm section it assumes no guitar. In cases where guitar is present but no piano, this is specified.
Publisher:	publisher of the chart.
Recording:	the original recording of the piece is listed. When out of print, newer releases or collections containing the exact piece are listed. CDs are favored over LPs. Multiple recordings are often listed to provide further options. Online recordings are listed when they are the main available source.
Highest written notes:	Ranges are given for lead brass. Ranges for non-lead parts are given when challenging. Occasionally bass trombone low ranges and saxophone or clarinet altissimo are listed.

The number of ledger lines is spelled out rather than the traditional octave lettering (C, c1, c2, etc.).

Solos:
are given in the order, with their length in parentheses.

Soli:
are given in the order, with their length in parentheses. The definition of soli as a *harmonized* passage for two or more instruments but less than full (*tutti*) ensemble playing the same rhythm is followed. Similar *unison* passages are listed as "unison line" though they are sometimes called "soli" in scores.

Introductory Notes:
any narrative information found at the beginning of the score.

At a Glance:
quick reference section in alphabetical order. Occasionally a voice is omitted if not relevant to that particular work.

Articulation:
articulation found in the chart.

Bass line:
whether the bass line is written or is to be improvised from chord changes.

Chords:
chord types with their chord extensions are listed. Modes and symmetrical scales associated with dominant type chords are listed when clearly relevant to their construction.

Chord progression:
main harmonic functions. Uppercase Roman numerals are used for major chords, lower case for minor (ex.: I and i). Chord symbols are always uppercase, whether major or minor (ex.: CMa7, Cmi7)

Dynamics:
all dynamic levels marked in the chart.

Edition:
layout, number of pages, measure numbering.

Expressive devices:
instruments or sections to which they apply listed in parentheses. See *Expressive Devices* chart in Appendix 1.

Form:
outline of the form. Numbers of measures for each section are listed in parentheses. This is treated in more detail in the *Form and Texture* section narrative.

Guitar:
whether the guitar part features written single lines or chords, or is to be improvised from chord changes.

Key:
key of the chart.

Modulations:
intended as a modulation of the *whole piece* to a different key and return to the original. Modulations to the bridge in an AABA song form or other temporary modulations are not listed here. When the piece ends in a different key than the initial one "progressive tonality" is added to the modulation key.

Mutes:
instruments or sections to which they apply, listed in parentheses.

Orchestration:
relatively uncommon or unique instrumental combinations and orchestration choices.

Piano part:
whether the piano part features written single lines or chords, or is to be improvised from chord changes.

Shout:
location of the shout.

Style:
style of the chart.

Tempo:
tempo of the chart.

Time feel:
time feels such as "in 2," "in 4."

Voicings:
listed by individual section. Combined brass or full ensemble voicings are also listed when featuring further voicing combinations of interests.

Form and Texture:
Narrative overview of formal and textural aspects. Tables added when needed. Specific rather than general features are favored when possible.

Melodic, Harmonic, and Rhythmic Materials:

Narrative overview of melodic, harmonic, rhythmic aspects. The three elements are often combined, and are discussed in varying proportions. General rhythmic aspects connected to performance such as creating swing feel or the placing of the upbeat are not discussed, but rhythmic aspects written in the score such as pedal points, hemiolas, and polyrhythms are. As with Form and Texture, the commentary is a starting point for further inquiry.

Technique Highlight:

short discussion of a specific technique relevant to the piece in the area of composing, arranging, harmony, rhythm, orchestration, notation, or texture.

Making Music:

suggestions in the areas of rehearsing, conducting, and approaches to rendering the chart musically. Because the music itself suggests the path of action (or inaction), score study is the beginning step to finding out what the chart needs and to develop an approach that might be different for each director, ensemble, or situation. Items specific to the chart are favored over general performance practices such as swing feel, articulation, and comping that are applicable to most jazz and can be reviewed in some of the manuals listed in the bibliography.

Self-Test Question:

one question for each chart. Answers are found in appendix E.

Lead Sheet:

Tunes are cross-listed with the Real Book series by Chuck Sher and Hal Leonard. These editions are favored because of their availability in C, Bb, Eb, and sometimes bass clef transpositions. Many directors agree that having the ensemble learn and perform the tune beforehand greatly enhances the understanding and rendition of the arrangement. Not all tunes are available in lead sheet format, especially when the charts are original works rather than arrangements.

For Further Reading:

Analyses in current publications are listed. This is not intended to be comprehensive, but rather to provide an indication of sources containing further discussion of the chart.

Abbreviations

A glance at many scores and books in print reveals the absence of standard abbreviation spellings: A.sx or as? t, tpt, or trpt? trbn or tbn? The following are used here:

Table F.1. Abbreviations

INSTRUMENTS		GENERAL TERMS	
Full name	Abbrev. (in score order)	Full name	Abbrev.
Vocals	voc	Ad libitum	ad lib
Flute	fl	Chorus	ch
Clarinet	cl	Chromatic	chr
Flutes	flts	Clusters	clus
Clarinets	clts	Constant Structure	con. struct
Horn	hn	Harmony	h
Horns	hns	Octatonic	octat
French Horn	f.hn	Octave above	8va
French Horns	f.hns	Octave below	8vb
Saxophones	saxes	Part	pt
Soprano	ss	Progressive Tonality	PT
Alto	as	"So What" chords	sw
Tenor	ts	Unison	unis
Baritone	bari	Upper Chromatic Dominant	ucd
Trumpet	tpt	Upper Structure Triad	ust
Trumpets	tpts		
Trombone	tbn		
Trombones	tbns		
Bass Trombone	b.tbn		
Valve Trombone	v.tbn		
Tuba	tba		
Guitar	guit		
Vibraphone	vibe		
Piano	pno		
Bass	bass		

INSTRUMENTS			
Full name	Abbrev. (in score order)		
Electric Bass Drums Percussion	el. b dms perc		

ARRANGEMENTS ALPHABETICALLY BY TITLE

A

ACROSS THE TRACK BLUES

Ellington, Duke 1940

Ellington, Duke

Grade:	3
Duration:	2:58
Instrumentation:	5, 3, 3, 4. Reed 3 on cl
Publisher:	Warner Bros. Publications, Jazz@Lincoln Center series
Recording:	Duke Ellington. *Never No Lament, the Blanton-Webster Band 1940–1942.* RCA Bluebird: 5659-2-RB. 3 CD set.

Highest Written Notes:

Cl:	F# (three ledger lines)
Tpt 1:	A (one ledger line)
Tbn 1:	B♭ (four ledger lines) (solo)

Solos:

(written out): cl (first and last chorus), tpt3 (one chorus), tbn 1 (one chorus)

Soli:

woodwinds (letter C)

Notes:

Cl player needs to be a medium to advanced player

Introductory Notes:

Original recording information, rehearsal notes by Brent Wallarab and Jon Faddis, notes from Wynton Marsalis.

Form and Texture:

Four-measure rhythm section introduction, followed by five 12-bar blues choruses with varied textures featuring solos, soli, and sectional accompaniments: clarinet and rhythm, trumpet with trombone background, woodwind soli, trombone with sax background, clarinet with trumpet background (see table A.1). The clarinet head in choruses 1 and 5 is freely improvised and frames the other choruses.

At a Glance:

Articulation:	• – > ∧ slurs
Bass:	written
Chords:	Ma6 (9), Ma7, mi7 (9, 11), Dom7 (♭9, 9, ♭13, 13), dim7
Chord progression:	Ma blues with reharmonizations
Dynamics:	*mp, mf, f, cresc, dim*
Edition:	8 1/2x11 oblong, 11 pages. Rehearsal letters every chorus. Measure numbers on first bar of every page.
Expressive devices:	lift, portamento, bend, short fall, + O, subtone
Form:	intro (4), five blues choruses, coda (2)
Guitar:	chord symbols
Key:	D Ma
Modulations:	none
Mutes:	plunger w. pixie (tpts), solotone mute (tbn solo)
Piano:	written
Style:	ballad
Tempo:	quarter=90, medium slow
Time feel:	swing
Voicings:	sax: 4-pt close, drop3, drop4, spreads, 5-pt tpts: triads tbns: triads and 3-pt structures (9-♭7-3)

The woodwind soli at letter C features clarinet lead over mostly four-part close saxes. The clarinet forms variable intervals with the top note of the sax voicing, including minor 7th, 5th, and tritone. The occasional doubling of the clarinet an octave below by the baritone sax creates a four-part texture (mm. 30, 32, 34, 40).

Melodic, Harmonic, and Rhythmic Materials:

A two bar figure played by the piano is featured at the beginning and end of the piece (mm. 1–12 and mm. 63–66). The clarinet plays only the first few bars of the head in a similar manner. Compare first five measures

Table A.1. "Across the Track Blues" outline

Letter		A	B	C	D	E	
Form	Intro	Ch 1	Ch 2	Ch 3	Ch 4	Ch 5	Coda
Number of measures	4	12	12	12	12	12	2
Solo	pno	cl	tpt	ww soli	tbn	cl	pno
Back-ground	rhythm section		tbns		saxes	tpts	rhythm section

Table A.2. Turnarounds on the last two bars of choruses 2 and 3

chorus 2	chorus 3
|D6 Em7 A7|D6 C D Em7|	|D9 |G7 E7 A7|

in choruses 1 and 5. The three-part trombone backgrounds (letter B) feature harmonizations in triads, mostly in second inversion, and three-part structures that outline 3, ♭7, and 9 of the chord. The three-part trumpet backgrounds (letter E) feature harmonizations in triads. Like the trombone backgrounds, they are built on a short distinctive rhythmic motive.

The soli chorus at letter C uses two motives: x (sustained note attacked on the end of one), and y (series of eighth notes beginning on the end of one). Motive y is alternatively displaced to begin on the end of three. Following the blues lyric pattern aab, motives x and y are arranged in two similar 4-bar phrases (mm. 29–32 and mm. 33–36) and a conclusion (mm. 37–40) that features a triplet figuration.

Much of the melodic writing contains blue notes. The harmony features the basic blues progression with some reharmonizations: I, IV V, ii V, or V are found on measure 2, I or sub.V7 on measure 3, IV or iv on measure 6, and various turnarounds on the last two bars (see table A.2).

Technique Highlight:

Second Inversion Triads with Blue Notes
Here is an occurence of the trombone section harmonized mostly in triads. Begin by having your trombone players play the top line (tbn. 1) at letter B in unison. It goes: A–F♯–A F♯–A–B–C♯–F♯, and so forth. Background lines are just as important as the main tune. Then have your trombonists harmonize in root position triads. This means that the top note will always be the fifth of the chord. Think D major but adjust to changing harmonies (C natural on D9,

B♭ on G minor). Use the same rhythm or explore other ones. You will be hearing something like the example fig. A.1.

Once familiar with the sound you just created, play Ellington's music. What is the difference?

His approach is to use 2nd inversion triads and to harmonize them at the outset by using blue notes F and C (minor 3rd and minor 7th) so all the triads in the first three measures are consistently major and deliver a nice tension resolution: FMa (tension because of the non-diatonic blue notes), DMa (resolution) and so on.

Making Music:
Letter C is the climactic chorus. It is the keystone of the arch form and is surrounded symmetrically by two choruses on each side plus the introduction and the coda. Open the dynamic lid slowly in choruses 1–2 and revert the process for choruses 4–5. Doing so will help chorus 3 have the desired *forte* impact, since it is played by the reed section alone rather than with the brass. Play it without the clarinet. Many of the sax voicings are four-part close. Listen to them by themselves, then add the clarinet.

The clarinet adds color and tension resolution. Study the intervals between clarinet and alto 1: m. 29=minor 7th, m. 30 (first chord)=minor 7th, m. 36 (last chord)=tritone. Notice how the dissonant minor 7th D–E in m. 29 "resolves" to a more consonant major 3rd F♯–D in m. 30 beat 4+. The clarinet part is a genuine fifth voice that is doubled only at the end of phrase (m. 30, m. 34, and m. 40 beat 4+ with bari, m. 32 beat 2+ with bari, and m. 36 beat 2+ with tenor). There are then many tension resolution patterns at work in this short passage: through dissonance/consonance, through density (from five-part to four-part) and, perhaps more obviously, through melodic curve (from high to low). Ellington wrote the music clearly; it is always a challenge and a pleasure to try and render his musical intentions.

Figure A.1

Figure A.2

Self-Test Question 1

Let's look at the harmonies in the introduction. The bass plays diatonically in the key of D major and outlines 1–3–5–6 of the I and IV chords. But what is the piano doing? It may be useful to review the scales that express various dominant chords and are used in conjunction with them. Let's see four of the most common ones:

Which of the scales in figure A.2 would fit the A chord on m. 2 beat 2+?

1. a
2. b
3. c
4. d

∽

AIREGIN

Rollins, Sonny 1963

Abene, Michael 1992

Grade: 5
Duration: 5:14
Instrumentation: 5, 4, 4, 3 (doublings: as1=ss, fl, or picc; ts1=ss; ts2=ss)
Publisher: Hal Leonard
Recording: *GRP All-Star Big Band. GRP, 1992.*

Highest Written Notes:

Tpt 1:   D (two ledger lines)
Tbn 1:   B (four ledger lines)

Solos:

pno (36), ts1 (28+36), as2 (36), ts1 and as2 trade fours (36+28+28)

Introductory Notes:
None

Form and Texture:

Intro (16), nine ABAC choruses (36), coda (16). An 8-bar vamp is added to introduce the head (mm. 45–52) after the piano solo, and so is a 2-bar break at the end of the head (mm. 89–90). The form of the original tune is followed: A (8), B (12), A (8), C (8). The introduction features unaccompanied tutti concerted ensemble. It returns verbatim as the coda (m. 321) with the drums playing time and the rhythm section adding two chords on the final bar.

The head and its counterline use unison couplings across sections (head=fl, as, tpt; counterpoint=ss, ts, bari, tbn). The first A section of the third chorus (mm. 91–98) features a constant structure tutti concerted passage that also returns verbatim as the second A section of the head out (mm. 303–10). A tenor solo on BAC ABAC follows and leads to an interlude (chorus 5, mm. 163–98) featuring canonic and unison saxes and concerted brass passages and punctuations, and to an alto solo (chorus 6). Choruses 7 and 8 feature the two soloists (tenor and

At a Glance:

Articulation:	• > ∧ ≥ slurs
Bass line:	written and chord symbols
Chords:	Ma6/9, Ma7 (♭5, 9), mi, mi7 (9, 11), mi7(♭5), Dom (♭9, 9, ♯9, ♯11, ♭5, ♭13, 13, sus, octatonic, altered), intervallically conceived vertical structures
Chord progression:	as the original, with secondary dominants (V/iv), upper chromatic dominants, and transient tonic "key of the moment" sequences
Dynamics:	*pp, p, mp, f, ff, cresc, dim*
Edition:	8 1/2x11 oblong, 36 pages. Measure numbers every bar, with boxed numbers highlighting sections
Expressive devices:	gliss (all)
Form:	intro (16), nine ABAC choruses (8, 12, 8, 8), coda (16). There is an additional 2-bar break at the end the head choruses and an 8-bar vamp between choruses 1 and 2.
Key:	A♭Ma
Modulations:	none
Mutes:	harmon-no stem (tpts), hats (brass)
Piano:	written and chord symbols
Orchestration:	SATTB and SASB saxes
Style:	swing
Tempo:	quarter note = 240
Time feel:	open, spacey feel (bass in 1 and 2), and 4
Voicings:	saxes: uni, 2-pt (4ths and 5ths), 3-pt (inverted 4ths), 4- and 5-pt constant structures tpts: uni, 2-pt, 3-pt, 3-pt (inverted 4ths), 4-pt close, clus, constant structures tbns: uni, 3-pt (inverted 4ths), 4-pt closed and open, constant structures brass: 5-6-7-pt chords ens: inversions, triads over bass note, slash chords, constant structures

alto) trading fours with the ensemble taking over (mm. 255–62), and punctuating (mm. 263–83). The head is recapitulated exactly (other than the second A, replaced by the constant structure passage previously found in m. 91), and is followed by the coda. Enter "remove hat" in tpt 3 at m. 16.

Melodic, Harmonic, and Rhythmic Materials:
The A section melody arpeggiates the relative minor (F minor) and is sequenced up a fourth in the second four bars. The chord progression follows the same pattern and tonicizes F minor and B♭ minor. The B section uses a two-bar motive over a descending sequence of transient "key of the moment" tonics beginning with IVMa7 and ending on IMa7(D♭ Ma, CMa, BMa, B♭ Ma, A♭ Ma). The C section features a similar sequence, compressed to eight bars, with the melody introducing a syncopated motive and closing on the tonic note.

The introduction features newly composed material. The lead emphasizes the pitches E♭ and E (mm. 1–2, mm. 13–15) found in the original melody. It is harmonized with constant structures (fourths with added half step between part 3-4 in the trumpets, and between part 1-2 in the trombones, mm. 1–3), inversions, triads over bass note, and slash chords (m. 4), trichords (B♭–B–E♭, mm. 9–10), and vertical sonorities built on intervals of the 4th and minor 2nd (mm. 11–15) producing 5- and 7-part clusters.

The passage at mm. 91–98 features a chromatic wedge between the upper and lower ensemble. The initial chord (m. 91) is a symmetric intervallic structure. Both of these intervallically conceived passages feature carefully regulated amounts of dissonance and strong linear writing that creates harmonic depth and forward motion. The A section accompaniment features constant structure inverted fourths ascending chromatically.

Cross rhythms are featured in the introduction (3/8 over 4/4, mm. 11–12; 3/4 over 4/4, mm. 13–15), and in the passage at m. 91 (3/4 over 4/4), and hockets are used in mm. 85–86.

Technique Highlight:

Intervallic Constant Structures with Clusters
Constant structures are harmonies that feature the same intervallic makeup. Playing the triads of a major scale does not produce constant structures, since the

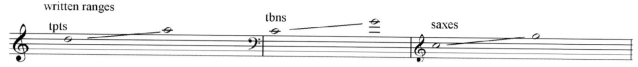

Figure A.4

triads change from major to minor to diminished (Ex: CMa, Dmi, Bdim). Clusters are voicings made up of seconds, often with a larger interval such as a third between the top two parts.

The structure in mm. 1–3 is (from the top) trumpets: 4th, step, half step; trombones: half step, Ma 3rd, 4th. Saxes are a composite of the brass structure. The example figure A.3 is in D minor.

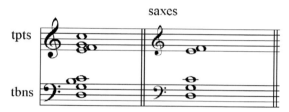

Figure A.3

Have each of the sections (saxes, trumpets, trombones, rhythm) play the structures individually. Each section should play the first type and then the second. Guitar players might want to edit out one or two of the notes to play comfortably. Have the bari play with the piano. Play the structures as fermatas, hold and listen, and proceed up the chromatic scale. Then play as whole notes/half notes and so on in slow tempo with full ensemble. To avoid low range muddiness or high range challenges, begin by staying within the ranges shown in figure A.4.

Why is the second structure so dissonant? Play now the two structures together. How does it sound? Add the sax doubling. See also "Stolen Moments" for constant structures over a pedal and "Blues and the Abstract Truth" for constant structures over an ostinato.

Making Music

The original tune originates in the 1950s and 1960s hard bop era. *Airegin* is *Nigeria* spelled backward. Listen to any of the combo recordings by Sonny Rollins,

Art Blakey, Horace Silver, and other recording artists found on the Blue Note and Prestige recording labels. You will notice that a rhythm section technique widespread during this period is the alternation of eight-bar segments featuring Latin feel in the drums and pedal in the bass with straight ahead time and walking bass.

Hard bop tunes that feature alternation between Latin and swing feels:

Horace Silver: "Yeah!" and "Nica's Dream"
Hank Mobley: "Split Feelings"
Max Roach-Clifford Brown Quintet: "Cherokee"

Here the alternation follows the form of the tune, with the bass pedal outlining tonic and dominant. Have your rhythm section practice these switches so they are comfortable and maintain an even tempo.

To warm up to the cross rhythms in mm. 11–15 have the whole ensemble practice 3/8 over 4/4 patterns and 3/4 over 4/4 patterns as in figure A.5. Initially the drummer can play a simple 4/4 beat with the hi-hat on 2 and 4, then they should play the same figures as the ensemble. Use any scale, begin with unison, progress to two part, triads, other structures. Stay within comfortable ranges. This is a rhythmic exercise. Begin patterns on different beats.

Self-Test Question 2

Review the discussion of constant structures with clusters in the Technique Highlight.

Which of the following structures is used in the trumpet passage at mm. 11–15?

a. 4th, mi 2nd, Ma 2nd
b. Ma 3rd, mi 2nd, mi 2nd
c. 4th, Ma 2nd, Ma 2nd
d. 4th, mi 2nd, mi 2nd

3/8 over 4/4   3/4 over 4/4

Figure A.5

Lead Sheet

The New Real Book. Sher Music Co., 1988.
The Real Book. 6th ed. Hal Leonard, 2004.

————

ALL OF ME

Simons, Seymour, and Gerald Marks 1931

Byers, Billy 1963

Grade:	5
Duration:	2:42
Instrumentation:	5,4,4,4, aux perc opt
Publisher:	Hal Leonard
Recording:	Count Basie Orchestra. *Count Basie: The Standards*. Verve CD841197-2. also on Fred Sturm. *Changes over Time: The Evolution of Jazz Arranging*. Advance Music, 1995. CD.

Highest Written Notes:

Tpt 1:	F (three ledger lines)
Tbn 1:	B (four ledger lines)
Tbn 4:	one C (four ledger lines)

Solos:

piano feature

Introductory Notes:

None

Form and Texture:

This is a classic two-and-a-half chorus Basie medium swing chart under three minutes long. A four-bar tutti intro ushers in a soft rhythm section chorus with the piano jazzing the tune in the sparse, swinging, and witty Basie style. An ensemble punctuation and a soft saxophone sustained background articulate the form.

The second chorus (letter E) is a recomposed variation of the changes and the melody. Basie 4-part voicings are used consistently, with the occasional deviation into 6- and 7-part voicings. It builds to a climax at letter H m. 4 and is followed by a soft reprise variation on the second A at letter I. C follows, shortened by two bars, at letter J and merges directly

At a Glance:

Articulation:	• – > ∧ slurs
Bass line:	written
Chords:	Ma6/9, Ma7, mi (Ma 7), mi7 (9, 11), mi7 (♭5), Dom (♭9, 9, ♯9, ♯11, ♭5, ♭13, 13, sus, octatonic, altered), dim, dim7
Chord progression:	as the original (with secondary dominants V/vi, V/ii, V/V), and with reharmonizations using chromatic planing (minor 7th and dominant chords) and upper chromatic dominants
Dynamics:	*pp, p, mp, f, ff, fz, cresc,*
Edition:	8 1/2x11 oblong, 11 pages. Rehearsal letters for each section.
Expressive devices:	in stand, spill (brass), short connecting gliss, turn, bend (all)
Form:	intro (4), ABAC (two choruses), AC (16), coda (6)
Guitar:	chord symbols
Key:	C Ma
Modulations:	none
Mutes:	hats (brass)
Piano:	written
Orchestration:	part crossing (tbns 3-4), tbn 4 has a high C lead (letter H6)
Shout:	two before G, H
Style:	swing
Tempo:	quarter note=152
Time feel:	in 4
Voicings:	saxes: 4-pt close (lead doubled 8vb), 5-pt open, 5-pt spreads tpts: 2-pt, triads (lead doubled 8vb), 4-pt close, sw tbns: triads (lead doubled 8vb), 4-pt close, 4-pt spreads brass: 5-, 6-, 7-pt ens: "Basie" 4-part voicings

into the coda (same as the introduction), followed by a Basie-type piano blues lick over stop time and a final ensemble chord. Most of the chart features tutti concerted texture.

Melodic, Harmonic, and Rhythmic Materials:
The descending 1–5–3 arpeggio from the melody is used for the introduction, the middle of the ensemble chorus (F mm. 7–8), and the coda, repeated in a 3 over 4 rhythm over a descending chromatic bass. Much melodic material is created anew, treated as a riff and developed. The reharmonizations use chromatic planing (minor 7th and dominant chords), upper chromatic dominants, passing diminished chords, and interpolated ii-7 chords. Trombones 3 and 4 cross parts.

Technique Highlight:

Four-Part Basie Voicings
So called four-part Basie voicings are found in the work of important arrangers such as Neal Hefti and Sammy Nestico, who wrote for the Basie band. The technique consists in the trombones and top four saxes doubling the trumpet parts an octave below. The bari sax doubles the lead trumpet two octaves below. Voicings are in close position (see figure A.6).

Parts move parallel to the lead using passing diminished chords and chromatic planing. See letters F mm.1–6 and G mm. 2–7. Notice in this otherwise textbook example that there are a few minor adjustments due to practical reasons:

Table A.3. Dynamic contrasts in Basie's "All of Me" recording

Intro	A	B	C	D	E	F	G	H	I	J	K
ff	pp	sfp–ff on pp last bar				p cresc. m.3 to f m.7		continue f ff at m. 4	pp		ff

- Trumpet 4, F mm. 2–3: 9th in place of 1 (referred to as "nine for one") B concert instead of A, to avoid low trumpet range.
- Trombone 3, F m. 4: 13th instead of ♭7th, F♯ instead of G, for better line.
- Trombones, F m. 6: F♯–E–A instead of E–C–A–F♯ (duplication of trumpets 8va below), beacuse it would sound muddy with the minor third intervals so low in the range.

The occasional expansion into six-part voicings can also be found for weightier articulation and fuller harmony (letter G, m. 3, last chord).

Making Music:
The exhilarating dynamic range of the Basie band is well documented in their studio and live recordings (see table A.3). Exaggerate the dynamics. Watch for intonation in ffs and maintain good swing feel in pp. Listen to and duplicate the Basie rhythm section style with piano left hand comping, "Freddie Green" one-per-beat guitar comping, walking bass, and ride cymbal drum patterns.

Select a passage with four-part Basie voicings such as letter F. With the rhythm section, rehearse the main melody (first trumpet, first trombone,

Figure A.6: Four-part Basie voicings

first alto, and bari sax) to solidify the interpretation set by the lead trumpet. Then run one section at a time so each can listen for consistency in attacks, dynamics, and pitch. Lean into the dotted 8th/16th figures on beats two and four on mm. 1–4.

Self-Test Question 3

Trombones and other instruments sometimes exchange parts. This is generally done to create better musical lines or for color variety. Trombones 3 and 4 exchange parts at:

a. Letter F mm. 1–3
b. Letter G mm. 2–8
c. Letter F mm. 4–8
d. Letter F mm. 4–6 and letter G mm. 2–7

Lead Sheet

The New Real Book. Sher Music Co. 1988.
The Real Book. 6th edition. Hal Leonard, 2004.

For Further Reading

Fred Sturm. *Changes over Time: The Evolution of Jazz Arranging.* Advance Music, 1995.

B

BACK BONE

Jones, Thad 1965

Jones, Thad 1965

Grade:	6
Duration:	4:00
Instrumentation:	5, 4, 4, 4
Publisher:	Kendor Music
Recording:	

Highest Written Notes:

Tpt 1:	E (three ledger lines)
Tpt 2:	D (two ledger lines)
Tbn 1-2:	C (four ledger lines)

Solos:
pno (two choruses), tbns 1-2-3 (one chorus each), dms (8 bars or extend ad lib)

Soli:
saxes (one chorus, letter I)

Introductory Notes:
none

Form and Texture:
Intro (8), 12 choruses of 12-bar blues, coda (8). The introduction alternates tutti concerted passages and unison lines in eighth notes accompanied by sustained harmonies. Choruses 1 and 2 feature a piano solo accompanied by the rhythm section, with the ensemble playing a concerted passage on the first turnaround.

The head (choruses 3–4, letters C and D) is played by saxes in unison, accompanied by trombones, joined on chorus 4 by the trumpets. Chorus 5 is an interlude that features a unison line in the low register (bari, trombones, bass) answered by the ensemble. A stop time launches the first solo: trombones 1-2-3 play a chorus each (choruses 6–7–8); saxes accompany the third chorus with concerted, active, eight-note lines that develop into a sax soli (chorus 9, letter I). The shout (choruses 10–11, letters J, K) features concerted tutti and concerted brass against unison saxes playing an elaboration of the head. The head out is played once (chorus 12, letter L). The coda is a 7-bar drum solo (that can be extended), and a final ensemble chord.

Melodic, Harmonic, and Rhythmic Materials:
The head phrasing follows the traditional blues AAB statement, restatement, and conclusion pattern (four bars each). It uses the blues scale with major and minor third, flat 5, and flat 7. C pentatonic minor is used in the first turnaround, over an ascending chromatic bass (trumpets, A mm. 11–12). Lines in moving eighths use diatonic and chromatic approaches. Riff-like figures and sequences such as minor thirds descending in whole steps are found in the brass (letter J).

Much harmony is derived from modes or chord scales, including the lydian, lydian ♭7, altered, and octatonic scales. The tonic chord is harmonized alternatively as a C7(♯9) (octatonic, letter C m.1),

At a Glance:

Articulation:	– > ∧ ≥ slurs
Bass line:	written, chord symbols
Chords:	Ma6, Ma7 (9, #11, 13, lydian), mi7 (9, #11), Dom7 (♭9, 9, ♯9, #11, #5, ♭13, 13, alt, lydian ♭7, octatonic), dim
Chord progression:	major blues with secondary and chromatic dominants, dominant chains, and chords borrowed from the parallel minor (♭IIMa7, ♭IIIMa7, ♭VIMa7, and their dominants)
Dynamics:	*mp, mf, f, cresc, dim*
Edition:	8 1/2x11 vertical, 10 pages. Rehearsal letters every twelve bars. No measure numbers. Single sided.
Expressive devices:	bend (saxes), shake (br), spill, gliss, fall (all)
Form:	intro (8), 12 choruses of 12-bar blues, coda (8)
Key:	CMa
Modulations:	none
Mutes:	none
Shout:	choruses 10–11 (J, K)
Style:	medium blues
Tempo:	moderato (moderate)
Voicings:	saxes: 4/5-pt close and open, spreads, clusters tpts: triads (lead doubled 8vb), 4-pt closed, clusters, fourths, and inverted fourths tbns: 4-pt open, spreads
Upper structure triads:	II, ♭V, ♭VI, VI, V

C7+(♯9) (altered, letter D m. 1), and C (lydian, letter E m. 1).

Voicings are dense, comprising frequently 6–7, or 8 different pitches: major chords use six notes of the major scale without the fourth degree (Ab, C, letter A m. 12), or use modes (F♯Ma7=Lydian, all 7 notes, letter A m. 12), dominants use the altered scale (D7+ and G7+, 6 notes, letter A mm. 11–12), lydian ♭7 (F7, 6 notes, letter E m. 5), or octatonic (C7, final chord, using all 8 pitches of the scale).

Upper Structure Triads are used extensively, for example in the trumpet section passage at letter D mm. 6–12 (see table B.1). All major triads in the trumpets are set over the chord sound [1–3–♭7] and one tension played by the trombones:

Saxes use variable voicings including closed, drop2 and drop3 (letter H mm. 1–3), and open voicings ranging from a Ma 9th to a Ma 7th plus an octave on the sax soli (letter I).

The turnarounds are varied in distinctive ways: chorus 1 features an ascending bass connecting chromatically the V/V chord (D7) to the ♭VIMa7 (Ab) and then cadencing to the tonic through an appoggiatura ♭IIMa7 (D♭); each quarter note is harmonized with a major or dominant structure (letter A mm. 11–12). Chorus 3 (letter C mm. 11–12) uses chords from the parallel minor: C E♭ A♭ G7 (I, ♭III, ♭VI, V7). Chorus 10 (letter J mm. 9–12) uses dominant chords descending in whole tones: G7, F7, E♭7, D♭7 (V7, IV7, ♭III7, ♭II7).

Rhythmic variety is pervasive. The brass backgrounds on the head contain many eighth note delayed attack figures and anticipations. The ensemble shout features strong fourth beats (letter J), and three over four cross rhythms (letter K).

Technique Highlight:

Upper Structure Triads
Upper Structure Triads are triads containing one or more non-chord tones. In jazz ensemble writing they

Table B.1. Upper Structure Triads in the trumpet section passage at letter D mm. 6–12

Letter D	m.6	m.7	m.8	m.9	m.10	m.11	m.12
Chord symbol	G7+(♯9)	F9	E7+(♭9)	D7+(♯9)	G7+(♯9)	E♭	D♭
Upper Structure Triad	♭VI=E♭	II=G	♭V=B♭	♭VI=B♭	♭VI=B♭	(SW) "So What" voicing	V=A♭
Chord sound	1–♭7–3–♭13	1–♭7–3–13	1–♭7–3–♭13	1–3–♭7–♯9	1–♭7–3–♭13		1–5–3–13
Mode of derivation	altered scale	lydian ♭7	altered scale	altered scale	altered scale		mixolydian

Figure B.1

are frequently found in the trumpets, in close position, with the 4th trumpet doubling the lead an octave below. They are supported by chord sound (1–3–7 or 6). The most common USTs are on dominant chords and are related to the mode or chord scale of derivation. They are indicated by upper-case Roman numerals: IIMa (from Lydian ♭7), ♭VIMa (from altered scale), VIMa (from octatonic scale). On major chords IIMa (from Lydian) is common (see figure B.1).

Making Music

The blues in its major form is the rare genre where the tonic chord is a dominant quality chord. This opens a range of possibilities from the simpler, more consonant, to the larger and more dissonant voicing (see figure B.2). Assign pitches to the ensemble proceeding from the bottom up and hold as fermatas. Piano does not need to play root, assign root to bass. Use as warm up.

The turnaround is a chord pattern (usually two chords per measure) found in the last two measures of the form. Its function is to lead harmonically back to the top of the form. A common turnaround is the diatonic I–vi–ii–V pattern. Assign numbers to the turnarounds in table B.2 and others you make up. Give them to your players. Have the soloist turnaround (no pun intended) and the rhythm section select turnarounds at random during solos, agreeing through a hand gesture indicating the number. Train so everyone can recognize the different patterns by ear. Then play the chart.

Self-Test Question 4

Adding a part to a voicing without duplicating it increases the density of the voicing. While many chords have four or five parts (possibly chord tones 1–3–7 and a couple of other pitches), chords with more parts are not uncommon. How many parts does the chord at letter D measure 1 have?

a. 4
b. 5
c. 6
d. 7

Table B.2. Four turnarounds in the key of C major

	1			2	3	4
Emi7	Ami7|	Dmi7	G7	E7 E♭7 |D7 D♭7	C E♭ |A♭ G7	G7 F7 E♭7 D♭7
iii		vi	ii	V7	chromatic dominant pattern	I ♭III ♭VI V7	V7 IV7 ♭III7 ♭II7

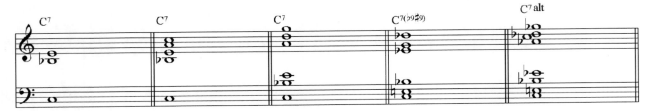

Figure B.2

For Further Reading

Rayburn Wright. *Inside The Score.* Kendor Music. Features a detailed analysis of three Thad Jones charts.

Ken Pullig and Ted Pease. *Modern Jazz Voicings.* Berklee Press and Mark Levine. *The Jazz Piano Book.* Sher Music. Both feature discussion and examples of upper structure triads.

BALLAD FOR BENNY

Nelson, Oliver 1962

Nelson, Oliver 1962

Grade: 3.5
Duration: 2:34
Instrumentation: cl solo, ATTB, 4, 4, 4 (optional f.hns 1–2)
Publisher: Sierra Music
Recording: Oliver Nelson. *Jazz Masters 48.* Verve 314 527 654-2, CD, 1995.

Highest Written Notes:

Tpt 1:   A (one ledger line) (E with three ledger lines in an optional unison passage for tpts 1-2)

Tbn 1:   B♭ (four ledger lines)

Solos:

Clarinet feature. Written part, moderate difficulty, highest note C above staff.

Introductory Notes:

Director's notes and General Performance Comments by Bob Curnow

Form and Texture:

Straight forward AABA swing ballad with abbreviated return from the bridge (B and last A sections). The 2-bar introduction features piano unison with brass in pairs in an interlocking 16th-note pattern. The A sections feature a dominant pedal in the first five measures (mm. 3–7) and supertonic and sub-

At a Glance:

Articulation:	• – > slurs
Bass line:	mostly written, three bars of chord symbols
Chords:	Ma6 (9), Ma7 (9), mi7 (9,11), Dom (♭9, 9, ♯9, ♯11, ♯5, 13, sus, alt)
Chord progression:	first A: V, iii, I6/4, V7sus, excursion to mediant major (I–vi–ii–V in DMa [III]). Second A: ii, vi, V7sus, same excursion to mediant major. Bridge: to key of FMa (V). Chords borrowed from the minor (♭VIMa7, ♭IIMa7) in the coda
Dynamics:	*p, mp, mf, f, ff, cresc, dim*
Edition:	8 1/2x11 oblong, 7 pages. Measure numbers every bar, with boxed numbers highlighting sections
Expressive devices:	portamento (bari sax), bend, portamento (tpts)
Form:	intro (2), AABA (32+2), BA (16), coda (2)
Guitar part:	written and chord symbols
Key:	B♭ Ma
Modulations:	none
Mutes:	cup, bucket (tpts), bucket (tbns)
Orchestration:	bari lead (mm. 18–22), tbn 3 above tbn 2 (mm. 36–40)
Piano part:	written and chord symbols
Shout:	mm. 35–44
Style:	ballad (swing and even eighths)
Tempo:	quarter=88
Time feel:	in 2 and in 4
Voicings:	saxes: 4-pt close, 4-pt spreads tpts: unison, triads with lead doubled 8vb, 4-pt close, clus (last chord) tbns: unison, 4-pt close, 4-pt spreads, clus ens: 4-pt close with saxes doubling tbns at the unison and tpts 3-4 on unison melody (doubled 8vb in bari and tbn4)

mediant pedals (C and G) in the first four measures of the other A sections. Pedals are released in the second four bars. There is a 2-bar codetta at the end of the chorus (mm. 35–36) and a 2-bar coda at the very end. Time feel is in "2" for the A sections and in "4" for the B.

The clarinet is featured throughout over sustained pads and counter lines. The ensemble takes over the melody for a climactic statement of the B at its return at mm. 35–44. The baritone sax takes the lead in mm. 18–22, though still playing the lowest voice in the 4-part harmony.

Melodic, Harmonic, and Rhythmic Materials:

The melody is basically diatonic to the key with some interesting departures. The first is an F♯ (♭9) on the Fsus 7 chord at m. 5 beat 4. The second is an excursion to the mediant major (DMa) in measures 6–7 of the A sections. The first occurrence can be found in table B.3.

The melody of the B section is also diatonic to the key (FMa), similarly departing in the last four measures to reflect the sequence of II–V chord patterns. Constant structures over pedal are featured in the rhythm section (mm. 11–14). Here the temporary modulation is to the supertonic C minor and the constant structures are C minor and G minor (see table B.4).

The minor chord voicing of the constant structure (see figure B.3) is found often in the music of Nelson (see *Stolen Moments*). Though here it is a simple version without the ♭7th, the ♭7th is found in the melody for both the C minor and G minor chords.

A chord borrowed from the parallel minor (♭VIMa7) and one derived from the parallel Phrygian

Figure B.3

mode (♭IIMa7) are used for the final cadence in the coda (m. 53).

The tonic chord B♭ is found only in two places: at m. 35, where it marks the conclusion of the first chorus, and in the last measure, where it closes the piece. The avoidance of the tonic chord and the frequent modulations make the harmony quite adventurous and unpredicatable.

Technique Highlight:

Chords borrowed from the parallel minor
A parallel minor key shares the same tonic with a major key. Using chords from the parallel minor key provides novel harmonies beyond the chords diatonic to the major scale (see figures B.4 and B.5). The examples are in B♭. The same procedure can be applied to modes.

Making Music

In addition to the caliber of the soloist, the quality of the rhythm section's playing will enhance the rendition of this piece. Its role alternates between backround accompanyiment of the clarinetist, accompaniment of the sax section, and propelling the tutti ensemble statement at mm. 35–44. The bass is almost fully written out (other than measures 37–39) and switches between pedals, written figures, and walking. The drums works in tandem with the bass. While the bass is playing the F pedal in the first few bars, the drummer plays simple time (see figure B.6).

The drummer joins the bass in the concerted kicks that underscore the modulation (mm. 8–10), reverts to simple time at the next bass pedal (mm. 11–14), and proceeds to full-fledged 4/4 time accompanying the sax section soli on the ride cymbal (mm. 19–22). Note that on the recording the switch to sticks occurs at m. 17, while in the score it is marked at m. 33. Both ways would probably work. The tutti at mm. 35–44 is a climactic statement that needs powerful support from the drummer.

Table B.3. Excursion to the mediant major in "Ballad for Bennie"

Measure number	7	8		9	
Chord	F7sus	DMa7	Bmi7	Emi7	A7
Roman Numeral	V7	I	vi	ii	V7
Key	B♭	D (=mediant major III)			

Table B.4. Modulation to the supertonic C minor

Measure number	10		11	12
Chord	D7	G7	Cmi	Gmi
Roman Numeral	V/V	V7	i	v
Key			C minor (=supertonic ii)	

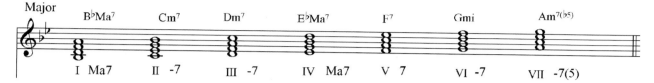

Figure B.4

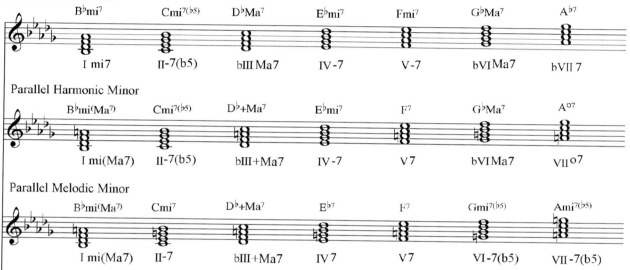

Figure B.5

Figure B.6

Self-Test Question 5

E♭ Ma7 is ♭IIIMa7 in the key of:

a. C natural minor
b. B♭ harmonic minor
c. C major
d. E♭ melodic minor

BASICALLY BLUES

Wilson, Phil 1959

Wilson, Phil 1959

Grade:	IV1/2
Duration:	5:25
Instrumentation:	5, 4, 4, 4
Publisher:	Kendor Music
Recording:	Buddy Rich. *Swingin' New Big Band*. BGO Records. CD169 (abridged version).

Highest Written Notes:

Tpt 1:	E (three ledger lines)
Tpt 2-3:	D♭ (two ledger lines)
Tbn 1-2:	C♭ (four ledger lines)
Tbn 3:	B♭ (four ledger lines)

Solos:

tbn2 (mm. 29–48, two choruses minus first four bars) and ts1 (mm. 54–72, two choruses minus first four bars)

Soli:
rhythm section (mm. 1–12 and mm. 73–84, choruses 1 and 8), saxes (mm. 49–53)

Notes:
A mine of Basie style blues riffs, voicings, and dynamic practices. Challenging tbn writing.

Introductory Notes:
none

At a Glance:

Articulation:	• – > ∧ slurs
Bass line:	chord symbols with some written passages (mm. 18, 26–28, 49–52, 119–20, 130–32)
Chords:	Ma6, Ma7 (9), mi7 (9), Dom (7, 9, #11, #5), dim
Chord progression:	basically blues with additional passing dominants.
Dynamics:	*pp, mp, mf, f, ff, fp, cresc, dim*
Edition:	8 1/2x11 vertical. 8 pages. Measure numbers every bar, circled numbers highlighting sections (every 12 bars)
Expressive devices:	doit (br m. 28), long gliss (saxes m. 53, br m. 73), scoop (m. 84) shake (br mm. 101), short gliss (tpts mm. 16, 20, 24; br m. 2; saxes m. 27), subtone (saxes mm. 37–48), trill (saxes m. 101), wa wa (tpts-tbn1 mm. 71–73)
Form:	12 choruses of blues
Guitar part:	chord symbols and a short written stop time (mm. 26–27) and ending (mm. 130–32) passage.
Key:	GMa
Modulations:	to A♭ Ma (♭II) mm. 109–20 (chorus 11) for one chorus
Mutes:	plunger (br mm. 71–73)
Orchestration:	triple lead (3 octaves, tpt1, as1-tbn1, bari, mm. 97–108), lead exchange(tbn 2 on tbn section lead mm.

	97–100, 103, 107)
Piano part:	chord symbols and a short written stop time (mm. 26–27) and ending (mm. 130–32) passage
Shout:	mm. 97–120 (choruses 10 and 11)
Style:	easy swing (Basie style)
Tempo:	quarter=100–112
Voicings:	saxes: 4-pt close double lead 8vb (mm. 84–118, with occasional clusters [m. 84], 3-pt [m. 85], 5-pt [m. 88–89], and unisons), 5-pt drop2 constant structures (mm. 13–20, 121–28) tpts: 4-pt close (mm. 97–120, alternating with unison) br: 6-pt voicings (mm. 97–100) ens: Basie 4-pt close bari dbl lead 8vb (mm. 92–95),

Form and Texture:
12 choruses of medium blues. The first four bars of choruses 4 and 6 feature a stop time send off for the soloist. Choruses 9 and 10 are a tutti concerted section that builds from *pp* to *ff*. The climactic chorus (chorus 11, m. 109) is underscored by a modulation a 1/2 step higher to A♭. The last two bars of this chorus (mm. 119–20) feature a decrescendo followed by a *ff* unison D punctuation that articulates the end of the shout section. The return of the initial sax riff in the key of G follows. Two contrasting gestures (*ff* and *pp*) used previously conclude (see table B.5).

Melodic, Harmonic, and Rhythmic Materials:
There are three main riffs, each featuring different bar lengths and harmonization: (1) saxes (mm. 13–22) 2-bar, 5-part and then unison, choruses 2, 3, and 12; (2) trumpets (mm.13–22) 4-bars, unison, chorus 3, varied then by saxes in chorus 5, and by trumpets in chorus 7; and (3) saxes (mm. 49–53) 1-bar, 5-part soli.There is also a 2-bar unison blues riff in the brass (mm. 25–28), a call that is answered by the saxes. It launches the trombone solo, and appears only once. The tutti choruses 9 through 11 use variations of the first two riffs.

Table B.5. Basically Blues outline

Chorus	1	2	3	4	5	6	7
Form	Intro	Head					
	rhythm section	sax 5pt ----------- tpts uni		br uni call sax 5pt response sax bkg stop time 1st 4 bars		sax soli brass bkg stop time 1st 4 bars	
Solo	pno			tbn2-------------		ts1-----------	
Key	G						

Chorus	8	9	10	11	12
Form		Shout			Head out
	rhy section	tutti concerted-----------------------------------			sax 5pt tutti ending
Solo	pno				
Key	G			A♭	G

Melodic and harmonic material uses blue notes. The first riff uses a double chromatic approach into the target chord (F7, F♯7, to G7) with the top line outlining a ♭7–7–1–5 line in the key of G. The second riff uses the minor pentatonic with passing ♭5 descending blues scale shown in figure B.7.

An ascending line cliché 3–4–♯4–5–6–7–8 ends the piece (mm. 131–32 bass and piano). This is found as a closing gesture in many pieces, generally in the bass part (see figure B.8).

The harmonic progression displays many variations of the blues changes. To the standard I–IV–V chords it adds a IV7 (m. 6) and a series of chromatic dominants (mm. 7–8). In choruses 2–3, 10, and 12 the harmonies use a ♭VII7 to I cadence (sometimes with a passing chromatic approach) that provides a "down home" character. Five different turnarounds (without counting the modulation chorus) are encountered (see table B.6).

See "Back Bone" for further discussion of the turnaround.

Technique Highlight:

Riff

A riff is a short motive, generally 1 to 4 bars, that repeats. It can repeat unaltered or it can adapt to the changing harmonies. The Basie band created whole arrangements through riffs devised by ear by the band members (see "Moten Swing"). Using multiple, contrasting riffs creates exciting back-

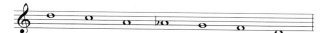

Figure B.7

grounds to solos or climactic ensemble sections as in Basie's "One O'Clock Jump." Other musicians used riffs as the basis for their compositions (see "Harlem Airshaft," "In a Mellow Tone," "Intermission Riff," "Main Stem").

Making Music:

Sudden, highly contrasted dynamic changes are crucial to the character of the piece: *fp cresc* in chorus 2 (tpts), sudden *ff* in brass (mm. 25–28), *mp* to *f* (saxes mm. 48–49), decrescendo *f* to *p* and sudden *ff* (mm. 119–20), and *ff–pp–ff* (mm.128–32). Gradual dynamics are also encountered (saxes mm. 37–39), and the slow build *pp–mp–mf–f–ff* in choruses 9–10–11. Marking all choruses with a consecutive number (1–12) and all dynamics with two different color erasable pencils (I use red and blue), helps keep track of the overall dynamic shape of the piece (see also "All of Me").

Figure B.8

Table B.6. Five different turnarounds in "Basically Blues"

1	iii	V7/ii	ii	V7
2	♭VII I7	♭VII I7	ii	V7
3	iii	subV7/ii	ii	subV7
4	I6	V7/ii	V7/V7	V7
5	I6	iii ♭iii dim	ii	V7

To have a reference point for the maximum loudness of your ensemble in a particular hall, select and play the loudest passage such as the shout in chorus 11. Other dynamics can then be set in relation to this. Are the 5-part chords in mm. 109–10 louder than the unison/octaves in mm. 111–12, or vice versa? Have each student create a riff and teach it by ear to other band members.

Self-Test Question 6
Review discussion of 4-part Basie voicings in "All of Me"
In "Basically Blues" 4-part Basie voicings are found at:

a. mm. 85–86
b. mm. 92–95
c. mm. 13–14
d. all of the above

BIG DIPPER

Jones, Thad 1965

Jones, Thad 1965

Grade: 5
Duration: 5:52
Instrumentation: 5, 4, 4, 4
Publisher: Kendor Music
Recording: Thad Jones-Mel Lewis Jazz Orchestra. *Central Park North*. Blue Note 7243 5 76852 2 1, CD.
Thad Jones-Mel Lewis Big Band. *Opening Night*. www.alangrantjazz.com. CD.

Highest Written Notes:
Tpt 1: E (three ledger lines)
Tpt 2–3: E (three ledger lines, on unison passage with tpt 1, 2 bars before letter J)
Tbn 1: G (three ledger lines)

Solos:
pno (16 bars), tpt2 (two choruses), ts1 (one chorus +12 bars)

Introductory Notes:
Brief Thad Jones biography

At a Glance:

Articulation:	– > ∧ slurs
Bass line:	written ostinato
Chords:	Ma6, Ma7 (9, 13), mi7 (9, 11), Dom (7, 9, #11, #5, #13, 13, mixolydian, alt, lydian, lydian ♭7, octatonic)
Chord progression:	I–IV–V blues with dominant chain and chords borrowed from the parallel minor
Dynamics:	*p, mf, f, ff, cresc, dim*
Edition:	8 1/2x11 vertical, 8 pages. Letters every 16 bars. No measure numbers.
Expressive devices:	bend, fall (saxes), squeeze, short gliss up, doit, lift, short and long gliss down (brass)
Form:	11 choruses of 12-bar blues with four bar extension (12+4=16 bars). Chorus 10 is 12 bars. Intro (8), interlude (8+4), and coda (4)
Guitar part:	chord symbols and rhythm slashes
Key:	G Ma
Modulations:	none
Mutes:	none
Piano part:	chord symbols and rhythm slashes
Shout:	none
Style:	bass ostinato groove
Tempo:	quarter=136–140
Time feel:	in 4
Voicings:	saxes: 4/5-pt spreads, 5-pt open (no root) tpts: triads (dbl lead 8vb), 3-pt (dbl lead 8vb), 4-pt closed, clusters, whole tone clusters tbns: 4-pt, spreads (chord sound and one tension) upper structure triads: II, ♭VI

Form and Texture:

The form comprises 11 choruses of 16-bar blues (12 bar blues +4 bar extensions), with chorus 10 being 12 measures long. There is an intro (8 bars), a 12 bar interlude (8+4) following chorus 10, and a coda (4).

The introduction is 8 bars, with unaccompanied saxes for four bars and rhythm section ostinato with trombone section "comping" figures on "2 and" for the next four. The first chorus features the piano soloing with the rhythm section. Saxes enter at m. 13 of the form (in the tonic), sounding for a moment as the head. A break on m.16 ushers in the brass unison pick-up to the actual head A that features antiphonal brass melody and saxophone responses. This first chorus is followed by a contrasting tutti concerted chorus B (letter C). Its last four bars feature a climactic two-bar figure repeated and varied that helps launch the trumpet solo. Theme B returns unchanged at letter F with the trumpet playing solo fills during the various sustaining or resting portions of the ensemble statement.

The tenor saxophone solos for three choruses at letter G and H. The interlude (letter I) serves as the apex of the form (trumpets 1–3 on written E above the staff). It leads into a 4-bar interlude where the bass figure of the introduction returns and to a *dal segno* to letter C. The B head is repeated with its last two bars displaced by an interpolated drum solo. The displaced closing phase is then brought back in the four bar coda.

Melodic, Harmonic, and Rhythmic Materials:

The saxophone introduction uses blue notes (♭3, ♭5, ♭7) with chromatic approaches as outlined in table B.7. The 13th is avoided so its impact in measure 5 (lead trombone, baritone, and bass) is heightened.

Melodic material in the first two chourses, though contrasting, stems from the same basic scale (G mixolydian with blue notes, see table B.8). The contrast is rhythmic and textural (call-and-response in the first, and tutti concerted in the second chorus).

Melodic material is sequenced and varied (B mm. 8–11, C, mm. 8–11 and mm. 13–16). The bass alternates an ostinato 1–5–6–5 with walking.

Table B.7. Saxophone introduction with blue notes (♭3, ♭5, ♭7) and chromatic approaches

G	Ab		A	B♭	B	C	C♯	D	F	F♯
1	Chr. Appr.		2	♭3	3	4	♭5	5	♭7	Chr. Appr.

Table B.8. G mixolydian with blue notes and chromatic approaches

G		A	B♭	B	C	C♯	D	E	F
1		2	♭3	3	4	♭5	5	13	♭7

Table B.9. Turnarounds in "Big Dipper"

Chorus	Letter	Chords in last two bar turnarounds			
1	A 15	A7	D7	G	
2	B 15	A7	D7		B7 E7 A7 D7
3	C 15		B♭Ma7		E♭Ma7 A♭Ma7 G7
4	D 15	A7	D7		G B♭ A A♭

While the first 14 bars of the blues remain unvaried throughout, the last two bars are reharmonized, acting as a turnaround and clarifying the form (see table B.9).

For a discussion of Thad Jones' harmony see "Back Bone."

The piece drives forward to the last four bars of letter C. These climactic four bars (C mm. 13–16) launch both solos, and wrap up the coda. They are the only places featuring a tutti ensemble with long values (half note) on a strong beat (beat 3), in a wide voicing. All preceding material emphasizes upbeats, figures on weak beats (saxes: 2+, letter B, mm. 1–11), or tutti concerted on a weak beat (beat 2, letter C, m. 1).

Chorus ten (letter H) features a 24-bar section that includes the main progression and much through composed melodic, and harmonic material: the trombone "comping" figure from the introduction returns and is developed, the trumpet A melody is recomposed and merged with the saxophone response. At letter I, a two-bar figure is sequenced four times, providing a retransition to the bass ostinato found on mm. 5–8 of the introduction.

Technique Highlight:

Expressive Devices

Expressive devices are also called articulations and special effects. For our discussion here, they do not include articulations such as accents, staccato, tenuto, marcato (see "Wind Machine"), and mainly pertain to wind instruments. They enhance the sound of the ensemble, add expression to the music, and convey the jazz tradition, both vocal and instrumental.

The list found in table B.10 is only meant to serve as a reference since special techniques are many and are specific to the instruments and players that produce them. To explore the many possibilities, consult

Table B.10. Expressive devices

Alternate (or false) Fingerings	Gliss	Rip
Bend	Ghost note	Shake
Doit	Growl	Smear
Fall	Hum	Spill
Flip	Lift	Squeeze
Fluttertongue	Plop	Tongue slap
Half Valve	Portamento	Turn

dictionaries or individaul manuals for flute, clarinet, saxophone, trumpet, trombone, French horn, and tuba instrumental study. The descriptions of the effect and how to produce it need to be matched with listening to the actual sounds. In addition to the recordings, refer to the bibliography, where many excellent manuals that contain audio demonstrations of these devices are listed.

Jones here uses bend and fall in the saxes and squeeze, short gliss up, doit, lift, short and long gliss down in the brass.

Making Music

Focus on dynamics, accents, expressive devices, and the rhythm section. Most dynamics are marked, but it might be useful to enter in the score all of the ones found in the recording. All long notes attacked on the end of four are played *sfp* crescendo (A m. 14, C m. 2), saxes need a dynamic curve at letter B, where they begin *p*. Sudden drop in dynamics in the Basie tradition is found at letter C m. 1. Here the first note is played *f* followed by a sudden *p*.

Listening to recordings that demonstrate accents and expressive devices will help imitate and duplicate the many found here, such as tenuto (–), accent (>), marcato, or hat (∧), and slurs and devices such as bend, fall (saxes), squeeze, short gliss up, doit, lift, short and long gliss down (brass). See discussion above.

The rhythm section plays in a combo style, in particular during solos. Experiment with leaving the anchor of the ostinato here and there. The bass walks on the first four bars of letter D and the rhythm section drops to a sudden *p* on bar 5 of the second trumpet solo chorus (on the first recording). The bass creates tension with a high register pedal (G, mm. 1–4), second chorus of tenor solo (first recording).

Compare the two recordings listed on the title page. There are some minor differences that might provide ideas for performance. In *Opening Night* (a live recording) there is an unaccompanied alto and trumpet duet

before the actual introduction begins and then later both solos are shortened by one chorus.

Self-Test Question 7

The voicing technique found in the saxophones at letter A, mm. 13–15 is:

a. close position
b. drop 2
c. drop 3
d. 4–5 part spreads with root at the bottom

BIG JIM BLUES

Williams, Mary Lou, and Harry Lawson 1939

Williams, Mary Lou 1939

Grade:	3
Duration:	2:54
Instrumentation:	4, (cl 1–2, ts 1–2) 3, 2, 4
Publisher:	Warner Brothers
Recording:	Andy Kirk. *Andy Kirk and His Twelve Clouds of Joy 1939–40*. Classics 640 CD. Also in *Big Band Jazz*, Vol II. The Smithsonian Collection of Recordings, RD 030-2, 1983, CD.

Highest Written Notes:

Tpt 3:	G on top of staff (all trumpets within staff)
Tbn 1:	F (two ledger lines)

Solos:
(written out): guit (4), tbn 1(11), ts1 (2)

Introductory Notes:
Instrumentation, Original Recording Information, Music of the 1930s: An Introduction and Big Jim Blues by Loren Schoenberg, Notes for the Performer by Brent Wallarab.

Form and Texture:
The four-bar introduction features a guitar solo with rhythm section accompaniment. It is followed by

At a Glance:

Articulation:	• – > dot under tenuto, slurs
Bass line:	written, with additional chord symbols
Chords:	triads, Ma6, mi6 (9, 11), Dom7 (♭9, 9, ♯5), dim, dim7
Chord progression:	Ma blues with passing diminished chords
Dynamics:	*mp, mf, f, sfz, dim*
Edition:	81/2x11 oblong, 8 pages. Measure numbers every bar, with boxed numbers highlighting sections
Expressive devices:	bend, slide (clts), rip (ts2), bend, slide (guit), bend, rip, slide (tbn)
Form:	intro (4), three blues choruses (18, 12, 18), coda (5)
Guitar part:	written melody, chord symbols
Key:	DMa
Modulations:	None
Mutes:	cup (tpt3), hat (tpts 1-2, tbns 1-2)
Orchestration:	writing across sections (clts 1-2+ muted tpt, ts1-2 + tpt)
Piano part:	written, with additional chord symbols, ad lib comping
Shout:	none, coda is climactic
Style:	med slow blues
Tempo:	quarter=72
Time Feel:	in 4
Voicings:	brass: 4pt close ens: 2-pt (thirds), triads, 4-pt close (lead or 2nd part doubled 8vb), 5-pt open

three blues choruses, the first and last 18 bars in length, the middle one 12. The expanded form is derived by a natural repetition of the customary chord changes as they follow the melodic line freely phrased in the tradition of rural vocal blues (see table B.11).

Table B.11. Eighteen-bar harmonic structure of choruses one and three in "Big Jim Blues"

Chord Function	I	IV	iv	I	V	I and turnaround
No. of measures	7	2	1	4	2	2

Textures are sparse and economical, giving this piece a chamber ensemble quality. Much of the character of this piece is derived by its orchestration and voicings: the first chorus features a dialogue between guitar and a trio of two clarinets and cup-muted trumpet. In the second chorus the trio's first and second voices are doubled 8vb by the tenor saxes, producing a new tone color, while the trombone solos. The third chorus opens with a new trio orchestration (open trumpet and two tenors, mm. 35–38), to then revert to the initial trio (mm. 39–42), add a unison counterline (mm. 43–48), reintroduce the orchestration of the second chorus (trio + two tenors 8vb, mm. 48–50), continue with a two-measure tutti (the only such passage in the piece, mm. 51–52), and launch the climactic contrapuntal coda (mm. 53–57), where the only dynamic *forte* in the piece is found.

Melodic, Harmonic, and Rhythmic Materials:
The main lines reflect the blues tradition, with blue notes (♭3, ♭5, and ♭7), descending chromatic triplet cadences (5–3–5, ♭5–♭3–♭5, 4–2–4, etc. . . . mm. 3–4, mm. 21–22), repeated notes (mm. 10–11), note bends and other expressive devices. A traditional blues lick in triplets is shown in figure B.9.

The first phrase (mm. 5–6) is repeated and then balanced by a contrasting ascending phrase. The melodic material is developed from a handful of motives through rhythmic variation, extensions, and elisions.

The trio voicings are always triadic (featuring major, minor, and diminished triads), with the muted trumpet as the second voice, sandwiched between the clarinets. The linear nature of the three individual lines that make up these chords (lines a b c, from the top down, mm. 5 ff.) is underscored by their rearranging at mm. 35–38. When present, tenor saxes always double 1st and 2nd voices 8vb. The short tutti at mm. 51–52 prepares the coda in at least two different ways: the brass in hats remove the mutes, and the voicings progress from four-part close to five-part open by adding tenor sax 2 (both at m. 52, beat 4).

Figure B.9

Table B.12. Voicing across sections examples

Composer/arranger	Mary Lou Williams	Duke Ellington	Duke Ellington	Gil Evans
Piece	"Big Jim Blues"	"Cottontail"	"Mood Indigo"	"King Porter Stomp"
Instrumental combination	Cl Tpt (in cup mute) Cl	As Tpt w. plunger Tbn Bari	Tpt w. plunger Tbn Cl	Cl As Tbn

Technique Highlight:

Voicing Across Sections
This technique consists in assigning passages to a small group of instruments belonging to different sections of the ensemble. The purpose is generally to exploit timbral combinations or to create lighter or heavier textures. Many writers have experimented with this. A few examples can be found in table B.12.

Making Music
There are excellent Notes for the Performer by Brent Wallarab included in the score.

Self-Test Question 8
The order of the three melodic lines found initially at m. 5 in the two clarinets and the trumpet are rearranged at m. 35. If we call the lines at m. 5, from the top down, a (cl), b (tpt), and c (cl), their order, from the top down, at m. 35 is:

    a. a c b
    b. b c a
    c. b a c
    d. none of the above

For Further Reading
Schuller, Gunther, and Martin Williams. *Big Band Jazz: From the Beginnings to the Fifties*. The Smithsonian Collection of Recordings, 1983, pp. 23–24 (booklet).

BLACK, BROWN, & BEAUTIFUL

Nelson, Oliver 1970

Nelson, Oliver 1970

Grade: 5
Duration: 2:34

Instrumentation: 5, 4, 4, 3 (no guit)
Publisher: Sierra Music
Recording: Oliver Nelson. *Black, Brown, and Beautiful*. RCA Bluebird 6993-2-RB.

Highest Written Notes:
Tpt 1:   E (three ledger lines)
Tpt 2:   E (three ledger lines)
Tbn 1:   A (three ledger lines)

Solos:
as1 feature. Bari (written two-bar solo mm. 19–20)

Soli:
trpts mm. 43–46

Notes:
trumpet unison at mm. 43–46 can be played an octave lower (tpts 1–2). Tpt 1 top note for the rest of the chart is B (one ledger line).

Introductory Notes:
director's notes, performance comments by Bob Curnow

Form and Texture:
A deceivingly standard, one-chorus AABA ballad with reprise from the bridge, and a framing introduction and coda. Length of sections varies: intro (8 bars), A (10 bars: 6+4), A1 (8 bars: 6+2), B (8 bars: 4+4), A2 (8 bars: 6+2), B (8 bars: 4+4), A2 (6 bars), coda (5 bars). Pedals contribute to the formal outline: intro and coda share the syncopated pedal figure emphasizing all the upbeats shown in figure B.10.

Figure B.10

At a Glance:

Articulation:	• – > slurs
Bass line:	written pedal, written line with additional chord symbols, chord symbols
Chords:	Ma7, mi7 (9), Dom7 (♭9, 9, ♯9, ♯11, +5, alt, oct, sus), lydian, mixolydian, oct, minor blues scale; triads and 7th chords over bass note, 7- and 8-note modal chords
Chord progression:	mix of functional and linear harmony. Extended dominant chains, chromatic bass sequences, pedals.
Dynamics:	*mp, mf, f, ff, cresc, dim*
Edition:	8 1/2x11 oblong. 10 pages. Measure numbers every bar, with boxed numbers highlighting sections
Expressive devices:	no vib. in stand (m. 57)
Form:	intro (8), A (10), A1 (8), B (8), A2 (8), B1(8), A3 (6), coda (5)
Key:	E♭ Ma key signature throughout, though progresses to FMa
Modulations:	FMa (progressive tonality)
Mutes:	bucket (tpts and tbns)
Piano part:	written and chord symbols
Style:	ballad
Tempo:	quarter=76
Time feel:	even eighths (mm. 1–8 and mm. 57–61) and swing eighths (mm. 9–56), dbl x feel (mm. 33–34, mm. 49–50)
Voicings:	sax: uni, 3–4pt, spreads tpts: uni, triadic (tertian), 4-pt close, clus tbns: uni, 2-pt, 3-pt over bass, 4-pt close, in 5ths, spreads, spreads with bari, clus. brass: concerted 5–6–7-part

Figure B.11

The endings of the A sections (after the first six bars) feature a syncopation on 2 and 4 (m. 15, m. 25, m. 41) (see figure B.11).

The last A section leads directly into the coda, without featuring the pedal (m. 57). The intro features unison altos accompanied by concerted brass/tutti over pedal. The first alto is then featured throughout with accompanying textures ranging from trio rhythm section, to brass, saxes, trombones, saxes/trombones, and tutti. There are short foreground passages (bari solo mm. 19–20; unison saxes mm. 25–26; unison trumpets m. 34, mm. 43–45, m. 50). The coda features a three-part texture: trumpets on melodic fragment, trombones in sustaining pads, and saxes on the pedal with piano and drums (please see outline in table B.13).

Melodic, Harmonic, and Rhythmic Materials:
The alto unison in the introduction displays a rising line (E, F♯) leading to the note G (m. 7) that anticipates the first note of the A section melody. The A section melody is based on the C minor blues scale, while the harmony is in E♭ Ma. They both cadence to C at m. 15, where the melody reaches the note C and the harmony a C7sus chord and C pedal. The motive in the saxes at m. 25 is based on the C blues scale. It is sequenced a minor third up at m. 26. The B section melody features a contrasting melody (solo alto, accompanied by trombones and saxes). On the return of B at mm. 43–46 the trumpets provide a climactic statement of the melody, before the alto picks it up again. In the coda the trumpets sound the A section initial motive.

The introduction features oblique motion, with the ensemble sustaining over a descending chromatic and scalar bass leading to V7. The chords feature brass clusters outlining complete 7 or 8 note modes: A mixolydian (m. 1), E7 (octatonic) m. 3, and B♭7 (octatonic) m. 8, interspersed with voicings with upper structure triads (m. 5, G Lydian) and 4-part close over stacked fourths (m. 7).

Table B.13. "Black, Brown, & Beautiful" outline

Measure	1	9	27	35	43	51	57
Form	Intro	A A1	B	A2 B1		A2	coda
Key	Descending chromatic bass leading to V7 (B♭7)	E♭Ma	Transient keys beginning with iv (A♭mi)	FMa as before		FMa	FMa Ending with a deceptive cadence on vi (Dmi)

Table B.14. "Black, Brown, & Beautiful" time feels and dynamics

Measure	1	9	19	27	35	43	51	57
Form	Intro	A	A	B	A	B	A	Coda
Brass	Bucket mutes					open		in stand
Drums (w. sticks)	Pedal w. Bass	Ride w. rim slap						Pedal w. bass
Feel	Even	Swing Ballad		Double time feel mm. 33–34	Swing Ballad	Apex Triplets Double time feel mm. 49–50	Swing Ballad	Even
Dynamics	mp			mp mf f		ff	mp	mp

The harmony features extended dominants (G7–C7–F7–B♭7, mm. 11–12), third relationships (E♭ to C, C to A♭, mm. 13–16), harmonies built over a chromatic bass (mm. 30–31, 31–33), secondary and substitute dominants, II–Vs, IV–Vs resolving down a fifth (mm. 40–41), and up a half step (mm. 56–57), and a final deceptive V–vi cadence (mm. 60–61).

Technique Highlight:

Progressive Tonality
Progressive Tonality denotes a modulation without the return to the original key: the piece ends in a different key or mode than the initial one. Reasons for modulations can be many, such as having the music in an optimal range for the singer or for the ensemble, creating momentum (when the modulation ascends), or for contrast. For a list of other pieces using progressive tonality see the Indexes of Musical Features.

Making Music
The voicings in the introduction are especially dense. They might be played as fermatas adding one instrument at a time. Try both directions. Then add the pedal, and finally the alto saxes.

The overall shape of the piece is aided by the brass muting and unmuting, attention to the dynamics in the score, and by the drummer. Brass begins in bucket mutes. They are removed at m. 39, just before the apex

of the piece. The ff dynamic in this passage lasts only three measures before decrescendo to mp at m. 46: make the most of it. The brass plays mp the last A (m. 51) and then the coda *in stand*, returning to the soft dynamics of the beginning (see outline in table B.14).

Dynamics are carefully marked and are meant to support the alto solo throughout. The only passages where the ensemble is on its own are the apex (mm. 43–46) mentioned above and the coda. The short foreground passages (bari solo mm. 19–20; unison saxes mm. 25–26; unison trumpets m. 34) remain subordinate to the solo. Achieving a good combo balance (rhythm section and alto solo) allows you to then balance the rest of the ensemble in relation to the dynamics set by the combo.

The drum set part includes written passages, ad lib parts, and a variety of feels. They contribute to the shaping of the piece.

Self-Test Question 9
After establishing the new key of FMa, the coda (mm. 57–61) wraps up the piece with the melody emphasizing the tonic F. The five chords in the harmony are:

a. IV–I–IV–ii–I
b. ii–V–I–V–I
c. IV–I–IV–V7sus–vi
d. ♭VI–♭III–♭VI–vi–i

BLUES AND THE ABSTRACT TRUTH

Nelson, Oliver, 1964

Nelson, Oliver 1964

Grade: 6
Duration: 5:11 (original recording)
Instrumentation: 5, 4, 4, 3
Publisher: Sierra Music
Recording: Oliver Nelson. *More Blues and the Abstract Truth*. Impulse IMPD-212.

Highest Written Notes:

Tpt 1:   D above staff (F♯ in final three bars)
Tpt 2:   D above staff
Tbn 1-2:   B (four ledger lines) on head, D (five ledger lines) on solo section background

Solos:

ts1 (two 30-bar choruses), drums (open).

Solo Section:

any player can solo, backgrounds on cue.

Introductory Notes:

director's notes, performance comments by Bob Curnow

Notes:

Multimeter work: conducting patterns in 1, 2, 3, 4, 5, and 6 are needed.

A sequel to "Blues and the Abstract Truth," the original recording features outstanding solos by Roger Kellaway (pno), Phil Woods (a), and Pepper Adams (b). The original is scored for septet (tpt, a, t, b, and rhy) and features some minor differences: mm. 51–52 are added in the big band version, and three fermatas ending on C lydian replace the six-bar D minor coda of the septet version. The septet version has been arranged for sax quintet (aattb) and rhythm by Ramon Ricker (Advance Music). This big band version is by the composer.

At a Glance:

Articulation:	• > slurs
Bass line:	written melodic line (mm. 1–20), written bass line (mm. 21–47), chord symbols for solo section, written for shout (mm.75–82)
Chords:	Ma, mi7 (9), Dom (♭9, ♯11, ♭5, alt, wt, oct, sus), dim.
Chord progression:	modal (dorian) 22-bar minor blues with modulating tonal progression on last 6 measures (mm. 41–46), non-modulating II–V progression in solo section (mm. 69–74)
Dynamics:	*mf, f, ff, dim*
Edition:	8 1/2x11 oblong, 14 pages. Measure numbers every bar, with boxed numbers highlighting sections
Expressive devices:	no vib. (m. 25)
Form:	A (20+4), B (22), A1 (6), solo section (22+8, B chords), open drum solo, A (20), coda (3).
Key:	D minor key signature throughout, though only the B section is in D dorian. The A sections are intervallically constructed around a CMa tonal center.
Modulations:	CMa (m. 1), to D minor (m. 21), to CMa (m. 47)
Modes:	dorian, phrygian, lydian
Mutes:	none
Orchestration:	four-part brass chorale in paired (two per part) tpts and tbns (m. 25)
Piano:	written treble line (mm. 1–20), written bass line (mm. 21–47), chord symbols for solo section, written for shout (mm. 75–82)
Shout:	mm. 75–82
Style:	swing
Tempo:	quarter=212 (fast)
Voicings:	triads, 4-pt close (tpts mm. 45–46), clus (m. 21, 44, 75–82), ust, (mm. 41, 105–07), 4-pt Ma7 constant structure chords over bass ostinato (mm. 25–40)

Whole tone scales mm. 1-2

Figure B.11

Whole tone scales mm. 18-20

Figure B.12

Form and Texture:

The form is a hybrid of blues and ternary ABA. Two contrasting sections (A, mm. 1–24, and B, mm. 25–46) supply the main material. They overlap at mm. 21–24, where the ending of A is also the introduction to B. The 24 measure A section can be divided in 6+6+5+3+4. The unison melody is treated canonically upon repeat (m. 13).

The ensemble is divided into two groups: (1) trumpets and altos, (2) trombones, tenor and bari saxes, rhythm section (mm. 1–9). A concerted texture (mm.10–12), canon (mm. 13–17), and unison pyramid (mm. 18–20) follow.

The B section is an abbreviated 24-bar blues. It is a 22-bar (8+8+6) modal blues in d dorian (mm. 25–40) followed by a short return of the initial A theme (m. 47) closing on the note d, here a unison rather than a chord as in m. 21 (mm. 51–52) (see table B.15).

The solo section is based on the 22-bar blues B section, transposed to c dorian, with an 8-bar climactic tutti concerted passage at the end (mm. 75–82). After the drum solo, mm. 85–105 are an exact recapitulation of A, with the final chord expanded to a three chord final cadence (mm. 105–107).

Melodic, Harmonic, and Rhythmic Materials:

A is a unison line (mm. 1–12) and its variation (mm. 13–24). The variation begins as a unison canon at a half note lag. The line spells out the two whole-tone scales: C–D–E–F♯–A♭–B♭ is outlined on the down beats, while its complement F–G–A–B–C♯–D♯ is on the upbeats (mm. 1–3) and proceeds in a pattern of ascending fourths and descending minor thirds (see figure B.11).

The patterns that follow continue to use predominantly thirds and fourths (mm. 3–5), ending with a full C dorian collection (mm. 6–7). This overlaps with the entrance of the second group of instruments now outlining an ascending D minor tetrachord (D–E–F–G, m. 7, beats 3, 5, and m. 8, beats 1, 2). This is followed by two diminished tetrachords (A♭–G–F–E, mm. 9–10; and G♭–F–E♭–D, m. 11). A chain of descending fourths (A–E–B–F♯–D♭) links back to C for the varied restatement. The pyramid at mm. 18–20 is

Table B.15. "Blues and the Abstract Truth" head outline

Measure number	1	7	13	18	21
Form	A				
# of measures	6	6	5	3	4
Texture	unison 1st group unaccompanied	2nd group w. rhythm section	unison canon tutti	pyramid	vamp
Meter	4/4 2/4 4/4	6/4 3/4 4/4	4/4	5/4	6/4

Measure number	25	33	41	47
Form	B			A
# of measures	8	8	6	6
Texture	Constant structures over bass ostinato	sectional imitation		
Meter	6/4			4/4 2/4 4/4

Table B.16. Constant major 7th structures harmonizing dorian lead over ostinato in mm. 25–26

Melody	D dorian→										
Measure	25					26					
Beat	2	3	4	5	6	1	2	3	4	5	6
Structure	FMa7	GMa7	FMa7	GMa7	GMa7*	FMa7*	GMa7*	CMa7	B♭Ma7	CMa7	CMa7
Bass ostinato	D		E			F		E			

Chords with an asterisk (*) feature a 9 for 1 substitution (9th replaces root).

Table B.17. "Blues and the Abstract Truth" conducting patterns

Measure	1	5	6	7	11	12	17	18	21
Half note conducting	2	1*	2*	3	1 longer by a quarter (=dotted half)	2	3	2 (=dotted half+half)	2 (=dotted half+dotted half)
Quarter note conducting (rehearsal)	4	2	4	6	3	4	6	5 (3+2)	6 (3+3)

a variation on the opening two measures and outlines the two wholetone scales with the same intervallic pattern of fourths and minor thirds (see figure B.12). It ends on a cluster (A–G–F–E) over D pedal, introducing the B section.

Section B features 4-bar phrases in D dorian (the third phrase, mm. 33–36, is transposed up a fourth), concluding with three 2-bar phrases using c minor pentatonic (mm. 41–46). The first sixteen bars are a four-part chorale style for brass. Trumpets and trombones are two on each part. While the lead and the four note bass ostinato outline D Dorian, the lead is harmonized with Ma7 constant structuresl in close position. See discussion in the next section. The harmony changes at the end of phrase (to minor mm. 28, 36; to dominant m. 32).

A modal inflection colors the tutti concerted section (mm. 75–82), where a Cmi chord alternates with a Phrygian ♭II chord (C–D♭–E♭–F–G–A♭) over a C pedal. A whole-step relation between C and D can be found in thematic and structural places. The opening theme: C (m. 1) to D (m. 6), with its repetition at m. 13 and 21, the relation between the A and B sections (C–Dmi), and the changes in the solo section (Cmi7–Dmi7, mm. 53–58).

Technique Highlight

Constant Structures over Ostinato Bass
Constant structures have been discussed in "Airegin." The difference is that here they are over an ostinato. Instead of being built from a specific sequence of intervals, they are built down from the melody. Each melody note of the D dorian lead is assigned a major 7 chord in close position. The inversions vary (the melody note can be 1, 3, 5, or 7 of the chord) (see table B.16 and the example in figure B.13).

Making Music
While multimeter is relatively rare in jazz, with the early exception of Dave Brubeck, it is frequent in twentieth-century music (Igor Stravinsky's *Octet* and *Histoire du Soldat*, Leonard Bernstein's *Prelude, Fugue, and Riffs*). The A section of this piece features meter changes, with the speed of the basic pulse remaining unvaried. Given the tempo, conducting is in half notes, but for a slower rehearsal tempo conducting in quarter notes might be useful. Therefore conducting patterns in 1, 2, 3, 4, 5, and 6 are needed (see table B.17).

The 1 and 2 patterns with the asterisk * in mm. 5–6 (and the 2 and 1 pattern later in mm. 49–50) can be grouped into a 3 pattern.

Figure B.13 Example of major 7th constant structures over ostinato bass in D dorian

Selections from Nelson's *Patterns for Improvisation* (Jamey Aebersold) can be used as a warm-up to introduce the sound of his intervallic patterns. The canon at mm. 13–17 can be rehearsed one part at a time (leaders and followers). Creating constant structures over a pedal tone (on the piano, or assigning chords to the ensemble) will introduce their characteristic sound. The notes that change under the sustaining melody need to be brought out: rehearse the chords as fermatas (mm. 28, 32, 36, all on beat 4). Experiment with details found on the recording such as the drummer continuning to play on the recapitulation (m. 85–90) and then switching to hi hat (mm. 97–101), rather than dropping out.

Self-Test Question 10

On the recording each end of phrase of the first 12 measures of the B section (mm. 28, 32, 36) is enhanced by:

    a.   piano fills
    b.   piano fills and a change of harmony
    c.   a change of harmony
    d.   a bass fill

BODY & SOUL

Green, John 1930

Stone, George 1992

Grade:	4
Duration:	4:00
Instrumentation:	5, 4, 4, 4 (tpts double on flugs; mallet aux. perc. optional)
Publisher:	Hal Leonard

Highest Written Notes:

Tpt 1:	G (on top of staff)
Tbn 1:	Gb (three ledger lines)

Solos:
as1 (written melody and written solo, 8 bars each), ts1 (written solo, 8 bars)

Soli:
saxes (8 bars)

At a Glance:

Articulation:	● – > ∧ slurs
Bass line:	written
Chords:	Ma (6, 9), Ma7 (9, ♯11), mi7 (9, 11), Dom (7, 9, ♯11, ♯5, ♭13, 13, sus, mixo, alt, octatonic), dim
Chord progression:	secondary dominants (V7/ii, V7/vi), substitute dominants (subV7/iii), passing diminished (♯iio), ♭IIMa7
Dynamics:	*mp, mf, f, cresc, dim*
Edition:	8 1/2x11 oblong, 14 pages. Measure numbers every bar, with boxed numbers highlighting sections
Expressive devices:	none
Form:	two choruses: A, A1, B, A2, (64); A, A1, B1; codetta (3); A1; coda (5)
Guitar part:	chord symbols, melodic line with the ensemble
Key:	D♭ Ma
Modulations:	to FMa on B1 (second bridge)
Mutes:	none
Orchestration:	voicing across sections (opening duet)
Piano part:	written chords with and without additional chord symbols
Style:	swing
Tempo:	quarter=120 or faster (medium)
Time Feel:	in 2 and in 4
Voicings:	saxes: unison, 4-pt close and open, 5-pt (tertian and quartal), spreads
	tpts: unison, 2-pt, 3-pt (triads, dbl lead 8vb and at the unison), 3-pt open, 4-pt closed
	tbns: unison, 2-pt, 3-pt, 4-pt closed (tertian, quartal, and sw), spreads
	brass: 6pt, ust (II, bii)

Introductory Notes:
None

Form and Texture:
No introduction. Two choruses with codetta and coda. The original ballad tune is rendered as if in double time feel, with the number of bars doubled from 32 to 64.

Table B.18. Intervals of the 2-part counterpoint in "Body & Soul"

Measure	1	2	3	4
Interval between two lines	M6	m6 5 +4 m3	M6 m6 5 +4 4	M3 4 +4 m6

The first A features a duet (flugelhorn and trombone, doubled by alto and tenor saxes) in counterpoint and concerted. The second A (m. 17) is voiced in four-part close with trumpets and trombones in two part pairs, saxes doubling the four-part brass, and baritone on root. The ensemble is concerted, with some connecting lines and counterpoint. The B section (m. 33) features sax soli, followed by the tune shared between saxes and trumpets. The last A (m. 49) features the alto sax on the melody (first 8), followed by tutti concerted ensemble. The first two A sections of the second chorus (m. 65) are an "arranger's chorus," alternating ensemble passages with solos by alto and tenor saxes. They are followed by the bridge (m. 83), where the tune is fragmented and tossed around the trombone and sax sections, leading to a concerted tutti. A three-bar codetta (mm. 99–101) connects to a repeat of A1 (*dal segno*), followed by a coda (m. 103).

Melodic, Harmonic, and Rhythmic Materials:
The original ballad tune is reworked as a medium swing through the use of eighth note lines, anticipations, delays, and other rhythmic and melodic manipulations. The harmonic rhythm features one chord per bar rather than the original two.

The first A section is scored in two part counterpoint in contrary and oblique motion, neatly merging into a concerted texture at the beginning (m. 1), middle (mm. 8–10), and end (m. 15) of the section. Moving lines under a sustaining lead (m. 18, m. 31, mm. 47–48), and inner parts moving within a stationary harmony (mm. 65–68) are present.

The chord progression remains close to the original, and retains the key of D♭ major, and the bridge in D major. The second chorus opens with a dominant pedal (mm. 65–68) and then modulates to F rather than D major for the bridge (m. 83). The codetta modulates back to the A section through a substitute V7 of ii ("sub V7 of two") E7 chord (mm. 100–1) leading to the E♭ minor 11 at m. 17.

The first chorus is in "two" feel, with the bass walking parts of the bridge (mm. 37–40). The second chorus (m. 65) alternates "four" feel in the drums in tandem with the bass on a pedal or walking, and "two" feel (8

bars each) for the A sections. On the B section (m. 83) the drums plays time in "four" and the bass walks.

Technique Highlight:

Counterpoint: Two Part
Counterpoint is the combination of two or more melodic lines. It has a horizontal and a vertical component: the two lines are rhythmically independent while also having variable intervallic relations (same rhythm or constant intervallic relations yield parallelism rather than counterpoint). In general, when one line holds the other moves and the amount of consonance and dissonance in the intervals is exploited for tension resolution. The intervals in the first four measures (mm. 1–4) are shown in table B.18.

In this arrangement the contrapuntal presentation of the A theme by the quartet is followed by a contrasting tutti concerted texture for the second A. Counterpoint is used in both written and improvised jazz.

Making Music
Review time feels and dynamics. Avoid drowning solos at mm. 73–80 with the backgrounds. Apex is at mm. 83–98. The many textures need balancing, whether they are small group duet counterpoint (mm. 1–16), sectional counterpoint (mm. 83–88), or tutti passages. The many cascading effects (trumpets, mm. 38–48) also might be isolated since going from unison to 4-part harmony or vice versa in a few bars might require additional awareness on the part of the players in the areas of tuning and balancing.

Self-Test Question 11
The drums switches from brushes to sticks:

   a. for the solo section
   b. for the D.S.
   c. for the apex
   d. never

Lead Sheet
The New Real Book. Vol. 2. Sher Music Co., 1991.
The Real Book. 6th ed. Hal Leonard, 2004.

C

C JAM BLUES

Ellington, Duke 1942

Ellington, Duke 1942

Grade:	4
Duration:	2:37
Instrumentation:	5, 3, 3, 4. (tpt 2 doubles on vln., ts1 doubles on cl.)
Publisher:	Warner Bros. Publications, Jazz@Lincoln Center series
Recording:	*The Blanton-Webster Band*, Bluebird (RCA/BMG) 5659-2.

Highest Written Notes:

Tpt 1:	A above staff
Tpt 2-3:	Bb above staff (solo)
Tbn 1:	A (three ledger lines)
Tbn 2:	C (four ledger lines) (solo)

Solos:

(written out): pno (12 bars), vln. (4+12, cue written out for tpt. 2), tpt 3 (4+12), ts 2 (4+12), tbn 2 (4+12), cl (4+12).

Introductory Notes:

Notes on Playing Ellington, Glossary, The Four Elements of Music, Instrumentation, Original Recording Information, Rehearsal Notes by David Berger. Note from Wynton Marsalis.

Form and Texture:

Twelve-bar blues, with each solo chorus (choruses 3–7) featuring an additional four-bar break, bringing the form to sixteen bars. The first head is stated by the piano, the second by unison saxes with piano improvisation. The last solo (clarinet) has an ensemble background (a brass four-bar riff). The final chorus is the only full ensemble section in the piece, featuring sectional writing with harmonized brass and saxophones in unison and harmony. It is also climactic, with the only *f* and *ff* markings in the piece.

Melodic, Harmonic, and Rhythmic Materials:

The melody is a four-bar riff built on just two pitches (scale degrees 1 and 5 in the key). The two eighth-

At a Glance:

Articulation:	• – > ∧
Bass line:	written
Chords:	Ma6, mi7, Dom (♯5, ♭9, 9, 13), dim
Chord progression:	Ma blues with some additional chords. *See* narrative
Dynamics:	*mp, mf, f, ff*
Edition:	8 1/2x11 oblong, 19 pages. Rehearsal letters every chorus. No measure numbers
Expressive devices:	fall, gliss, ½ valve, lift, ya–ya (tbn)
Form:	eight blues choruses: head twice (12+12), five solo choruses (4 bar break + 12 bar blues), final chorus (12)
Guitar part:	chord symbols
Key:	CMa
Modulations:	None
Mutes:	closed plunger w. pixie (tpt3 solo), plunger w. mute (tbn solo)
Orchestration:	AATB saxes in stacked thirds with cl. color coupling lead
Piano part:	written solo, written chords w. additional chord symbols
Shout:	last 12 bars (G)
Style:	swing
Tempo:	quarter=188 (medium)
Voicings:	saxes: unison, 4-pt close with clarinet lead tpts: 3-pt (tertian and quartal) tbns: 2-pt, 3-pt (mostly tertian) brass: 4-, 5-, 6-part

note rhythm is stated in the first bar, intensified by repetition in the second, and released in the third through elongation and pitch change. A one-bar rest follows. The remainder of the ensemble's melodic material centers on the C triad with added 6

Table C.1. "C Jam Blues" outline

Chorus	1	2	3	4	5	6	7	8
Letter		A	B	C	D	E	F	G
Form	Head		Solos					Ending
Instrumentation	Rhythm section	Saxes	Vln.	Tpt.3	Ts.2	Tbn.2	Cl.	Tutti
Number of bars	12	12	4+12	4+12	4+12	4+12	4+12	12

(C–E–G–A) and ♭3, ♭5, and ♭7 blue notes (E♭, G♭, B♭). The brass riff in chorus 7 neatly adapts to the blues harmonies by changing a few pitches while maintaining its basic shape intact.

The harmony uses the major tonic chord rather than the dominant (I7) type. The IV chord is a dominant quality chord (IV7). The upper chromatic dominant to the tonic chord (♭II7) is used frequently on mm. 2, 10, and 12 of the form. The last three choruses feature additional harmonies such as secondary dominants (V/V), supertonic (ii–7), and upper chromatic dominant to the subdominant chord (subV7 of IV).

Chorus 8, the climactic ending, features 4-, 5-, and 6-part brass voicings in thirds, with the trumpets voiced in fourths at measures 1, 5, and 10–12 of letter G. The bari is scored in its high register, and the clarinet plays the lead of the sax section and solo fills.

Technique Highlight

Riff
See discussion of Riff in "Basically Blues."

Making Music

There are thorough notes on playing Ellington and rehearsal notes in the score. This is essentially a combo chart, and it can be used to practice soloing on the blues. The violin solo can be substituted by any other instrument. If you want to keep the same string instrument sound, choose guitar. After the violin solo Ellington alternates a brass and a reed for the next four solos (tpt, ts, tbn, cl). This creates variety in a 2'37" recording. Solos can be rearranged and opened up for more choruses. When practicing improvisation try the piece in different keys, and close with the initial head in unison. When you play the chart as written, drive relentlessly to the last chorus and make the most of it. Ellington uses a similar end-accented form in "Harlem Airshaft" and "Cottontail."

Self-Test Question 12

At letter A the main riff spells scale degrees 1 and 5 of the tonic harmony C. On bar 5 of letter A, as the chord changes to F7 the melodic function of the riff is scale degree:

    a. 1
    b. 5
    c. ♭7
    d. 2

For Further Reading

Schuller, Gunther, and Martin Williams. *Big Band Jazz: From the Beginnings to the Fifties.* The Smithsonian Collection of Recordings, 1983, pp. 34–35 (booklet).

—— ✸ ——

CARAVAN

Ellington, Duke, Juan Tizol, and Irving Mills 1937

Ellington, Duke 1937

Grade:	4
Duration:	3:30
Instrumentation:	5, 5, 3, 4 (reed three plays clarinet, tbn3 opt.vtbn)
Publisher:	Warner Bros. Publications, Jazz@Lincoln Center series
Recording:	Duke Ellington. *The Great Chicago Concerts.* MusicMasters Jazz/BMG; 01612-65110-2.

Highest Written Notes:

Tpt 1:	F♯9 (in staff, on 5th line)
Tbn 1:	C (four ledger lines) on solo
Tbn 2:	F (two ledger lines)

Solos:
(written out): tpt 2 (4+4), tbn 1(16 solo +32 solo fills), cl (32), bari sax (32)

Introductory Notes:
Instrumentation, Original Recording Information, Rehearsal Notes, Notes from Wynton Marsalis.

At a Glance:

Articulation:	• – > slurs
Bass line:	written
Chords:	mi6 (9), Dom7 (♭9)
Chord Progression:	V7 i (A section), dominant chain to ♭III (B section)
Dynamics:	*pp, mp, f, sfz, poco, sfz, cresc, dim*
Edition:	8 1/2x11 oblong, 18 pages. Rehearsal letters every 16 bars. No measure numbers
Expressive devices:	portamento (bari sax solo), portamento, smear (tbn1 solo)
Form:	A (16), A (16), B (16), AB (cl solo), AB (bari solo), A (16), A (16)
Guitar part:	chord symbols
Key:	F minor
Modulations:	None
Mutes:	plunger o + (tpt2 and tbn2 solos), metal derby hat (brass)
Orchestration:	parallel 5-part dominant 7th (♭9) chords with tpt lead doubled 8vb by bari and tbn3
Piano part:	written, including fills, flourishes, and stride passages
Shout:	none
Style:	jungle groove
Tempo:	half=88
Time Feel:	ostinato in 2
Voicings:	saxes: 4pt close
	tpts: 4-pt close
	tbns: 2-pt
	ens: 5-pt parallel structures

Form and Texture:
Form is AAB (sixteen bars each) followed by clarinet and bari sax solos on AB, and head out on AA. No introduction or coda. The first trombone plays the bridge over three-part sax pads, and returns with solo fills on the head out. The piano contributes to the atmosphere of the piece with coloristic fills such as the two Cs in extreme ranges of the piano, six octaves apart, in the second A (letter B), and seven octaves apart at letter F, repeated note patterns in thirds (mm. 15–16, mm. 29–32), tremolos (letter C and H), a stride passage (letter G), and a 6-part cluster outlining F natural minor in the final four measures.

Melodic, Harmonic, and Rhythmic Materials:
This piece is considered part of Ellington's "jungle" music style. The title that Ellington gave it puts this piece a bit at odds with that terminology. Caravans are best known for crossing deserts rather than jungles. The camel is the mode of transport of choice here, elephants and all other jungle animals would quickly die of thirst. An astute traveler and program music composer, Ellington also selected the Middle Eastern sounding harmonic minor scale for the melody to paint his picture. He spices it up with a ♭5, a passing chromatic, and a double chromatic approach to the tonic note (mm. 12–13) as shown in figure C.1. Would "desert" music work?

The melody is tripled (tpt, with bari and tbn 3 one octave below) and harmonized with a 5-part constant structure voicing. The structure changes at the resolution to Fmi (m. 13). Both structures are kept within the span of one octave by having the lead trumpet written in the staff and the bari in a mid to high range (see figure C.2). Notice the whole step between the top two parts and the half step between the lower two parts: the melody always "grinds" with the adjacent voice. Fifth trumpet is above fourth and brasses, except lead, are in derby hats.

There is a large-scale dominant-tonic resolution to m. 13 of the A section (C7 ♭9 to F minor). This is paralleled by the melody that also descends from scale degree 5 to 1, and is additionally emphasized by the change from ostinato to "two" feel in the bass, by the second trumpet plunger fills, and by the voicing changing to a different structure.

The B section melody uses F pentatonic major (mm. 33–36) and F dorian with added chromatics (mm. 37–47). The ostinato also changes rhythm and uses a tonic-dominant pattern outlining the cycle of fifths chord progression.

Harmonic minor scale with added chromatic approaches

Figure C.1

Technique Highlight

Constant Structures over Ostinato Bass
See discussion in "Blues and the Abstract Truth."

Making Music

Rehearsal comments by Mark Lopeman and Jon Faddis can be found in the score.

Piece begins right with the melody: this gives one more reason to establish the groove first. Listen to recording and imitate. Drum set is played with mallets on tom-tom, bass has a two bar ostinato, and guitar plays upbeats: their parts need to interlock nicely. The switch to comping (m. 9), to two-feel (m. 13), and the addition of the piano (m. 10) need to happen seamlessly, without the tempo waivering.

Rehearse the melody in unison/octaves (tpt, bari, and tbn 3) and then add the harmonization. The parts that rub against the melody (tpt 3, tbn 2, ts 2) need to be played in tune and must not overwhelm the melody note dynamically. Have tenor 2 and bari play by themselves so they can tune-in to the half-step parallelism. Do the same with trombones 2 and 3. Then play each structure as a fermata, and finally the whole head in tempo.

Self-Test Question 13

In his varied and colorful comping and soloing Ellington inserts a stride piano style passage at letter G. The bass of mm. 106–8 outlines the:

    a. Major scale
    b. Harmonic minor scale
    c. Whole tone scale
    d. Diminished scale

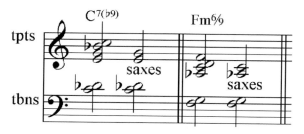

Figure C.2

Lead Sheet

The New Real Book. Vol 3. Sher Music Co., 1995.

CHERRY JUICE

Jones, Thad 1977

Jones, Thad 1977
Grade: 6
Duration: 5:45
Instrumentation: 5, 4, 4, 3, solo flug. ss1 and ss2 throughout (opt. as2 part provided for ss2)
Publisher: Kendor Music
Recording: The Mel Lewis Jazz Orchestra. *The Definitive Thad Jones, vol. 2: Live from the Village Vanguard.* Ocean, N.J. MusicMasters, 1990, CD out of print.
New Life. A&M Horizon #p-707. LP out of print.

Highest Written Notes:

Tpt 1–2: E (three ledger lines), and a couple of Gs (four ledger lines)
Tpt 3: E (three ledger lines)
Tbn 1: Bb (four ledger lines) one D (five ledger lines)

Solos:

pno (8 bars), solo flug (two choruses), ts 2 (24 bars + one chorus), pno (16 bars)

Soli:

saxes (one chorus)

Introductory Notes:

Brief Thad Jones biography

At a Glance:

Articulation:	• – > ∧ slurs
Bass line:	written and chord symbols
Chords:	Ma7 (9, ♯11), mi7 (9, 11), min7 (♭5), Dom (7, ♭9, 9, ♯9, ♯11, ♯5, ♭13, 13, mixolydian, alt, lydian, lydian ♭7, octatonic)
Chord progression:	II–V–i in minor with secondary dominants. Bridge in subdominant.
Dynamics:	*mf, f, ff, fp,* cresc
Edition:	8 1/2x11 vertical, 14 pages. Letters every 16 bars. No measure numbers.
Expressive devices:	gliss, spill, fall (saxes), gliss, spill, fall (brass)
Form:	intro (16), seven AABA choruses, recapitulation from the bridge (BA), coda (8+3)
Key:	G minor
Modulations:	none
Mutes:	none
Orchestration:	SSTTB saxes, lead exchange (tpt2 lead, tpt1 plays 4th, letter L)
Piano part:	chord symbols and rhythm slashes
Shout:	IJKL and QR
Style:	fast swing
Tempo:	quarter=224
Time feel:	in 4
Voicings:	saxes: unis, 2-pt, 3-pt, 4-pt (closed, open, and sw), 5-pt (open, over root and inversions, ust II and ♭VI over 3rd and ♭7) tpts: unis, triads (dbl lead 8vb, ust II and ♭VI), 4-pt closed (7thchords), 5-pt open with flug lead tbns: unis, 4-pt (open, over root and inversions)

Form and Texture:

The 16-bar introduction features a tutti concerted with connecting saxophone passages (8 bars), and a piano solo groove with brass rhythmic figures (8 bars).

The AABA head is presented by the saxophones in unison and then in 3rds and 4-part harmony on the bridge, accompanied by brass punctuations and riffs (letters A and B). Two choruses of flugelhorn solo follow, accompanied by a saxophone background the first time and a call and response passage the second (letters D and E). A passage with brass and saxes in counterpoint begins the next chorus, taken by the tenor sax solo (letters E and F). During the second chorus of the tenor sax solo the ensemble builds by adding sections one at a time playing strong rhythmic figures. The order is trombones, trumpets, saxes, intensifying to the high D (letter H, m. 8).

Chorus six is a tutti concerted shout, with occasional unison runs by the saxes (letter I). Chorus seven features a sax soli with brass punctuations in the second half, and a unison 4-octave brass pyramid on the last two bars. Another tutti passage with sax section unison runs is found in the first half of chorus eight (letters Q and R), with a piano solo wrapping up the last sixteen bars before the return to the bridge of the head. The coda features saxes with double-time figures, over glissing brass, tutti concerted chords, and four short ensemble holds before the final chord (see outline in table C.2).

Melodic, Harmonic, and Rhythmic Materials:

Theme A (unison saxes) is predominantly in eighth notes and outlines the minor key (g minor, using both the natural and flat 7th), the ♭VI7 (E ♭7, using the lydian ♭7 mode) and V7 (D7, using the minor 7th arpeggio on the dominant). It features a pattern of ascending thirds, descending 4ths and 5ths, scales, and arpeggios. The lines contain chromatic and diatonic approaches.

The shout (chorus 6, letter I), is a powerful arranger's chorus by Jones, where a different harmony is assigned to each melody note and substitute and chromatic chords are used to create forward motion, through a process called tonicization. See technique highlight on page 35. Here melodic material develops from the transformation of a few motives such as the descending D minor triad (letter I mm. 1–2, and then at J1 and J3), and the motive B♭–A–G–E (letter K) that is varied twice, sequenced, and extended. The sax soli (letters M–P) features 4- and 5-part SSTTB harmony. For more on Jones's harmonic language see "Back Bone" and other arrangements of his.

Many 3 over 4 cross rhythms are present throughout. In the introduction trumpets and trombones share

Table C.2. "Cherry Juice" outline

Letter		A B	C D	E F G H	
Chorus	Intro	1 Head	2–3	4–5	
Form		A A B A	AABA	AABA	
Number of bars	16	32	32+32	32+32	
Texture	Tutti and sax 8th-note lines	Sax section w. brass accompaniment	Backgrounds at letter D	Tutti at letter E Ens. build at letters G–H	
Solos	Piano (last 8 bars)		Flug. solo	Tenor 2 solo	

Letter	I J K L	M N O P	Q R S	B	
Chorus	6 Shout	7	8	Head	Coda
Form	A A B A	A A B A	A A B A	BA	
Number of bars	32	32	32	16	8+3
Texture	Tutti, mostly concerted	Sax section soli w. brass punctuations at letters Q and P	Tutti with sax section unison runs, piano solo		Tutti + short holds
Solos		Sax soli	Piano (last 16 bars)		Drum fills

Figure C.3 3 over 4 pattern (mm. 13–16)

a 3 over 4 pattern for four bars at mm. 13–16. Other passages can be found at (I7, J7–8, K5–8, L7–8).

Technique Highlight:

Reharmonization of each Note of the Melody with a Different Harmony
This is achieved by creating new harmonies that work with the lead and enhance forward motion.

Among the added harmonies used are II–Vs secondary IIs and secondary dominant chords, substitute II–V patterns (often referred to as secondary IIs and upper chromatic chords), and upper chromatic major 7th chords. The added harmonies create momentary or transient tonics, a process known as tonicization. An example applied to a well-known tune can be seen in figure C.4.

Reharmonization of each note of the melody with a different harmony has been used by many in jazz and classical music. Thad Jones uses it here at letter I and in other pieces such as "Three and One," and his classic arrangement of "All of Me."

original

reharmonization using secondary and substitute dominants and upper chromatic Major 7th chords

Figure C.4

Making Music

The sax section is showcased throughout, in consistent SSTTB orchestration. This is a fast tempoed, virtuosic piece. Depending on the level of your players, a sax sectional might be beneficial. On the positive side, many of the sax passages are in unison and eighth-note based. Listen to recording for crescendo and decrescendo emphasizing the natural contour of the melody. Follow phrasing and slurs in the score.

Self-Test Question 14

Compound rhythm is the rhythm resulting from two or more rhythmic strands played together. In a measure of eighth notes there are eight places where a note can be attacked (four downbeats and four upbeats). At letter K m. 5 brass and saxes interlock their attacks, resulting in a compound rhythm of:

a. all 8 beats
b. beats 2+, 3+, 4+
c. beats 1, 2+, 4+
d. beats 1+, 2, 3+

A CHILD IS BORN

Jones, Thad 1969

Jones, Thad 1969

Grade:	3
Duration:	4:04
Instrumentation:	5, 4, 4, 4 (optional a.flts. for a.saxes and flts for t.saxes and bari)
Publisher:	Kendor Music
Recording:	Thad Jones/Mel Lewis. *Consummation.* Blue Note 7243 5 38226 2.

Highest Written Notes:

Tpt 1:	G above staff
Tbn 1:	B♭ (four ledger lines)

Solos:

piano (written, 30 bars), flugelhorn/tpt 3 (written, 30 bars)

Notes:

Thad's flugelhorn (written as tpt. 3) solo at letter A is very jazzed up, and the bass duets freely. Their parts are written out in the score only as a guide. They should be played in an improvisatory way or the tune will sound very square. The flugelhorn part is intended for an additional player. Saxes play flutes throughout on the original. They are in unison other than their final five bars. Bass plays arco at letters F and G.

Introductory Notes:

None

At a Glance:

Articulation:	– ∧ slurs
Bass line:	written
Chords:	Ma triad, Ma triad (add 9th), Ma7 (9), mi triad, mi7 (9), mi7(♭5), Dom (♭5, ♭9, 9, ♯9, ♯11, ♭13, 13, sus)
Chord progression:	centered around B♭ and its relative minor
Dynamics:	*p, mp, mf, cresc, dim*
Edition:	8 1/2x11 vertical, 5 pages. Rehearsal letters every 8 bars
Expressive devices:	long gliss (all)
Form:	three 30 measure choruses with a 2-bar interlude, and a 6-bar coda ABAC with strophic melody
Guitar part:	chord symbols
Key:	B♭ Ma
Modulations:	none
Mutes:	harmon, cup, hat (tpts), hat (tbns)
Orchestration:	sectional
Piano part:	written and chord symbols
Style:	¾ ballad
Tempo:	quarter= 68
Voicings:	saxes (flutes): unison, 2–3–4–pt on coda tpts: unison, triads, 4-pt close, clus tbns: triad over bass, 4-pt close, 4ths, spreads, clus

Table C.3. "A Child Is Born" outline

Measure	1	2	3	4	5	6	7	8
Chord progression	B♭	E♭ mi/B♭	B♭ Ma7	E♭ mi/B♭	B♭ (add C)	E♭ mi/B♭	Ami7 (♭5)	D7 (♯9)
Pedal	B♭						pedal moves	
Roman Numeral	I	iv	I	iv	I	iv	vii–7(♭5)	V7/vi

Form and Texture:

The tune is presented immediately by the unaccompanied piano (8 bars), joined by the bass and light cymbal fills in the drums at measure 8 (as per recording), settling into time at letter B. On repeat the flugelhorn varies the 30-bar tune and the bass duets with it (see notes).

Two bars before letter C the ensemble enters with a dual function conclusion/interlude: these two measures serve as a harmonic conclusion (the tonic is sounded for the first time at the end of the 8-bar phrase), and formal balancing (they yield a 32-bar form). It serves also as an introduction, articulated by the ensemble entrance, to the ensemble statement of the tune that begins at letter C. The coda at letter G supplies a similar function of conclusion and extension, and is based on the same I–iv progression and melody of the first four bars. The ensemble chorus features unison saxes (flutes on recording) over harmonized brass, unison trumpets in counterpoint with the saxes, and concerted passages.

Melodic, Harmonic, and Rhythmic Materials:

The theme is comprised of four statements that begin identically (other than the first note of statement four) and conclude differently. The eight-bar melody can be divided into two segments, the first stationary (initial five bars) and the second variable (last three bars). The last statement is shortened by two bars by avoiding repetition of measures 2–3 of the melody, and concludes in the same way as the first statement. The melody is strophic (a, a1, a2, a3).

The theme uses scale degrees 1, 3, 4, and 5 for the first 7 bars, and then adds scale degrees 2, ♯4, and 6 beginning at m. 14.

The harmony follows the plan of the melody: the first five measures feature a one- or two-note pedal, while the last three measures move away from it (see table C.3).

The last of the four statements does not feature a pedal, so the return to the initial pedal at the top of the form is more effective.

Technique Highlight:

Hybrid Form

In a standard AABA tune both chord progression and melody follow the formal design. They will be similar in the A sections and contrasting in the B section. Mixing forms leads to hybrids. Two types of form are at work here: ABA1C for the chord progression and strophic form (a a1 a2 a3) for the melody. The a3 is a shortened a1. The interplay between melodic and harmonic material provides a subtle balance of repetition and contrast (see table C.4).

Making Music

The flugelhorn part is intended for an additional player. In the score it is written for tpt3. If it is played by tpt3 on flugelhorn, the player will need to have the trumpet in harmon ready to go at the last two measures of letter B. If this cannot be accomplished comfortably have them play those bars and the first one of letter C on flugelhorn and then switch to cup muted trumpet at measure 7 of letter C. Two out of three choruses are combo with flugelhorn solo. Feature your strongest ballad player who has a good sound and can embellish the melody and work with the rhythm section in creating the mood of this piece.

Phrasing and breathing spots on the recording don't match the ones in the score (saxes and trumpets letters C, D, E, F).

Self-Test Question 15

The breathing spots (end of phrases) for the counterline played on the recording by the trumpets in cup mutes at letter C mm. 7–8, and letter D mm. 1–4 are:

Table C.4. Melody-harmony relation in "A Child Is Born"

Measure	1	9	17	25
Melody	a	a1	a2	a3 or a1
Harmony	A	B	A1	C

a. Letter C, m. 8, after beat 2; Letter D, m. 4, after beat 2

b. Letter C, m. 8, after beat 2; Letter D, m. 2, after beat 2

c. Letter C, m. 8, after beat 2; Letter D, m. 2 and m. 4, after beat 2

d. Letter D, m. 2, after beat 2, and m. 4, after beat 2

Lead Sheet

The New Real Book. Vol 2. Sher Music Co., 1991.
The Real Book. 6th ed. Hal Leonard, 2004.

COTTONTAIL

Ellington, Duke 1940

Ellington, Duke, and Ben Webster 1940

Grade:	4
Duration:	3:08
Instrumentation:	5, 3, 3, 4. ts1 doubles on clarinet
Publisher:	Warner Brothers-Jazz@Lincoln Center
Recording:	Duke Ellington. *Never No Lament.* The Blanton-Webster Band. Bluebird (RCA/BMG) 5659-2. 3 CDs. Also on *Smithsonian Collection of Classic Jazz,* rev. ed. CBS special products RD 033, 1987. CD III.

Highest Written Notes:

Cl:	D (two ledger lines) plays only 16 bars (ensemble lead on letters G, H)
Tpt 1:	C (two ledger lines)
Tpt 2:	D (two ledger lines)
Tbn1:	B♭ (four ledger lines)
Tbn 2:	C (four ledger lines)

Solos:

(all written) tpt 2 (8 bars), t 2 (two choruses), bari (8 bars), pno (8 bars)

Soli:

br (M, N), saxes (Q, R, S, T)

Introductory Notes:

Notes on playing Ellington and rehearsal notes by David Berger, glossary, the four elements of music, instrumentation, original recording information, notes from Wynton Marsalis.

Form and Texture:

AABA form, no introduction or coda. The only form modification occurs in the first chorus where the last A is shortened to four bars. Climax is at letter W; it is the final B section, and is followed by the recapitulation of the A theme once (letter X). The work opens and closes with small band featuring trumpet with plunger, alto and baritone saxes, and trombone (letters A and X).

Table C.5. "Cottontail" outline

Chorus	1				2				3			
Letter	A	B	C	D	E	F	G	H	I	J	K	L
Form	A	A	B	A	A	A	B	A	A	A	B	A
# of measures	8	8	8	4	32				32			
texture	small band—		sax tutti bkg		br/cl bkg				br bkg			
Solo			tpt 2—		t2---							

Chorus	4				5				6 shout			
Letter	M	N	O	P	Q	R	S	T	U	V	W	X
Form	A	A	B	A	A	A	B	A	A	A	B	A
# of measures	32				32				32			
texture									call+ resp	tutti	small band	
Solo	br soli—		bari—	pno-	sax soli—							

At a Glance:

Articulation:	– > ∧ slurs
Bass line:	written
Chords:	Ma6, Ma7, mi7 (9, 11), mi7♭5, Dom7 (♭9, 9, #11, ♭5, #5, 13, sus4), dim7
Chord progression:	"Rhythm" changes (based on the chord progression of "I Got Rhythm" by George Gershwin)
Edition:	8 1/2x11 oblong. 24 pages. Rehearsal letters every eight bars, no measure numbers
Expressive devices:	fall-short (br), ghost (ts2), growl (tpt2, ts2) no vib (br) portamento (saxes)
Form:	AABA (six choruses)
Guitar part:	chord symbols
Key:	B♭ Ma
Modulations:	none
Mutes:	plunger (tpt2 A, B, C, D, X)
Orchestration:	writing across sections: theme at A (tpt w. plunger, as, bari, tbn), cl lead over br (G), lead exchange (as2 lead at C; tpt2 lead at U, V, W; tbn2 lead at U, V)
Piano:	chord symbols, some written chords, written solo
Shout:	letters U, V, W
Style:	swing
Tempo:	quarter=234 (fast)
Voicings:	saxes: uni, 4-pt close w. bari dbl. lead 8vb (Q, R, S, T), 5-pt (mostly stacked thirds, close or partially open position) tpts: 2-pt, 3-pt (triads, tertian, 4ths) tbns: 3-pt (triads or chord tones and one tension) br: 3-pt (triads or chord sound w. cl lead on tensions, G) 3–4-pt close (H), 6-pt (K), 4–5–6-pt (M, N)

Textures feature backgrounds (saxes, letter C), tutti (letters D and W), brass punctuations (letters G and H), and sustained chords (letter K), soli brass (letters M and N), soli saxes (letters Q, R, S, T), and call and response (saxes/br, letter U and V) (see table C. 5).

Melodic, Harmonic, and Rhythmic Materials:
The main melody and the melody of the sax soli were written by Ben Webster.

The main melody is based on the B♭ pentatonic (letter A mm. 1–4), and then expands to outline the complete B♭ major scale (letter A mm. 5–8). The sustained E natural (letter A m. 5) is a ♭5 blue note, and the last two bars feature a series of double chromatic approaches in a descending whole step sequence outlining different chord relations (m. 7, beat 2+ A=9th of G7, m. 7, beat 4+ G=5th of C7; m. 8, beat 2+ F=1 of F7).

The sax soli (letters Q, R, S, T) has an improvisatory feel, with arpeggios, approach notes, syncopations, and sequences, and is an extension of the soloists's style. Letter W (the shout) sequences and develops a two-bar syncopated figure.

The chord progression is based on "I Got Rhythm" changes in B♭ with various reharmonizations and passing chords.

Technique Highlight:

Harmonization in Four-part Close with Lead Doubled 8vb. The sax soli at letters Q–R–S–T is a textbook example of harmonization in 4-part close with lead doubled 8vb. The technique consists of voicing the chords from the lead down without skipping chord tones (1, 3, 5, 7). Substitutions are commonly used to increase the musicality of under lines. Frequently found is the substitution of the root of the chord with the 9th (known as "nine for one"). The bari sax doubles the lead 8vb. An example in the key of C major is shown in figure C.5. It uses a couple of 9 for 1 and 13 for 5 substitutions and some passing diminished chords.

Making Music
There are thorough notes on playing Ellington and rehearsal notes in the score. Help players be aware of the many lead exchanges: alto 2 lead on the B section (pick up to letter C), tpt 2 lead at letters U, V, and W; and tbn2 lead at letters U, V. Also, clarinet lead over brass at letter G (see comments for "Across the Track Blues"). Driving to a climactic tutti at the end or just

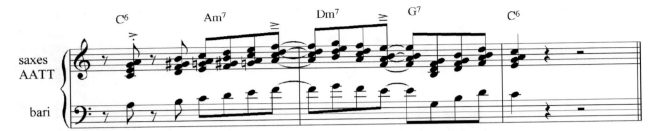

Figure C.5 Four part close saxophones with lead doubled 8VB.

before the end is a form that Ellington uses frequently in this period in his short three minute pieces (see "C Jam Blues" and "Harlem Airshaft"). Pacing is crucial to the dramatic ff call-and-response between brasses and saxes (letters U and V) that join in the climactic tutti concerted at letter W, followed by a drop to the mf combo head statement.

Self-Test Question 16
At Letter N, mm. 5–8, the cross rhythm in the tutti brass passage is:

    a. 5 over 4
    b. triplets against duplets
    c. 4 over 3
    d. 3 over 4

Lead Sheet
The Real Book. 6th ed. Hal Leonard, 2004.

For Further Reading
Gridley, Mark. *Jazz Styles: History and Analysis.* 8th ed. New Jersey: Prentice-Hall, 2003. Listening guide, pp. 109–110.

⸎

CUTE

Hefti, Neal 1958

Story, Mike 2000 (original is POP)

Grade:	2
Duration:	2:13
Instrumentation:	5, 3, 3, 4 (can be played with 3, 2, 1, 3) optional flute and tuba

Publisher:	Warner Bros.
Recording:	Count Basie and His Orchestra. *Corner Pocket.* Laserlight 15782 CD, 1992. Count Basie Orchestra. *Basie Plays "Hefti"* and also *The Best of the Roulette Years* (2 CDs) Roulette.

Highest Written Notes:

Tpt 1:	E♭ (on fourth space)
Tbn 1:	C (one ledger line)

Solos:
feature for drums

Introductory Notes:
The original is out of print. Given the high ranking of this chart in the multiple selection list, this version for young band is discussed instead since is gives a good representation of the piece. This arrangement can be played with as few as nine players: 3 saxes (as1, as2, ts1), two trumpets, one trombone, piano, bass, and drums. Two other arrangements are also available at this time.

Form and Texture:
Intro (4 bars) for solo drums, one AABA chorus (16 bars each section=64 measures), and a coda that repeats the last 8 bars of A adding an eighth-note run followed by the tonic note on beat four (last measure). Texture is tutti concerted (including the bass) in the A section where a pattern of call and response between drums and ensemble is followed. Phrasing is 2+2, compressed to 1+1 in measures 13–16.

    The contrasting B features the saxes accompanied by rhythm section time, with the bass walking, and brass punctuations. The brass is generally voiced in 3 to 5 parts, with the trumpets in unison or cascading to 2 and 3 parts (mm. 37–38).

At a Glance:

Articulation:	• – > ∧ slurs
Bass line:	written
Chords:	Ma triad, Ma 6 (9), mi6, mi7 (9), mi7 (♭5), Dom (♭9)
Chord progression:	secondary dominants (V/ii, V/iii, V/vi) and use of iv and v
Dynamics:	p, mp, mf, cresc, dim
Edition:	8 1/2x11 vertical, 8 pages. Measure numbers every bar, boxed numbers highlighting sections
Form:	intro (4), AABA (16 bars each), coda (8)
Guitar part:	chord symbols
Key:	B♭ Ma
Modulations:	none
Mutes:	none
Piano part:	written and chord symbols
Style:	swing
Tempo:	quarter= 138
Voicings:	saxes: 2-3-4-pt
	tpts: unison, 2-pt, 3-pt triads
	tbns: 2-pt, 3-pt triad, 4-pt.
	brass: 4/5-pt

Melodic, Harmonic, and Rhythmic Materials:

The main motive displays a characteristic rhythm beginning on the "and" of one (see figure C.6). This two-bar motive is compressed to one measure by eliding some of its inner values while maintaining the initial and final ones.

The drum response is similarly shortened to one measure (mm. 13–17). This creates an aaba phrasing design (the b is represented by the contrasting one-bar statements) within the AABA form.

There are six statements of the motive, with the melodic contours varying for each one; they work in tandem with the harmony to produce different cadences and melody-harmony relations (see table C.6).

As seen in the table, a perfect cadence (with root in the melody over tonic chord) occurs only in the final phrase, at the end of the section. The open harmonic design creates forward motion, propelling the dialogue with the drums.

The B section does not modulate but rather progresses from the subdominant back to the tonic (IV–iii–V/ii–ii–V7–I, mm. 25–31).

Technique Highlight:

Placement of the Upbeat
Placement of the upbeat determines where a rhythm or note on an upbeat is initiated.

Taking as an example two eighth notes on beat one in a 4/4 measure, the upbeat ("and" of one) can be attacked so that it is of the same length as the down beat (ratio=50/50) "even eighths,"or the upbeat can be placed higher so the ratio between length of downbeat and upbeat can change to 66.6/33.3 (generally indicated as "swing eighths), 70/30, 85/15, and so on. Most likely the two notes will still be notated as eighth notes, just they are played differently. The slower the tempo the higher the upbeat can be placed. Fast tempos with running eighth-note lines don't allow for maneuvering space for the application of this technique. The Basie band displays a vast range of interpretations of this principle, which is one of the factors for its prodigious swing feel.

Table C.6. Six statements of the motive in "Cute," with the melodic contours varying for each

Measure	6	10	13	15	18	22
Phrase	1	2	3	4	5	6
Final melodic note	third of chord	root	6th	minor third	5th	root
Harmony	B♭6	Fmi7	E♭mi6	Gmi7	D6/9	B♭6
Roman numeral	I	v	iv	vi	III	I

Two-bar motive   One-bar motive

Figure C.6 Characteristic rhythms in "Cute," beginning on the "and" of one.

Making Music

This is a showcase to feature your drummer's brush work, inventiveness with short solo breaks and setting up ensemble figures. The concerted chords need to be in balance. Play just lead and bass to hear their relation. Measure 57 is marked mp, then end with a whisper.

The Basie recordings feature generally faster tempos (half=96–120), the introduction is opened up for various choruses of piano and rhythm section (see "All of Me"), solo choruses are added (flute), sax soli, and additional head out. Brass is in cup mutes.

Self-Test Question 17

In the first eight measures of the contrasting B section (mm. 25–32) the saxes are voiced:

a. 3-part, in 3rds
b. 4-part in 4ths
c. 2-part, in 3rds
d. 4-part, in clusters

D

DAAHOUD

Brown, Clifford 1962

Taylor, Mark 2001

Grade:	3
Duration:	3:27
Instrumentation:	5, 4, 4, 4, aux perc.
Publisher:	Second Floor Music
Recording:`	Hal Leonard 2001-02 Demo Easy Edition, CD 2.

Highest Written Notes:

Tpt 1:	A♭ (one ledger line)
Tbn 1:	F (two ledger lines)

Solos:
tpt 1 and ts 1 (32 bars, as written or ad lib)

Introductory Notes:
None

Form and Texture:
Five-bar introduction, followed by a 36-measure form (32-bar AABA with a 4-bar tutti concerted section at the end). The concerted section is like the intro and begins on m. 31; it serves as a launching pad for the solos. The solo section is on the 36-bar form, with sax and brass backgrounds, and the concerted section at the end. After the solos there is a repeated 8-bar interlude that features a tutti ensemble passage based on the A section tune, followed by a four-bar solo by the drums. The *dal segno* is to the bridge (m. 16). The

At a Glance:

Articulation:	– > ʌ slurs
Bass line:	written
Chords:	Ma6, Ma7 (9), mi7 (9, 11), mi7(♭5), Dom (♭9, 9, ♯9, ♯5, 13)
Chord progression:	see Melodic, Harmonic, and Rhythmic Materials
Dynamics:	*mf, f, ff, cresc, dim*
Edition:	8 1/2x11 oblong, 11 pages. Measure numbers every bar, boxed numbers highlighting sections
Form:	intro (4), AABA (32), C (4, same as intro), AABAC (36) solo section, D (16) interlude, BA, Coda (4)
Guitar part:	melodic line, chord symbols
Key:	E♭ Ma
Modulations:	none
Mutes:	none
Orchestration:	unison head (tpt, ts, g, vib), voicings across sections (as, ts, bari, tpt, tbn, guitar on bridge mm. 16–22), (as, ts 1, ts 2, tpt, tbn backgrounds mm. 52–58)
Piano:	written throughout
Style:	bebop
Tempo:	quarter=160
Voicings:	saxes: uni, 2-, 3-, 4-pt tpts: uni, 2-pt, 3-pt, triads, triads with tpt 4 doubling lead 8vb tbns: uni, 3-pt, triads (closed and open), spreads

Table D.1. Chord progression in "Daahoud"

Measure	1	2	3	4	5	6	7–8
Section	A						
Chord Progr.	Eb-7 Ab7	Db-7 Gb7	BMa7	(Fmi7 Bb7 in original)	Ab-7 Gb7	F7 E6	Eb Ma7
Roman Num.	iii V/ii	ii V	I		iv ucd	V/V bII	I
Key	B (bVI)			Eb: (I)			

Measure	1	2	3	4	5	6	7–8
Section	B						
Chord Progression	Bb-7	Eb7	AbMa7		Ab-7	Db7	GbMa7
Roman Numerals	ii	V	I		ii	V	I
Key	Ab (IV)				Gb (bIII)		

four-bar coda begins with a drum solo fill followed by a unison figure by the soli line-up (trumpet, tenor, guitar, and vibraphone).

The A theme is presented in unison by trumpet, tenor, guitar, and vibraphone, with backgrounds on the repeat. The bridge features voicings across sections (alto, tenor, baritone, trumpet, trombone, and guitar). On the last A (m. 24) a trumpet counterline is added.

Melodic, Harmonic, and Rhythmic Materials:

The tune is in Clifford Brown's original key of Eb major, with eighth-note hard bop style lines using arpeggios, anticipations, and approaches. The bridge opens with a minor 7th ascending interval followed by a repeated note figure. The four-bar phrase is sequenced down a step. The introduction features a three note motive (Db, B, Bb) sequenced in descending fourths (mm. 1–3).

The A section harmony opens with a chord progression in the key of B major (bVI of the home key Eb). In the original, the tonic chord Eb is reached at m. 5 of the section, while here a detour beginning with Ab-7 (iv) delays the cadence on Eb to the last two bars of the form. The B section features a four-bar II–V–I sequence in Ab (IV) and Gb (bIII) (see table D.1).

Technique Highlight:

Small Group "Band Within a Band" Writing
Frequently a small group of instruments is extracted from the larger ensemble to play the main melody in a combo-style presentation. This technique of pitting a small group against the rest of the ensemble has many precedents such as the baroque era concerto grosso in Western music and many examples in musics from the world, and has parallels in other performing arts such as dance.

This is similar to *soli* writing, which features instruments rhythmically concerted and in harmony (see "Cottontail," "Cherry Juice," "Groove Merchant," and "TipToe"), though soli tend to showcase a section in an improvisatory sounding passage rather than present the main melody. When in unison as here, it is sometimes called *soli unison*. Most likely writing across sections it involved (see "Big Jim Blues"). For a harmonized example of "band within a band" presentation of the melody see "A Minor Excursion."

Making Music

Everything is clearly marked in this chart, including a thorough part for the drums, with many ensemble figures, solo fills, and one-bar breaks. The breaks highlight the pickups to the head (mm. 13–14) and to the interlude (m. 31), and are used also in the solo section. The apex is at m. 73. Bring down the volume for the D.S. to m. 16 so there is some contrast.

Self-Test Question 18

The bridge melody at mm. 16–22 features voicings across sections (alto, tenor, baritone, trumpet, trombone, and guitar). The voicings are:

a. 4-part close
b. clusters
c. Upper Structure Triads
d. 5-part with lead 8vb

Lead Sheet

The Real Book. 6th ed. Hal Leonard, 2004.

⚬⚬

DING DONG DING

Brookmeyer, Bob 1979

Brookmeyer, Bob 1980

Grade:	5
Duration:	6:00
Instrumentation:	5, 5, 4, 4 (as 1 on ss 1, as 2 on ss 2 with substitute part for as, tpt 5 on flug)
Publisher:	Kendor Music
Recording:	Mel Lewis Orchestra. *Bob Brookmeyer, Composer and Arranger.* Finesse, 1982, CD.

Highest Written Notes:

Tpt 1:	D (two ledger lines)
Tpt 2:	C (two ledger lines)
Tbn 1:	C (four ledger lines)
Tbn 2:	Bb (four ledger lines)

Solos:
ss 1feature, dms (8), pno (unaccompanied, 1 minute)

Introductory Notes:
Composer's biographical sketch

Form and Texture:
There is a four-measure introduction.The form is strophic variation. The main head is comprised of 16 bars with various modifications: the first presentation (mm. 5–20) is extended to 20 measures by a codetta, the second chorus (mm. 29–52) is 24, the third (letter A) is 35 (17 +18), and the fourth (letter C) is 22. Soprano sax solo form is five times at letter E and twice at letter F. At Letter G (22 bars) soprano plays around ensemble and wraps up solo. An unaccompanied piano solo for about a minute follows at letter H1.

After the piano solo the *dal segno* is to m. 29 and the soprano solo continues through the coda sign (letter J) and interacts with an ad libitum ensemble (letters K and L). The actual coda is at letter M, after the head is played both in Db (letter J) and "played loosely" twice in the key of F major in augmentation

At a Glance:

Articulation:	> ≥ ∧ slurs
Bass line:	written
Chords:	intervallic structures, Ma7 (9, #11), mi7 (9, 11), mi7(b5), Dom (b9, #11, b5, 13, sus)
Chord progression:	modal and intervallic construction over pedal points, functional tonality passages with ii–V–I temporary tonicizations
Dynamics:	*ppp, pp, p, mp, mf, f, ff, fff, sf, sfz, sfp,* cresc., *cresc. poco a poco,* dim., *gradual decresc.*
Edition:	8 1/2x11 vertical, 14 pages. Boxed numbers highlighting sections until measure 52, rehearsal letters from measure 53 to end.
Expressive devices:	bend pitch up and down, slow-medium-fast trill (all), gliss (bari), long drop (ss saxes), slow gliss/flutter tongue (tbn 2)
Form:	strophic with interludes
Guitar:	chord symbols
Key:	C Ma
Modulations:	to Db Ma and FMa, progressive tonality
Mutes:	in stand (brass)
Orchestration:	SSTTB saxes
Piano:	written, chord symbols, and ad lib with rhythm outlined
Tempo:	half note=140
Time feel:	even eighths
Voicings:	ens: 9-tone pyramid, 6-note clusters, 7-note "complete major scale" clusters

(letters K and L). Measure markings end at m. 52. Rehearsal letters continue from there to the end.

Various ad libitum sections add variety and improvisational quality to the mainly tutti concerted texture. First soprano sax ad libs on dal segno repeat (letter B), plays around or over the ensemble (letters G, J, and

Table D.2. "Ding, Dong, Ding" outline

Measure/letter	1	5		29	A	B
Material	Intro	A	A	Interlude/A	A	A
Number of bars	4	20	20	8+8+8	16+1	16+2
Texture	pno solo vamp	piano tune ens. pyramid		dms groove, bass and piano pedal	ss 1 and 2 soli unis. + rhy and ens.	tutti concerted
Key center	C					chord changes

Measure/letter	C	D	E	F	G
Material	A	A			A
Number of bars	8+8	6	24	8	
Texture	ss 1 and 2 canon, brass pitch bends	tutti	sustained bkgr	ss 1 and 2 soli unis. + rhy and ens.	tutti concerted
Key center	Db		C	Db	chr to E and other key centers
Solo			Soprano 1		

Measure/letter	H	H1	D.S. m. 29, A , B	J K L	M Coda
Material	A			A	A
Number of bars	16	6		16 +16+16	16
Texture	rhy. section	unaccompanied pno		tutti, ens ad lib	canon
Key center	C	ad lib		Db	F
Solo	Soprano 1	pno	Soprano 1 at B	Soprano 1	

Figure D.1 "Ding, Dong, Ding" rhythmic motive

L), and ad libs notes while following the rhythmic motive of the melody (letter H). The melody is "played loosely" at letter K, and players not playing the melody ad lib while following the indicated rhythm.

Other devices such as progressive bending of the pitch up and down on the Ab pedal and progressive slow-medium-fast trills add textural variety (letter C) (see table D.2).

Melodic, Harmonic, and Rhythmic Materials:
The main melody is diatonic to C major and features a characteristic two-bar rhythmic motive (the "Ding, Dong, Ding" motive: half, dotted quarter, eighth tied over to a whole note) (see figure D.1).

It outlines C major by beginning on the pitch C (m. 5), and by cadencing on C, preceded by the leading tone (m. 20). The open fifth G–C piano ostinato reinforces the C tonality. Beginning at measure 8 the ensemble introduces a 9-part pyramid structure on F#–Ab–F–E–Eb–B–Bb–A–C# that builds to a triple forte (m. 28).

At letter A, m. 9 the trombones in fifths (C–G–D) support a seven note "complete C major scale" cluster in the ensemble. Sections over pedal points are contrasted with sections featuring harmonic progressions (letters B, D, and G) that provide variety to the static pedal points. These harmonic progressions feature tonicizations of various key areas and lead to modulations: the first to Db, the second and third back to C. The third passage features a descending and ascending chromatic bass that leads to and away from the key of E major.

Pedal points are on C and Db. The Db pedal at letter C is reinforced by a dominant pedal on Ab in the ensemble. The C pedal becomes a dominant pedal in the recapitulation of the head in the key of F at letter K. Progressive tonality is used, with the piece ending in F major.

Technique Highlight:

Clusters: 7-Note
Clusters are voicings predominantly in seconds (see "Airegin"). Here complete scales such as the com-

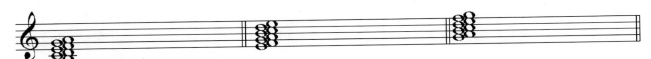

Figure D.2 Seven-part cluster voicings using the C major scale

plete C major scale are used at letter A m. 9. The voicing spans one octave and is a "verticalized" scale or "white note" collection (see figure D.2). Modes are similarly used.

Making Music

Careful score study will help navigate this chart, paying attention to dynamics (in clusters, canons, pads), effects (piano blurred music box effect, bending of pitch up and down, progressive slow-medium-fast trills, long drops), ad lib ensemble parts, and the setting of the overall mood. Soprano and piano can really stretch out.

Self-Test Question 19

The seven-note cluster at letter M m. 9 outlines the complete:

    a. C major scale
    b. C mixolydian mode
    c. C minor scale
    d. F diminished scale

DON'T GIT SASSY

Jones, Thad 1970

Jones, Thad 1970

Grade:	5
Duration:	7:20
Instrumentation:	5, 4, 4, 4 (as1 doubles on ss)
Publisher:	Kendor Music
Recording:	Thad Jones/Mel Lewis Orchestra. *Live at the Village Vanguard.* Blue Note 7243 5 60438 2 4 CD. Reissued in *The Complete Solid State Recordings of the Thad Jones/Mel Lewis Orchestra.* Mosaic Records MD5-151,

five CDs, 1994. Out of print. The first minute (then fades out) is also on Thad Jones/Mel Lewis Orchestra-Woody Herman & His Swinging Herd. *Ralph Gleason's Jazz Casual.* Koch Jazz KOC CD-8563.

Highest Written Notes:

Tpt 1:	D♭ (two ledger lines), E♭ (three ledger lines, on final chord only)
Tbns 1-4:	A♭ (three ledger lines)

Solos:

tpt 2 (16 bars, open), tpt 3 (8 bars), tpt 4 (8 bars), ts 2 (16 bars, open, + 8 bars),

Soli:

saxes (16 bars)

Introductory Notes

Brief Thad Jones biography

Form and Texture:

The basic section is 8 bars. The eight-bar tutti introduction is derived from A1 (it shares with it its last two bars). An open "groove" section for rhythm section and piano solo follows (letter A, played six times on the live recording). The head is organized melodically as A B C A1 over the basic 8-bar progression that undergoes much reharmonization (letters A, B, C, D)

The solo section chorus for trumpets begins with an open section (letter F), followed by two 8-bar sections with backgrounds (letters G and H), and another ad lib section (letter I). The A1 head acts as an interlude (letter J) that sets up the tenor solo that has an ad lib section (letter K), and one with call-and-response tutti ensemble (letter L).

A sax section soli (letters M and N) leads to the shout (letter O) in call and response between unison brass and harmonized saxes (letter O), two restatements of A (letter P) and a climactic coda.

At a Glance:

Articulation:	– > ∧ accent over tenuto, slurs
Bass line:	written walking bass with obbligato melodic lines with the ensemble, chord symbols and written walking bass for solo sections.
Chords:	mi7 (9, 11), Dom (7, 9, ♯11, ♯5, ♭13, 13, alt, octatonic), dim
Chord progression:	centered around D♭7 (blues inflected I7), IV7, secondary dominants, and chromatic dominant sequences (both ascending and descending). Characteristic bass line (I7, IV7, ♯IV diminished, I7 over its 5th) featured on first two bars (letters B and E).
Dynamics:	*p, mp, mf, f, cresc*
Edition:	8 1/2x11 vertical, 10 pages. Letters every 8 bars. No measure numbers.
Expressive devices:	bend, lift, fall, trill, gliss (saxes), bend, short gliss up, gliss down, fall, shake (brass)
Form:	the basic chord progression is 8 bars. Head is 32 and is recapitulated as 16, intro, and coda. Mostly through composed, see Form and Texture.
Guitar part:	chord symbols and rhythm slashes
Key:	D♭ Ma
Modulations:	none
Mutes:	none
Orchestration:	SATTB : soprano lead on sax soli (letters M, N)
Piano part:	chord symbols and rhythm slashes, written voicings (letter A)
Shout:	letter O, continuing to the end through the restatement of the head and the coda
Style:	shuffle
Tempo:	quarter=148
Voicings:	saxes: 4-pt/5-pt open (no root and over root)
	tpts: unis, triads (dbl lead 8vb), 4-pt closed, clusters,
	tbns: 4-pt closed, spreads (chord sound and one tension)

Table D.3. "Don't Git Sassy" outline

Letter	A	B C D E	F G H I	J	K L
Material	Intro	head	solos	head	solos
Number of bars	8+ 8 with open repeats	32	32 with open repeats	8	16 with open repeats

Letter	M N	O	P	
Material	sax soli	shout	head	Coda
Number of bars	8+ 8 open repeats	32	16	8

Melodic, Harmonic, and Rhythmic Materials:

The tune is constructed on D♭ pentatonic, with the ♭5 as a lower neighbor (last bar of letter B), and the added 4th and ♭3 degrees (G♭ and E, second to the last bar of letter E). The difference between sections A and A1 is in the last two measures: A features a repeated D♭–A♭ fanfare-like motive in the trumpets where the note A♭ (5th degree) remains unresolved. A1 resolves the A♭ to the tonic D♭, closing melodi-cally the section. This closure is reinforced by the harmony that remains open (last chord is always V7 or subV7) at the end of the first three 8-bar sections (letters B, C, D), but closes in the tonic D♭7 in the final section (letter E).

The D♭–A♭ motive is extended through the coda with trumpets and trombones in canon at the octave featuring shakes on the A♭, culminating with the resolution to high D♭ in the final bar.

Table D.4. The basic eight-bar chord progression at letter F

D♭7	G♭7 Go	D♭7 B♭7	E♭7 A♭7	D♭7	G♭7 Go	D♭ C♭7 B♭7 E7	E♭7 A♭7 D♭

The basic eight-bar chord progression is constantly reharmonized often using the reharmonization of each note of the melody with a different harmony approach (see "Cherry Juice"). It is illustrated in table D.4 in its simplest form for the solo at letter F.

Much material is through composed, though A1 does return as an interlude between the two solo sections, and A returns twice at the end. A and A1 are connected by a sustained tonic pedal in the trombones (letters C and D).

Technique Highlight:

Hocket
A technique where a melodic line is distributed between two or more lines resulting in one sounding when the other ones pause. Traditionally involving two voices, here (mm. 1–5) it involves three (see figure D.3).

Making Music
This is a shuffle groove with a back beat. The solo section allows for solos by each of the four trumpet players, though any number can be used, so gear it to your trumpet section's strength. Same for the tenor sax solo (played 7 times on the recording). The piano at letter A grooves and introduces the melody; probably not the place to show off, but rather to establish these important elements at the outset. Go through all articulations with recording and mark exact durations in score.

Self-Test Question 20
On the *Live at the Village Vanguard* recording the trumpet at letter F improvises:

    a. twice
    b. three times

    c. four times
    d. seven times

DUKE ELLINGTON'S SOUND OF LOVE

Mingus, Charles 1974

Walrath, Jack 1993

Grade:	6
Duration:	7:36
Instrumentation:	5, 3, 3, 3 (doublings: as 1 to cl and ts 1-2 to flts on mm. 46–53 background)
Publisher:	Hal Leonard
Recording:	Mingus Big Band. *Mingus Big Band 93*. Dreyfus FDM 36559-2 CD.
	Original quintet recording on Charles Mingus's *Changes One*. Rhino 1993, CD (original LP released as Atlantic 1677, 1975).

Highest Written Notes:
Tpt 1:   F♯ (three ledger lines)
Tbn 1:   A♭ (three ledger lines)

Solos:
bass feature (one 32-bar chorus + cadenza)

Soli:
saxes (13 bars)

Introductory Notes:
None

Form and Texture:
32 measures long, the form features a unique rearrangement of melodic, harmonic, and rhythmic elements. Traditional points of articulation are also blurred or displaced. The original quintet version is followed. The

Figure D.3 Hocket

At a Glance:

Articulation:	slurs
Bass line:	chord symbols, short written passages including dyads (played as double stops)
Chords:	Ma7 (6, 9, #11), mi7 (9, 11), Dom (7, 9, ♭9, #9, #11, ♭5, #5, 13, mixo, oct)
Chord progression:	ii–V–I sequences, secondary dominants (V/ii, V/vi), substitute dominants (♭II7, sub V7/iii), chords borrowed from the minor (♭IIIMa7, ♭IIMa7)
Dynamics:	*pp, p, mp, mf, f, ff, cresc, dim*
Edition:	8 1/2x11 oblong, 14 pages. Measure numbers every bar, boxed numbers highlighting sections
Expressive devices:	+ O plunger (brass)
Form:	32-measure form, through composed with the exception of the last 5 bars that return after having been previously played.
Key:	D♭ Ma
Modulations:	none
Mutes:	plunger (brass), cup (tpts)
Piano part:	chord symbols, written final chord
Style:	ballad (swing and even eighths)
Tempo:	quarter=64
Time feel:	in 4, double time feel
Voicings:	saxes: unis, 3-pt close, 4-pt close and open, 5-pt open, spreads
	tpts: 2-pt (in 2nds), 3-pt (tertian, non-tertian, quartal)
	tbns: 2-pt, 3-pt (tertian, non-tertian, quartal, spreads)
	brass: 5-pt

first measure creates the first formal ambiguity: it has the character of an introduction (the tune and the rhythm section enter in measure 2), but it is also an integral part of the form (each subsequent chorus starts with it). A harmonically closed 12-bar section A follows (begins and ends in D♭ major). The contrasting B section is 14 bars (mm. 14–27), followed by A1 (restating only the last four measures of A: mm. 28–31=mm. 10–13), with an additional bar (m. 32). Considering the first bar part of the form rather than an introduction, the form reads as A (13), B (14), A1 (5) (see table D.5).

The two choruses that follow reinforce this design: the first begins with a bass solo (m. 33), and the second with a sax soli in double time feel (m. 65). The recapitulation is at m. 88 (pickup at m. 87) on the last four bars of the B section. The A1 of this last chorus features two additional measures: m. 94 is a bass cadenza, and the final chord is extended (m. 98).

Melodic, Harmonic, and Rhythmic Materials:
Melodic material is through composed with the exception of the last 5 bars. Beginning in m. 2, the A section phrasing can be read as a (2), a1 (2), b (2), b1 (2), c (2). Other readings are possible, given that the contrasting phrases are based on same rhythmic motive.

The harmony of the A section closes in D♭ major (m. 13), while in A1 the tonic chord is followed by D major (♭II), with the melody also ascending by a half step. This is also the final harmony, to which blue notes (♭3, ♭5, and ♭7) are added (m. 98). The B section features a series of ii–V–I tonicizations of transient tonics (EMa, DMa, CMa, A♭Ma). The return to D♭ major in the last four bars of the B section creates a strong formal articulation (a return to the tonic), that does not coincide with the melodic material (still part of the contrasting section), adding further possible interpretations to the design of the piece.

Technique Highlight:

Tonicization
Tonicization is the process of cadencing to major or minor chords beyond the primary tonic. This is accomplished by using cadential patterns such as ii–Vs and substitute ii–Vs (a tritone away) at the secondary dominant level, and upper chromatic Major 7th chords such as ♭II Ma7.

The chord patterns can be arranged in virtually any cycle: cycle 2 (down a step or half step, cycle 3 (in thirds), cycle 5, and so on. Mingus uses cycle 2

Table D.5. Duke Ellington's "Sound of Love" outline

Measure	1			33			65	88 (recap)	
Form	A	B	A1	A	B	A1	A	B	A1
Number of bars	13	14	5 (=32)	13	14	5 (=32)	13	14	5 +2 (cadenza and final chord (=34)

(down a whole step) in tonicizing the first three keys of the B section (EMa, DMa, CMa). Each cadential pattern creates a temporary or transient tonic:

| F♯ mi7 B7 | EMa7 | Emi7 A7 | DMa7 | Dmi7 G7 | CMa7 |

Though it is a type of modulation, tonicization differs from it because modulation is generally understood as a move to a new key and its establishment rather than touching on fleeting keys.

Making Music

This tune is more than a nod to Billy Strayhorn's "Lush Life," which can be played or given as a listening assignment. The bass is featured and the sax soli is a transcription and harmonization of Charles Mingus's solo by Jack Walrath.

In this arrangement there are three basic time feels: cadenza (no time), for the bass at m. 94, single time (ballad), and double time feel for the sax soli (m. 65). Transitions need to be seamless and not to drag or speed up. Practice the measures around the transitions.

On the recording there is a trumpet and piano cadenza before bar 1, where they play loosely the last nine bars of the tune; something you might want to adopt. The two main interpretations of the beat are triplet feel and even eighths. Make up exercises alternating the two. Also, see placement of the upbeat discussion in "Cute."

Self-Test Question 21

At the recapitulation (pickup to m. 88) the two trumpets carrying the melody play in:

a. octaves and switch to harmony at m. 91
b. harmony and switch to octaves at m. 91
c. two-part counterpoint
d. unison until the bass cadenza

Lead Sheet

Homzy, Andrew, ed. *Charles Mingus: More Than a Fake Book.* Jazz Workshop/Hal Leonard, 1991, p. 28.

E

ECCLUSIASTICS

Mingus, Charles 1961

Johnson, Sy 1993

Grade:	5
Duration:	5:58
Instrumentation:	5, 3, 2+ tuba or btbn, 3
Publisher:	Hal Leonard
Recording:	Mingus Big Band. *Mingus Big Band 93.* Dreyfus FDM 36559-2 CD.
	Original sextet recording on Charles Mingus's *Oh Yeah.* Atlantic Jazz, 1988, CD (original analog disc SD 1377, 1962).

Highest Written Notes:
Tpt 1:   D (two ledger lines)
Tbn 1:   C (four ledger lines)

Solos:
feature for tenor saxes: one chorus each (with optional repeat), tenor battle (open 8-bar section on two-chord vamp + 6 bars, and 7 final bars at the end of the piece). Tpt 1 plays a written 4-bar solo (mm. 19–22), and screech improvisation on the final 7 bars

Introductory Notes:
None

Form and Texture:
The 12-bar form is divided into four short sections (ABCD) of 4, 2, 3, and 3 measures by its melodic,

At a Glance:

Articulation:	> ≥ ∧ slurs
Bass line:	written, chord symbols, and rhythm slashes
Chords:	Ma triads, Ma7, mi7 (9, 11), Dom (7, 9, ♭9, ♯9, ♯11, ♭5, ♯5, 13 sus, alt, lyd ♭7)
Chord progression:	2-chord ostinato (I7–IV7), secondary dominants (V7/vi, V7/ii), progressions in minor thirds, chords borrowed from the minor (♭III, ♭VI, ♭VII). Tonic and dominant chords as triads and also as dominant quality chords derived from the blues
Dynamics:	*mp, mf, f, ff, fff, cresc, dim*
Edition:	8 1/2x11 oblong, 11 pages. Measure numbers every bar, boxed numbers highlighting sections
Expressive devices:	gradual smear, smear (saxes) gliss (bari sax, tuba), smear, doit, fall, shake (brass), portamento (tbn)
Form:	intro (2, opt open vamp), six 12-bar choruses (head twice, ts2 solo, ts1 solo, tenor sax battle, head out), coda (5). The tenor sax battle chorus adds an open section on the two-chord introduction and does not include the first six measures of the form
Key:	F Ma
Modulations:	none
Mutes:	plunger (tpt1, solo), harmon (tpts)
Piano part:	written chords and lines, chord symbols, and rhythm slashes
Shout:	none, but choruses 5 and 6 are climactic
Style:	eclectic (bluesy, churchy/gospel, jazzy), swing and even eigths
Tempo:	quarter=60–64
Time feel:	in 2, in 4, double time gospel feel, 12/8 feel
Voicings:	saxes: 2-pt (duet), 3-pt (tertian), 4-pt open
	tpts: unis, 2-pt (in 3rds), 3-pt (open and closed triads, non-tertian)
	tbns: 2-pt, 3-pt (open triads in root position), 3-pt spreads

rhythmic, dynamic, and time feel content. This design is followed throughout, with the exception of chorus 5 (m. 49), where only sections C and D are played, making the return of the A section head (m. 63) sound fresher.

The intro is a two-chord vamp. It is found again in chorus 5 as an open section for the tenor battle. The final D section (m. 72) is extended by a 5-bar coda using the same two chord pattern. A, B, C, and D feature contrasting styles (blues, double time gospel in even eighths and sixteenths, 12/8 triplet feel with strong back beat), and textures (sustained chordal with rapid arpeggios, contrapuntal with solo or duet improvisation).

Melodic, Harmonic, and Rhythmic Materials:
A (m. 1) is based on the pentatonic major scale (F–G–A–C–D) with a melodic contour that ascends and gradually smears into the major 7th E at the peak of the line, followed by the ♭7th E♭. The ♭3 and ♯5 are also included as approach and passing tones (pickup and m.1).

The B section (m. 5) features a hocket between open triads in the trombones and unison trumpets in descending arpeggios. The first three notes of the arpeggios are unvaried while the final one (and its approach notes) changes. One way to look at them is as a harmonic superimposition of the trumpets over the trombone major triads (B♭ triad /B♭ triad, G–7/D♭ triad, B♭7/E triad mm. 5–6) leading to the concerted GMa7 (m. 6, beat 3). Root motion here is in ascending minor thirds.

Section C (m. 7) features a melodic sequence in descending minor thirds over root motion in cycle 5. Section D (m. 11) emphasizes melodically the tonic note and the ♭3rd, and harmonically the blues I7 and IV7 chords first found in the intro (see table E.1).

Technique Highlight:

Expressive Devices
See discussion in "Big Dipper"

Table E.1. Chord progression mm. 1–12

m.1		2		3		4		5		6	
F	G-7	A-7	B♭		B7 E7	A-7	D7	B♭	D♭	E	GMa7
I	ii	iii	IV		G: V/vi V/ii	ii	V7	minor 3rd cycle			IMa7

7		8		9		10		11		12	
C	F	B♭	E♭	A♭	D♭	G-7	C7	F7	B♭7	F7	B♭7
F: V	I	IV	♭VII	♭III	♭VI	ii	V7	I7	IV7	I7	IV7

Making Music

The chart is a kaleidoscope of different feels, moods, and styles, packed into a 12-bar form. Expressive devices and stylistic approaches are clearly marked ("bluesy," "churchy," "jazzy," "gospel") and so are time feels (in 2, in 4, double time gospel feel, 12/8 feel). Each of the sections needs to have its own individual character, and it might be a challenge to switch quickly from one to another, as they are so short, and one does not want to be still feeling the mood of the previous one while the music moves on. Each section has it own dynamic curve and so does the main section, and the piece as a whole, driving to the climactic coda.

Self-Test Question 22

The harmony revolves around F major and the key of:

  a. A major
  b. G major
  c. D minor
  d. C major

Lead Sheet

The Real Book. 6th ed. Hal Leonard, 2004.

  Homzy, Andrew, ed. *Charles Mingus: More Than a Fake Book.* Jazz Workshop/Hal Leonard, 1991, p. 42

⏤⏤⏤

Duration:	5:35
Instrumentation:	5, 4, 4, 4
Publisher:	Kendor Music
Recording:	Bob Mintzer. *Art of the Big Band.* DMP 1991 CD.

Highest Written Notes:

Tpt 1:   D (two ledger lines), one G (four ledger lines)

Tbn 1:   A♭ (three ledger lines)

Solos:

open for solos (32 bars, for ts1, tpt4, tbn2), open for more solos (8 bars, same instruments), and for a drums and percussion section (m. 90)

Introductory Notes:
None

At a Glance:

Articulation:	• – > ∧ ≥ slurs
Bass line:	written ostinato and chord symbols
Chords:	triads (add 2), Ma7 (6, 9), mi7 (9, 11), Dom 7 (♭9, 9, ♯9, ♯11, ♯5, 13, sus, alt, oct)
Chord progression:	A section features four chords: I7sus, ♭VII7, IV, V7♯9; B section features a dominant cycle 5 chain (with one chord being major rather than dominant quality) and a ii–V back to the tonic F.
Dynamics:	*mp, mf, f, sfz, cresc, dim*
Edition:	8 1/2x11 vertical, 8 pages. Measure numbers every bar, boxed numbers highlighting sections

ELVIN'S MAMBO

Mintzer, Bob 1989

Mintzer, Bob 1989

Grade: 4

Expressive devices:	(all) fall, spill (out of tempo, on the final chord)
Form:	intro (16) AABB head (32, repeated), A1 (8, repeated), AABB (open for solos), A1 (8, repeated), C (8, repeated 4 times), A (8, open for more solos), AABB head out (32), A1 (8, repeated), coda (7)
Guitar part:	written ostinato, chord symbols, and melodic line with the ensemble
Key:	F Ma
Modulations:	none
Mutes:	none
Piano part:	written ostinato, chord symbols, and melodic line with the ensemble
Shout:	layered ostinato (mm. 90–107) is climactic
Style:	Latin jazz
Tempo:	half=120
Voicings:	saxes: unis, 2-pt
	tpts: unis, 2-pt, 3-pt (triads with lead doubled 8vb), 4-pt close, sw
	tbns: unis, 2-pt, 3-pt (tertian and quartal), 4-pt close, 4-pt spreads
	brass: 2-pt (unison tpts and unis tbns creating two part harmony)
	tbns: sus with Ma3rd above the 4th

Form and Texture:

32-bar binary form with each part repeated (AABB), and an A1 (8+8) section returning at various points throughout giving it a rondo quality. After the intro (mm. 1–16) the head is presented in two-part harmony by the saxes, with the brass joining on repeat also in two-part harmony. The B section features unison saxes accompanied by trombones, with the trumpets joining in on the repeat with a sustained unison line. A1 (m. 42) is a variation of A in 6- and 7-part harmony.

Solos are on the form (trombone plays two choruses on the recording). A1 returns (m. 82), and is followed by a contrasting C section (m. 90) repeated four times: (1) drum set and congas; (2) add saxes, guitar, piano, bass; (3) and (4) add brass punctuations and tenor sax solo fills. This layered ostinato builds to a climax and launches an A (8 bars) section open for more solos (tenor sax transitions from the previous fills to a full-fledged fifteen 8-bar chorus solo on recording). *Dal segno* brings the repeat of the AABB head, though on the recording the first A is omitted. A1 is repeated and leads into a 7-bar coda.

Melodic, Harmonic, and Rhythmic Materials:

The A section melody is based on the F mixolydian mode. The two-bar ostinato uses four pitches (C–D–Eb–F) in the bass and triads and quartal harmonies that yield a I7sus–bVII7–IV–V7 #9 progression. The bVII7 chord is a sus chord with the 3rd scale degree used as a tension tone a major 7th above the 4th scale degree.

The IV chord is a triad in first inversion with an added second scale degree. The B section melody is built from a two-bar motive based on a major triad arpeggio with added scale degree 2. This motive is sequenced through the harmonies moving in cycle 5. The harmonies are altered dominants (G7, C7, F7, from the altered scale), dominant 7 sus 4 (expressed as a major 7th chord over bass note: AbMa7 over Bb), dominant 7 chords derived from the octatonic scale (Bb13 b9, Ab13 #11, C13 b9 #11), and a major 7 chord in second inversion (EbMa9 over Bb) that is temporarily tonicized. The EbMa9 is followed by a pivot chord (Ab13, m. 36) that leads back to the tonic key through a II–V (mm. 38–41).

Technique Highlight:

Sus 4 Chord with 3rd of Chord above the 4th
Sus (suspended 4th) chords can be found in different voicings (see Figure 29). Their characteristic sound can be heard in tunes such as Herbie Hancock's "Maiden Voyage." Here Mintzer includes both the 4th scale degree and the 3rd scale degree voiced a major 7th above the 4th, adding a bit more dissonance (see figure E.1).

Figure E.1

Making Music

There are three elements in the intro: the rhythm section groove, the chords in the ensemble, and the unisons. Determine how to approach each and in what order. Establish the Latin jazz groove "à la Elvin" (referring to drummer Elvin Jones) in bass, drums, piano, and guitar. Chords (m. 1, 5, and 6) can be used for balance, dynamics, and tuning assessment. Play from bottom up, top down, section by section, down an octave, and so forth, as fermatas and in tempo. Use the unison passages to focus on tuning and articulation. Trombones join the rhythm section ostinato at m. 9, with the bass trombone adding body to the low end. With the intro in place the head will probably follow easily, the natural intensification is written in: unison altos,

tutti 2-part, unison saxes over 4-part harmony, add trumpet counterline, and finally tutti 6-part brass with 2-part sax counterpoint. Here (m. 42, the last A section before the solos) having both bari and bass trombone on the ostinato bass line provides a powerful bottom end to the culmination of the head presentation.

Self-Test Question 23

The very final chord, written as an eighth note, is played as a:

a. staccato ending
b. quarter note
c. fermata with a spill
d. undefined pitch

F

FABLES OF FAUBUS

Mingus, Charles 1975

Slagle, Steve 2001

Grade: 4.5
Duration: 10:00
Instrumentation: 5, 3, 3, 3 (no guit), (as2 doubles on ss)
Publisher: Hal Leonard
Recording: Mingus Big Band. *Gunslinging Birds*. Dreyfus FDM 36575-2, 1995.
The original recording is on Charles Mingus's *Mingus Ah Um*. Columbia Legacy, 1959

Highest Written Notes:

Ts 2: altissimo Bb
Tpt 1: Eb (three ledger lines), but mainly around C (two ledger lines)
Tbn 1: A (three ledger lines)
Tbn 3 (bass) lowest note: G below bass clef staff

Solos:

as 2 (one 71-bar chorus), tpt 2 (one 71-bar chorus plus 16 bars), optional ts 1 and tbn 1 (one 71-bar chorus)

Introductory Notes:
None

Form and Texture:
Two-and-a-half choruses of modified or non-standard AABA song form. The A section varies in length: 19 measures on the first chorus and the solo section, 17 measures in the "head out" chorus. The B section is always 16 bars in length. The 2-bar motive presented in the introduction returns once between the A and A1 sections and twice between B and the last A sections, but not in the solo section. It also returns to introduce the "head out."

Textures are contrasted, with the baritone sax and bass trombone on the 2-bar ostinato in the low register, beginning the introduction unaccompanied. They are gradually joined by the bass (m. 5), the rest of the rhythm section, and the band with theme A (m. 9). The second part of theme A (m. 17) features call-and-response, concerted, and canonical writing.

In the B section the tune is accompanied by two contrapuntal parts (baritone sax and first trombone, m. 46), followed by a tutti concerted (m. 54), and a layered ostinato with five different lines over an alternating Bb–E tritone in the bass and a screaming tenor sax in the altissimo register (m. 58) (see table F.1).

At a Glance:

Articulation:	• – > ∧ slurs
Bass line:	chord symbols and rhythm slashes, occasional written parts
Chords:	mi (ma7), mi7 (9, 11), mi (locrian), Dom (7, 9, ♭9, ♯9, ♯11, ♭5, ♯5, 13), dim
Chord progression:	2-chord ostinatos and chord progression using II–V–I in minor, dominant and substitute dominant chords
Dynamics:	*mp, mf, f, ff, cresc, dim*
Edition:	8 1/2x11 oblong, 26 pages. Measure numbers every bar, boxed numbers highlighting sections
Expressive devices:	short gliss up (brass), turn
Form:	modified AABA song form
Key:	F minor
Modulations:	none
Mutes:	none
Piano part:	treble clef only. Chord symbols and rhythm slashes, written parts (doubling melody)
Shout:	none
Style:	eclectic
Tempo:	quarter=144
Time feel:	in 2, in 4, double time swing feel, Afro-Cuban
Voicings:	saxes: 2-pt (3rds, tritone), 3-pt (tertian, non-tertian) tpts: 2-pt (in 3rds), 3-pt (tertian, non-tertian) tbns: 2-pt (7ths, 10ths), 3-pt (tertian, non-tertian) voicings across sections: ss, as, ts, tpts 2-3, tbn 1 (unison and 2-part) ss, ts 1-2, tbn 2-3 (4- and 5-part) polychords: E minor triad over F minor (Ma7) on final chord

Melodic, Harmonic, and Rhythmic Materials:

Melodic, harmonic, rhythmic, and time feel elements work together to create tension-release: the 2-bar ostinato motive in the introduction is based on the F minor blues scale. It is followed by a re-statement sequenced up a step. This 4-bar pattern is then repeated over a 2-chord vamp on B♭-7 and D♭7 creating a layering of functions (the motive is in tonic and super tonic, chords are on subdominant and sub.V/V). When the first part of the A theme enters (mm. 9–16) it reinforces the harmony rather than the ostinato.

The second part of the A section (mm. 17–25) brings a release to the tension build-up: it features a new theme, brings harmonic resolution (the tonic is now reached with a ii–V–I in F minor, mm. 17–19), there is a chord progression rather than a 2-chord vamp, and there is a change in time feel (from 2-beat to swing "in 4").

The two parts of A are also contrasting in length: while the first part of the A section is always 8 bars, the second part is 9 (6+3) bars, and 10 (6+4) bars in the A1 sections.

At the motivic level the importance of the minor third motive is readily apparent in m. 1. It is picked up by the 2-chord vamp on m. 5–8 (minor third relation B♭–D♭), and is inverted in m. 17 (ts1). In the B section two contrasting modes are used: jazz minor for the melody and natural minor for the trombone counterpoint. This section also features internal variety, contrasting Afro-Cuban (first 8 bars), double-time swing feel (4 bars), and a climactic layered ostinato (last 4 bars).

A shared 4-bar climactic stop time figure is used in the last four bars of both the A and the B sections (see figure F.1).

Technique Highlight:

Layered Ostinato

The repetition of short musical ostinato patterns in a layered fashion. Often they begin with one element and proceed in additive manner until all strands sound together. They are generally climactic in nature, since they naturally build rhythmically, melodically, and in density, range, and dynamics. The technique is used here from the beginning (the first two themes are superimposed at m. 9) and climaxes with the 5-part ostinato at m. 58 (see figure F.2).

Table F.1. "Fables of Faubus" outline

Section	Intro	Head					
Material	2-bar ostinato	A	2-bar ostinato	A1	B	2-bar ostinato	A1
Number of Measures	8	17	2	18	16	4	18

Section	Solo Section (open)	Last Solo Only	Collective Improvisation	Intro Recap	Head Recap	
Material	A A1 B A1	B1	cadenza	2-bar ostinato	A	A1
Number of Measures	19 18 16 18	16	no tempo	4	17	18

Figure F.1 Four-bar climactic stoptime figure

Making Music

Many of Mingus's pieces were not born as jazz ensemble works, but rather for the combos he played in. Listen to the original recording for the concept and spirit. As with "Ecclusiastics" and other tunes, an array of moods and styles coexist or are juxtaposed. Time feel switches are integral to this music: "2" beat to "swing" 4 in A sections and Afro-Cuban and double time swing feel in the B sections. There are also unaccompanied passages (one might want to conduct if necessary, with a small unobtrusive beat), breaks, and ostinato figures in the rhythm section.

Self-Test Question 24

The concerted theme that begins at m. 9 for the next eight bars is in:

    a. unison and two parts
    b. 4-part close
    c. unison
    d. triads

Lead Sheet

Homzy, Andrew, ed. *Charles Mingus: More Than a Fake Book.* Jazz Workshop/Hal Leonard, 1991, p. 44.

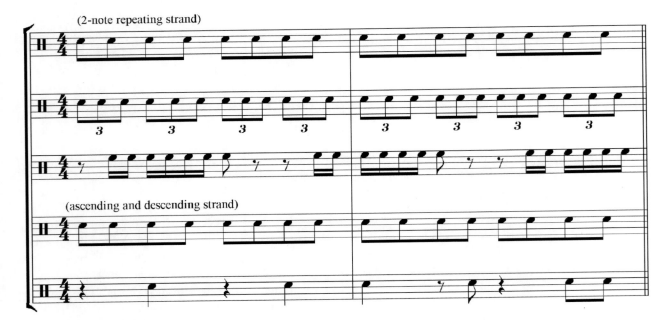

Figure F.2 Layered ostinato mm. 58–59

FOUR BROTHERS

Giuffre, Jimmy 1948

Giuffre, Jimmy 1948

Grade:	4.5
Duration:	3:13
Instrumentation:	cl, 4 (ts 1, ts 2, ts 3, bari), 5, 3, 3 (g opt), (opt. as for ts 2)
Publisher:	Hal Leonard
Recording:	*Big Band Jazz,* Vol. IV. The Smithsonian Collection of Recordings, RD 030-4, 1987. CD.

Highest Written Notes:

Cl:	F♯ (three ledger lines) (solo)
Tpt 1-2:	E (three ledger lines)
Tbn 1:	B♭ (four ledger lines)

Solos:
(all written out on part) ts 2, bari, ts 3, ts 1 (each 16 bars), cl (8), ts 1, ts 2, ts 3, bari (each 2 bars)

Soli:
saxes (mm. 142–49)

Notes:
Though ts 2 is written also for optional alto, 3 tenors and a bari are needed for the classic sound of this arrangement. Clarinet plays only 8 bars (the original Herman solo)

Introductory Notes:
None

Form and Texture:
A showpiece for the saxophone section of the Woody Herman band of the late 1940s, it featured the four "brothers": Herbie Steward, Stan Getz, and Zoot Sims on tenors, and Serge Chaloff on baritone. There are six AABA choruses, a 16-bar coda, and no introduction. The head is presented by the harmonized sax section accompanied by brass punctuations. Choruses 2 and 3 feature 16-bar solos by tenors and baritone saxes, with various backgrounds.

At a Glance:

Articulation:	• – > ∧ slurs
Bass line:	written
Chord progression:	diatonic harmony, passing diminished chords (♯I dim), secondary dominants (V/II, V/V), upper chromatic dominants (♭II7), II–V–I sequences.
Chords:	Ma6, Ma6/9, Ma7, mi7 (9, 11), Dom7 (♭9, 9, ♭5, ♯5, ♭13, 13, sus), dim
Dynamics:	*pp, mp, mf, f, ff, fp, cresc, dim*
Edition:	8 1/2x11 oblong, 19 pages. Measure numbers every bar, boxed letters every eight bars
Form:	AABA (6 choruses), coda (16)
Guitar:	chord symbols
Key:	A♭ Ma
Modulations:	to E♭ Ma, B♭ Ma
Mutes:	hat, plunger (tpts and tbns)
Piano:	written
Shout:	chorus 5 (mm. 109–33)
Style:	swing
Tempo:	quarter=200+
Voicings:	saxes: uni, 4-pt close (tenor lead)
	tpts: uni, 4-pt close with tpt 5 doubling lead 8vb, 5-pt open (last chord)
	tbns: uni, 3-pt, triads
	brass: 5-pt
	ens: block voicings

Chorus 4 features a call-and-response between unison brass and unison saxes, with a clarinet solo with sax background on the bridge. The fifth chorus is a tutti concerted shout, with saxes on the bridge. The last 16 bars are divided between 2-bar solos for each of the saxes punctuated by brass, a 4-bar sax soli break, and four more bars of rubato sax soli over the final chord.

Melodic, Harmonic, and Rhythmic Materials:
The melodic line is eighth-note based and features ascending and descending arpeggios linked by half

step. Double chromatic approaches, upper and lower neighbor tones, and passing chromatic notes are used.

The A section harmony makes use of diatonic chords and secondary dominants. The B section uses transient tonics (♭III, ♯IV, and III). Chorus three modulates to the dominant E♭, and chorus four to the supertonic B♭. The same chord progression is used for all keys. Chorus five returns to the tonic A♭. The last chord is a dominant type I7.

The "four brothers" voicings are in 4-part close, with the occasional triad (see "Cottontail"). The ensemble shout is in Basie 4-part close (see "All of Me"), though the bari plays mostly roots instead of doubling the melody two octaves below.

Technique Highlight

Sectional Writing

Other than the tutti shout, this arrangement features the sections of the ensemble in distinct roles, with the saxes spotlighted and the brass in an accompanimental role. Sectional writing was the main texture in the early days of the big band (see Fletcher Henderson). It is used to this day, though many other textures have been developed, such as writing across sections, layered ostinato, and counterpoint.

Making Music

The tempo needs to be close to the original or this chart will lose its verve. Saxes can work on it separately and join in when they are ready. Suggested solos are included. Brass figures and punctuations need to be exact and well accented. Rehearse with rhythm section, since the drummer catches many of the brass figures. Letter N is a classic shout tutti concerted with the drums adding power and fills.

Tenors exchange the lead repeatedly: players need to be aware of when they lead and where they play under parts and play accordingly. In the last four bars there is a caesura followed by a fermata that can be cued as a downbeat. The lead tenor can then lead or it can be conducted with a basic quarter note pulse and some allargando.

For a vocalese version that follows the original closely see the version by Manhattan Transfer.

Self-Test Question 25

In chorus 4 (letters J–M) brasses play many:

a. downbeats
b. upbeats and three over four figures
c. sustained notes
d. "ands" of four and three over four figures

Lead Sheet

The New Real Book. Sher Music Co., 1988.

For Further Reading

Gridley, Mark. *Jazz Styles: History and Analysis.* 8th ed. New Jersey: Prentice-Hall, 2003.
Listening guide, pp. 155–157.

FULL NELSON

Nelson, Oliver 1962

Nelson, Oliver 1962

Grade:	4
Duration:	2:47
Instrumentation:	5, 4, 4, 4 (optional fr.hns 1–2)
Publisher:	Sierra Music
Recording:	Oliver Nelson. *Jazz Masters 48.* Verve 314 527 654-2, CD, 1995.

Highest Written Notes:

Tpts 1-2:	E (three ledger lines, once in a unison passage at the end)
Tbn 1:	B♭ (four ledger lines)

Solos:

tenor saxophone feature

Introductory Notes:

Director's notes and General Performance Comments by Bob Curnow

Form and Texture:

Hybrid form based on the 12-bar blues, with 4-bar extensions (on the head only). After a 2-bar intro, the A theme (16 bars) follows with unison trumpet melody over trombone ostinato. The B theme (m.

At a Glance:

Articulation:	• – > slurs
Bass line:	written and chord symbols
Chords:	Ma6 (9), Ma7 (9), mi7 (9), mi7(♭5), Dom (♭9, 9, ♯9, ♯5, 13, sus)
Chord progression:	constant structures over I–IV–V pedal (A), one-bar dominant 7 ostinato (B), blues progression with upper chromatic dominants to I7–IV7–V7 (solo section)
Dynamics:	*mp, mf, f, ff, cresc, dim*
Edition:	8 1/2x11 oblong, 10 pages. Measure numbers every bar, with boxed numbers highlighting sections
Expressive devices:	bend (tpts), fall (brass), arco (bass)
Form:	16- and 12-bar blues variant. Intro (2), A (16), B (16), ts solo (three 12 bar choruses), A and B recap (10)
Guitar part:	chord symbols and two bars written
Key:	F Ma
Modulations:	none
Mutes:	none
Piano part:	chord symbols and two bars written
Shout:	mm. 59–70
Style:	swing
Tempo:	quarter=120
Time feel:	in 2 and in 4
Voicings:	saxes: 4-pt, 5-pt, 5-pt clus tpts: unison, 4-pt close tbns: unison, 4-pt close, 4-pt spreads brass: 5-pt and 6-pt ens: 5-pt voicing across sections (4-pt saxes + tbn4)

19, 16 bars) also features unison melody (only two trumpets rather than all four) over a new ostinato in the saxes and trombones. Three choruses of tenor sax solo on the 12-bar blues form follow, with a background figure on "one" and "two and." The third of the three choruses (m. 59) features an overlap: the

tenor solo is still in the picture (see recording), the first two phrases of the A theme are recapitulated and then interrupted by a climactic tutti brass (m. 67), before the last two phrases return (pick up to m. 71), followed by a brief restatement of the B section ostinato (m. 77) and a final chord.

I opted to use "theme" rather than "section" here because the two A and B themes, while highly contrasting, share a similar reworked blues progression. For more on Nelson's integration of the blues with other forms see "Blues and the Abstract Truth."

Melodic, Harmonic, and Rhythmic Materials:
Theme A is in F minor dorian. Theme B is also in F minor (scale degrees 1, ♭3, 4, 5, 6 in the first eight bars, then ♭5 and ♭7 are added).

The A theme ostinato is a four–quarter note pattern that uses constant major 7 structures (A♭ Ma7=♭III Ma7 and B♭ Ma7=IV Ma7) over F pedal. The same lead line (C–D–E♭–D) in the trombone ostinato is maintained (mm. 1–13), while the under parts change to adapt to the changing harmonies. The line then ascends to conclude on the tonic F (mm. 14–16). The ostinato at B features a variation of the previous ostinato lead (C–D–E♭–D), voiced in the saxes as a 5-part cluster (E♭–F–G–A–C) outlining the I7 chord. The trombones reiterate the tonic note on the upbeats.

In addition to sharing the lead line, the two ostinatos use a similar I to IV progression, though the A theme is in the tonic minor Fmi7 and the B theme in the blues dominant type tonic F7. When the ostinato returns four bars before the end (m. 77) the mode of the tonic chord is again modified, concluding the piece on a FMa7 (E–F–G–A–C cluster over F).

Technique Highlight:

Constant Structures over Ostinato Bass
See "Blues and the Abstract Truth."

Making Music
Phrasing is sophisticated in this piece. The first ostinato is really a one-bar pattern but is phrased in two measures, legato. The second ostinato is an actual one-bar pattern. For both take a breath at the end of phrase. The themes are in unison and need to sound like one instrument in terms of intonation and articulation. Notice the phrasing's progressive compression: theme A (4 phrases of four), theme B (4

phrases of two, then on to 1+1+2+1+3). Both themes have a nice dynamic curve that peaks toward the end (m. 15, and m. 31).

The tenor sax solo is continually backed by the background figure on "one" and "two and." Make this truly *ostinato* figure build slowly (*p, mf, f*) and progressively until it hits the *f* brass tutti release at m. 67. This is the climax, just before the return to pp. Notice that on the recording the tenor continues to play through m. 69 rather then ending the solo at m. 62 as in the score. Arguably this creates increased drama before the last two phrases of theme A are recapitulated. To be effective these last two phrases need to be played with the wide dynamic contrast (*pp* and *ff*) marked in the score.

Self-Test Question 26
The voicings of the solo backgrounds at m. 35 are:

a. 4-part close
b. 5-part spreads
c. Constant structures over bass pedal
d. Clusters

G

GOOD BYE PORK PIE HAT

Mingus, Charles 1959

Johnson, Sy 1980

Grade: 4
Duration: 5:30
Instrumentation: 5, 4, 4, 4
Publisher: Kendor Music
Recording: The original recording is on Charles Mingus's *Mingus Ah Um*. Columbia Legacy, 1959.

Highest Written Notes:
Tpt 1:   Db (two ledger lines)
Tbn 1:   Ab (three ledger lines)

Solos:
ts 1 feature

Introductory Notes:
None

Form and Texture:
Tenor sax plays an introductory improvised cadenza. The tune is then presented by unison saxes (alternatively, it can be played by solo tenor sax). The second chorus (m. 13) features brass in varying textures: trumpet unison (trumpet entrances are staggered, tpts1-2 are followed by tpt3 at m. 15, and by tpt 4 at m. 17) over trombone spreads, trumpets in 4-part harmony, concerted tutti brass with independent lead. Chorus 3 and 4 feature tenor sax solo (with a soft tutti background on chorus 4).

Chorus 5 is a varied reprise of the head, presented by unison trumpets over trombone and sax spreads, followed by unison saxes over sustained brass, saxes five part spreads with independent lead, and trumpets again in unison over trombone and sax spreads. The 4-bar coda features tenor sax solo over a tremolo-like triplet figure for alto 1 and tenor 2, a caesura, and a final chord with *arco* bass.

Melodic, Harmonic, and Rhythmic Materials:
The melody is based on the F pentatonic minor with added b5 (see "Basically Blues"). On mm. 6–7 other scale degrees from the minor mode are added (major 7, b6, 2, and b2). On mm. 8–12 the minor third ascending motive from mm. 1–4 (F–Ab) is inverted (Ab–F). The repeated tonic note F in the melody on the strong beats of mm.1–4 creates different relations with the shifting harmonies: 1/F7, Ma7/Gb Ma7, b5/B7b5, 9/Eb11, to return to 1/F7).

Most harmonies are from the minor mode, but I7 (dominant-quality blues tonic chord) is used on the head. The blues progression is reharmonized with secondary and substitute dominants. The first measures are:

| F7(#9) Db13 | GbMa7 B7(b5) | Eb11 Db9 | Eb11 F7(#9) | Bbmi9 |
| I7 V7/bII | bII subV/IV | bVII7 subV/V | bVII7 V/IV | iv |

The F minor (with major 7th) chord is used for the solo section, where the chord progression shifts

At a Glance:

Articulation:	– > slurs
Bass line:	written, chord symbols on solo section
Chords:	mi (ma7), mi7 (9, 11), mi7 (♭5) Ma7 (9, ♯11, 13), Dom (7, 9, ♭9, ♯9, ♯11, ♭5, ♯5, 13), triads, triads over bass note.
Chord progression:	12-bar minor blues with I7 (dominant-quality blues tonic chord) used on the head, and i minor (Ma7) for the solo section, iv minor used throughout as the subdominant chord on m. 5 of the form, IV7 used on m. 9 of the form. Secondary dominants (V/II, V/V), substitute dominants (subV/V, subV/IV), ♭IIMa7, ♭VII7.
Dynamics:	*pp, p, mp, mf, f, cresc, dim*
Edition:	8 1/2x11 vertical, 4 pages. Boxed numbers every 12 bars
Expressive devices:	gliss, breathy tremolo, no vibrato (saxes), bend (tpts), gliss, no vibrato (brass), four finger tremolo (bass)
Form:	12-bar blues (five choruses) and coda (4 bars)
Guitar:	chord symbols, short written part
Key:	F minor
Modulations:	none
Mutes:	harmon, no stem (tpts), bucket or in stand (tbns)
Piano part:	chord symbols, short written part
Style:	ballad, swing, and even 8ths
Tempo:	quarter=48
Time feel:	in 4, 12/8 feel
Voicings:	saxes: unis, 5-pt spreads, 5-pt spreads with independent lead tpts: unis, 2-pt, 3-pt triads, 3-pt close with lead doubled 8vb, 4-pt close (7th chords) tbns: 4-pt spreads brass: 5-pt (4-pt tbns with tpt 2 lead), 6-pt, 7-pt

to a tonic minor/subdominant minor one-bar pattern (mm. 25–27). Both the ii–V of V and sub ii–V of V tritone substitution are used as cadential patterns in measures 9 and 10 of the form: D-7 G7 and A♭-7 D♭7 to C7 (mm. 33–34). The soft background at mm. 37–40 features triads over a chromatic bass descending from F to C.

The tonic minor chord is also found in the first measure of the coda (m. 61), over its fifth in the bass trombone. The dominant pedal C continues under the next chord G♭Ma7 (=♭IIMa7). On the final C triad with added ninth the tenor sax adds E♭ (=♭3), ending the piece on the dominant chord with blue third.

Swing feel alternates with even 8th feel (m. 10 of the form and in the last chorus).

Technique Highlight:

Tremolo
Expressive devices can be reviewed in "Big Dipper." Here (m. 37) "breathy tremolo" is required from the saxes. It is achieved by touching lightly the reed with the tongue in a 16th-note sextuplet rhythm. This effect is encountered quite rarely. Here it is coupled with four-finger tremolo in the bass.

Making Music
This is a tenor feature in memory of Lester Young. Tenor soloist and ensemble should be familiar with Young's sound. If you use the sax section instead of the solo for the head, make sure it plays pp and no vibrato as marked.

This is ballad playing, with brushes for the drums and round, resonant quarter notes in the bass. The only *f* passage is the four bars at mm. 49–52, for the rest the ensemble plays mostly *pp, p,* or *mp*.

The bass trombone contributes to the low end by supplying mostly roots to the spread voicings. It gets some help from the bari on the last chorus (m. 49). Low end needs to be clear. The feel switches between swing eighths and even eighths (see discussion in "Cute").

Self-Test Question 27
The basic blues progression generally features the IV or iv subdominant chord on measure 5, the tonic I or i on measure 7 and the dominant V on measure 9 of the form. Here, on the main tune (mm. 1–12) the progression features:

a. subdominant, tonic, and dominant chords in the traditional places

b. subdominant, but not tonic and dominant chords in the traditional places

c. tonic, but not subdominant and dominant chords in the traditional places

d. dominant, but not tonic and subdominant chords in the traditional places

Lead Sheet

Homzy, Andrew, ed. *Charles Mingus: More Than a Fake Book.* Jazz Workshop/Hal Leonard, 1991, p. 52.

⸻⸙⸻

GROOVE MERCHANT

Richardson, Jerome 1967

Jones, Thad 1969

Grade: 5
Duration: 5:30
Instrumentation: 5, 4, 4, 4 (as 1 plays ss throughout, substitute part for as provided)
Publisher: Kendor Music
Recording: Thad Jones–Mel Lewis Jazz Orchestra. *Central Park North.* Blue Note 7243 5 76852 2 1, CD.

Highest Written Notes:

Tpt 1:   F (three ledger lines)
Tbn 1:   Bb (four ledger lines)

Solos:

solo fills around melody (piano, 16), 16-bar form open for solos for ss (as 1), tpt 2, tbn 1, pno, guit

Soli:

saxes (three choruses), brass (one chorus)

Introductory Notes:

Brief history of the Thad Jones/Mel Lewis Orchestra

At a Glance:

Articulation:	• – > ⋀ slurs
Bass line:	written walking bass and obbligato lines with the ensemble, chord symbols
Chords:	Ma (6, 9), mi7 (9, 11), Dom (7, 9, #11, #5, b 13, 13, sus, mixo, alt, octatonic), dim
Chord progression:	use of I Ma and blues inflected I7, IV7, secondary dominants, and chromatic and cycle of fifths dominant sequences. Characteristic chromatic ascending bass line Db –D–Eb –E–F (IV7, #IV diminished, I7 over its 5th, #>5 diminished, VI-7, featured in mm. 11–14 of the 16-bar form.
Dynamics:	*mf, f, ff, fp, cresc, dim*
Edition:	8 1/2x11 vertical, 8 pages. Letters every 8 or 16 bars. No measure numbers.
Expressive devices:	smear, gliss, fall (saxes), shake (tpts), rip, fall, turn (brass)
Form:	Intro (8), A (16), A1 (20), sax soli (three 16-bar choruses), open solos (16), brass soli (16), shout (16), A1 (20), coda (2)
Guitar part:	chord symbols and rhythm slashes
Key:	Ab Ma
Modulations:	none
Mutes:	none
Orchestration:	SATTB: soprano lead on sax soli (letters D E F)
Piano part:	chord symbols and rhythm slashes
Shout:	letter I
Style:	shuffle (swing and even eighths)
Tempo:	quarter=132
Voicings:	saxes: 4-/5-pt open (no root and over root), sw tpts: unis, 3-pt (triads, dbl lead 8vb, and in fourths), 4-pt closed, clusters tbns: 4-pt closed, spreads (chord sound and one tension) brass: 6-pt, 7-pt, 8-pt

Figure G.1 A♭ pentatonic major with passing chromatics

Figure G.2 A♭ pentatonic minor with ♭5

Form and Texture:

After an 8-bar introduction the basic A section is 16 bars (8+8), with A1 (chorus 2) adding a four-bar interpolation (letter B, mm.9–12) that brings it to 20 bars (8+4 interpolation +6+2). This is also used on the headout (letter B *dal Segno*). The A 16-bar form is used throughout for soli, solos, and shout.

Textures range from tutti concerted (letter B, mm. 9–12), shout (letter I), to call and response (letter B), and contrapuntal ostinato (letter C and letter H, mm. 7–16). The brass soli (letter H) features a two-part pick up in contrary motion, and the interweaving of unison and five- and six-part passages.

Melodic, Harmonic, and Rhythmic Materials:

The A section melody is based on the A♭ pentatonic major with passing chromatics between degrees 5 and 6, and the occasional ♭3 blue note (see figure G.1).

The closing descending line (letter A, mm. 15–16) veers to the A♭ pentatonic minor with added ♭5 (see figure G.2).

The second presentation of the melody (letter B) adds sax section answers, the first tutti concerted passage (letter B mm. 9–12, derived from letter A m. 9), repeats mm. 13–14 of letter A three times over a two-bar contrapuntal ostinato (letter C mm.1–6), and concludes with the last two bars of letter A (A mm. 15–16 = C mm. 7–8). At the coda sign measure 7 of letter C is augmented to two bars and followed by a conclusion in even eighths by the sax section.

The harmony uses I major and blues I7 tonic chords and IV7 subdominant chords, secondary dominants, and chromatic and cycle of fifths dominant sequences. A characteristic chromatic ascending bass line cliché (D♭–D–E♭–E–F) is featured in mm. 11–14 of the form (IV7, ♯IV diminished, I7 over its 5th, ♯5 diminished, VI–7), similar to the one in "Don't Git Sassy."

The full 8-pitch octatonic scale collection is used both vertically (letter B m. 9, beat 4), and horizontally (sax soli, letter F2).

For more on Jones's harmony and voicings see "Back Bone," "Big Dipper," and "Cherry Juice."

Technique Highlight:

Augmentation

Augmentation is the process of stating a passage in rhythmic values uniformily longer than those initially associated with it. A common ratio for augmentation is 2:1, where an eighth becomes a quarter, as Jones employs here. Augmentation is also referred to intervals, such as enlarging a perfect fourth to an augmented fourth.

Making Music

Articulation markings (• – > ∧) need to be matched to what is heard on the recording. *Tenutos* are not always held full value. See "Back Bone" for further discussion.

The three chorus sax soli might need a separate rehearsal. For the sound that Jones intended you would need a soprano lead, though an alternate part for 1st alto is provided. Other sax soli by Jones can be found in his "Cherry Juice" (SSTTB), "Don't Git Sassy" (SATTB), and "Three and One" (AATTB).

Jones provides peaks and valleys that articulate the form. Here are some of the peaks: intro m. 4, letter C m. 7, one measure before letter G, m. 13 of letter I. Peaks, as in mountains, are of different shapes and heights, and how one gets there determines how enjoyable the trip turns out to be.

Self-Test Question 28

The groove is medium shuffle. Which of the following statements is the most accurate?

a. eighths are always swung, except one short passage of even eighths
b. eighths are always swung, except two short passages of even eighths
c. eighths are always swung, alternating with many passages of even eighths
d. the tempo is too fast to swing the eighths

Lead Sheet

Real Easy Book. Sher, 2003.

H

HAITIAN FIGHT SONG

Mingus, Charles 1975

Johnson, Sy 1999

Grade: 5
Duration: 8:22
Instrumentation: 5, 3, 3, 3 (as 1 doubles on ss)
Publisher: Hal Leonard
Recording: Mingus Big Band. *Blues and Politics*. Dreyfus FDM 36603-2 CD, 1999.

Highest Written Notes:

Tpt 1:   E♭ (three ledger lines)
Tbn 1:   B♭ (four ledger lines)
Tbn 3:   low G (three ledger lines below staff, opt. 8va)

Solos:

ss (16+24+8), tpt 2 (12, open), any (open, on 12-bar blues), dms (24)

On recording bass plays unaccompanied solo introduction before starting the ostinato in m. 1, soprano sax plays four choruses of the blues at m. 73, trumpet and piano take four choruses each at m. 113

Introductory Notes:

None

Form and Texture:

Ternary form comprised of the main melody over the ostinato bass pattern (A), and a 12-bar minor blues (B) for solos. A is used also as an interlude between solos (mm. 97–112).

The introduction (12 bars) establishes the ostinato pattern (in the recording it is preceded by an open bass solo). Eight 8-bar choruses follow (except for chorus 6, which is 4 bars). B (m. 73) features a contrasting minor blues section open for soprano sax solo (four choruses on recording), followed by an ensemble chorus. A returns as an interlude at m. 97 (16 bars), followed by a second open section for solos (trumpet and piano play four choruses each on recording). After a two chorus drum solo, A is repeated exactly, and followed by an 8-bar coda (m. 149) (see table H.1).

At a Glance:

Articulation:	– > ∧ ≥ slurs
Bass line:	written ostinato, chord symbols
Chords:	mi 7 (11), Dom7 (♯9, ♯11, ♯5, 13, sus)
Chord progression:	ostinato, minor blues
Dynamics:	*mp, mf, f, ff, cresc, dim*
Edition:	8 1/2x11 oblong, 17 pages. Measure numbers every bar, boxed numbers highlighting sections
Expressive devices:	bends, grace notes, long fall
Form:	ostinato/minor blues. See Form and Texture.
Key:	G mi
Modulations:	none
Mutes:	none
Piano:	written, chord symbols
Style:	swing
Tempo:	quarter=176
Voicings:	saxes: uni, 4-pt tpts and tbns : uni, 2-pt and 3-pt fourths

Melodic, Harmonic, and Rhythmic Materials:

There are five main melodic elements: the ostinato (a, mm. 1–4), the quarter note descending triplet arpeggio (b, m. 11–12), the first phrase of the tune (c, mm. 13–16), the second phrase of the tune (d, mm. 17–20), and the low tonic pedal (e, m. 21).

The ostinato a is a four-bar pattern on the tonic triad with additional ♭5 (D♭), and it climbs to the ♭6 (E♭) on m. 4. Element b outlines the tonic arpeggio (with added ♭5), c is a call answered by a response (d) in repeated note triplets: both are based on the blues and are four bars in length.

The A section is created by the layering of c and d in unison in various instrumental combinations. After being presented separately, they are combined beginning on m. 25. Entrances are shortened from the initial 4-bar lag (m. 33), settling into a pattern of 2-bar lag entrances (as1/tpts, tbns1-2, bari/tbn3, as2/ts1-2). This texture builds progressively in intensity (aided by the brass repetitions at the octave) to

Table H.1. "Haitian Fight Song" outline

measure		13	21	29	37	45	53	57	65
chorus	intro	1	2	3	4	5	6	7	8
# of measures	12	8	8	8	8	8	4	8	8

measure	73	85	97	105	113	125		149
chorus	9 solo	10	11	12	13 solos	drum solo	D.C. intro and ch 1–8	coda
# of measures	12 (2x)	12	8	8	12 open	24		8

a climactic fortissimo section (mm. 57–112) where the brass is harmonized in fourths and all elements (a b c d e) are layered, with the soprano solo adding to the textural complexity (see discussion of layered ostinato in "Fables of Faubus").

The one-beat lag canons at m. 85 develop element d. The tune (c+d) is then presented in exact rhythmic augmentation in the interlude (values doubled, saxes, mm. 97–112) accompanied by shout brass figures.

Harmonized passages are reserved for climactic spots, such as the 6-part brass fourths (mm. 69–73). Three-part brass fourths are found at mm. 97–104. See Figure H.1 for examples of chords in 4ths.

Measure 96 features a D7sus chord on beat two (saxes) and a 6-part dominant chord with a prominent natural 11th in the lead (D7#9, 11).

Technique Highlight:

Layered Ostinato and Augmentation
Review the discussion of layered ostinato in "Fables of Faubus" and of augmentation in "Groove Merchant."

Making Music
Many of Mingus's pieces were not born as jazz ensemble works, but rather for the combos he played in. One of the original quintet versions can be found in the Smithsonian Collection of Classic Jazz, Vol. IV. Notice that all the basic elements of the composition are present, with just two winds (alto sax and trom-

bone) and rhythm section. This recording can provide ideas on how to play the arrangement. Among the elements present in the quintet recording are: vocal shouts by Mingus, double time feel on portions of the trombone and alto solos, tango like stop times on 1, 2, and 3, and slowing down (decelerando) over arco bass in the very final bars.

This last technique was used by Mingus frequently, most evidently on "Sue's Changes" (also available in the original quintet version and an arrangement by Sy Johnson). Though Mingus led accelerandi and decelerandi with his bass, you might want to conduct them here.

The recording also demonstrates Mingus's outstanding bass virtuosity. He plays an extended cadenza at the very beginning and then moves on to the ostinato groove, and takes another solo later, before the recapitulation. If you do want to feature your bass player you might want to add a solo spot in place or after the drum solo at m. 125.

Mark all entrances/reentrances in the score and try to memorize the sequence so you are turning toward the right group of players as they grow the layered ostinato and build in intensity and range (mm. 29–73).

Self-Test Question 29
Review discussion of constant structures in "Airegin," "Blues and the Abstract Truth," and "Caravan." The constant stucture used at mm. 105–7 is made up of:

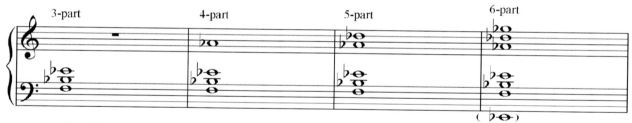

Figure H.1 Chords in fourths

a. pure stacked 4ths
b. 4ths and 3rds
c. two trichords in 4ths separated by a major 3rd
d. two trichords in 4ths separated by a minor 3rd

Lead Sheet

Homzy, Andrew, ed. *Charles Mingus: More Than a Fake Book.* Jazz Workshop/Hal Leonard, 1991, p. 54

THE HAPPY SONG

Mintzer, Bob 1988

Mintzer, Bob 1988

Grade:	5
Duration:	5:30 (4:19 on recording)
Instrumentation:	5, 4, 4, 4
Publisher:	Kendor Music
Recording:	Bob Mintzer Big Band. *Urban Contours.* DMP 467 CD, 1989.

Highest Written Notes:

Tpt 1:	E (three ledger lines)
Tbn 1:	C (four ledger lines)

Solos:

ts 1, tpt 4 (32 +36, open) dms (8). On the recording the bari solos 32+36 (instead of ts and tpt) with no repeats and no backgrounds, the drums solos for 6 bars instead of 8.

Introductory Notes:
None

Form and Texture:

The intro features concerted ensemble without drums (6 bars) followed by a 12-bar rhythm section groove. The head (m. 19) is a through composed abcd 32-bar form. Chorus two (m. 51) features a 44-bar variation that includes a new section over a dominant pedal (mm. 75–90), and a 4-bar modulating link. Chorus one and two can also be seen as parts of a larger two-part form. Chorus 3 spotlights a 38-bar a cappella

At a Glance:

Articulation:	• – > ≥ slurs
Bass line:	written ostinato and chord symbols
Chords:	Ma triads, Ma triads (add 2), Ma7 (6, 9), mi7 (9, 11), min7 (♭5), Dom 7 (♭9, 9, ♯9, ♯11, ♯5, 13, sus, mixo, oct)
Chord progression:	secondary dominants (V/ii, V/vi), substitute dominants (♭II7, ♭VI7), chords borrowed from minor (♭VII7), pedals and polychords
Dynamics:	*mp, mf, f, sp, cresc, dim*
Edition:	8 1/2x11 vertical, 16 pages. Measure numbers every bar, boxed numbers highlighting sections
Expressive devices:	fall (saxes)
Form:	six choruses, through composed 32-bar tune developed
Guitar part:	written ostinato, chord symbols, and melodic line with the ensemble
Key:	C Ma
Modulations:	to E♭ Ma and D Ma, progressive tonality
Mutes:	none
Piano part:	written chords, chord symbols, and melodic line with the ensemble
Shout:	mm. 233–48 (last chorus) are climactic
Style:	samba
Tempo:	half=120
Voicings:	saxes: unis, triads (with two pitches doubled), 4-pt close, 5-pt spreads, voicings in fourths tpts: unis, 3-pt (triads with lead doubled 8vb), 4-pt close tbns: unis, 3-pt (tertian and quartal), 4-pt close and open, 4-pt spreads brass: polychords, sus with Ma3rd above the 4th ens: inversions and slash chords

Table H.2. Polychords in the introduction of "The Happy Song"

measure	1	2		3		4		5
trumpets	A-7	Bb Ma7	G7	A-7		C triad (add2)	Bb triad	E-7	FMa7
trombones	Bb triad (C9sus)	Csus	Ab triad	Bb triad (C9sus)	C7sus		Ab triad	F triad	Ami triad
pno, bass, tbn4	C pedal							

ensemble in tutti concerted and homophonic passages. The solo section (choruses 4–5, mm. 133–200) is based on choruses 1 and 2 (the second chorus shortened by 8 bars). An 8-bar drum solo introduces the last chorus (modified 40-bar second chorus, mm. 209–48), and a 12-bar coda based on the introduction closes the piece (m. 249).

Melodic, Harmonic, and Rhythmic Materials:

A main rhythmic motive (half note, dotted quarter, eighth) unifies the 8-bar through composed abcd sections. It is varied and developed through syncopations and extensions, and sequenced through the changing harmonies. The second and sixth choruses feature a contrasting melody and counterline (mm. 75–90 and mm. 233–48). The introduction and coda feature a melodic sequence descending to the tonic note. Each of the abcd sections features its own characteristic chord progression. The tonic chord appears on mm. 1, 13, 15, 23–24 of the 32-bar form. The variation that follows closes on the tonic (m. 91) before modulating to Eb. This is the first of a series of modulations that lead the piece through the keys of Eb major (m. 95), a return to C major (m. 133) for the solo section, and ending in D major (m. 209) (see discussion of progressive tonality in "Black, Brown, & Beautiful"). Each modulation is prepared by a II–V or dominant harmony.

Dominant pedals can be found at mm. 75–90, mm. 103–109, mm. 189–200, mm. 233–48, and mm. 255–60. A double tonic-dominant pedal can be found in the piano part at mm. 249–53.

Technique Highlight:

Inversions, Slash Chords, Triads over Bass Note, Polychords
All of the above can be found in this piece. They provide harmonic variety and often a smoother bass line. The first three are marked by a diagonal slash between the two letters. Inversions feature a chord tone other than the root in the lowest voice. There are three inversions for any given 7th chord: 3rd, 5th, or 7th in bass. Slash chords are chords (not triads) over a non-chord tone in the bass, such as the 9th, 11th. Triads over bass note are major or minor triads over a bass note that is anything other than a chord tone.

Polychords are chords made up of two or more chords. They are marked by a horizontal slash between the two letters. Though not marked, the introduction (mm. 1–5) features brass polychords over a tonic pedal (see figure H.2)

Making Music

Create a good samba groove, since it does not change throughout the piece. Electric bass is preferred if you have a choice, with all the pops and slaps as you get into the chart. As with other unaccompanied sections, at mm. 95–124 you might want to rehearse slower, keep a drum click in rehearsal, and then conduct in performance. Mark all modulations two bars before the actual key change (where the ii–Vs are) and lead/help the ensemble articulate the modulation.

Self-Test Question 30

The six chords at mm. 48–50 are:

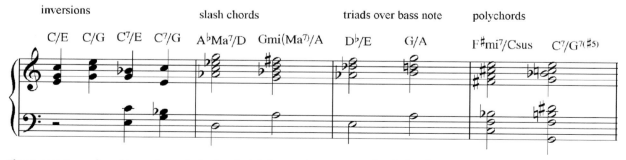

Figure H.2 Examples of inversions, slash chords, triads over bass note, and polychords

a. all slash chords
b. all triads over bass note
c. four triads over bass note, one inversion, and one root position chord
d. five triads over bass note and one root position chord

⟋⟋⟋

HARLEM AIRSHAFT

Ellington, Duke 1943

Ellington, Duke 1943

Grade:	4
Duration:	2:57
Instrumentation:	5, 3, 3, 4, ts 1 doubles on clarinet
Publisher:	Jazz@Lincoln Center
Recording:	Duke Ellington. *The Blanton-Webster Band*. RCA Bluebird: 5659-2-RB, 3CD set. Also on the *Smithsonian Collection of Classic Jazz*, CD III.

Highest Written Notes:

Cl:	G (four ledger lines) (solo)
Tpt 1:	D above staff (last note of piece only)
Tpt 3:	F above staff (solo)
Tbn 1:	C (four ledger lines)
Tbn 2:	C (four ledger lines) (solo)

Solos:
(written out): pno (mm. 4, 8), tbn 2 (8 bars), tpt 3 (one chorus + 16 measures at letter M), cl (one chorus + 16 measures at letter O).

Soli:
sax (E, F, G, H), tbns (Intro, I, J, L)

Notes:
Ts 1 needs to be a medium advanced cl player; if not, a cl player can be added and the part can be split between the two players.

The two brass soloists need familiarity with expressive devices and mute usage.

Tpt 3 plays repeated high Fs on solo.

Piano plays only a couple of motives in the entire chart. The director can play them if no pianist is available.

At a Glance:

Articulation:	• – > ∧ ≥ slurs
Bass line:	written
Expressive devices:	bend, fall (short), ghost, growl, hum, half-valve, portamento (ascending and descending), shake
Form:	12-bar intro, four 32-bar AABA choruses, 3-bar coda
Chords:	Ma, mi, Dom (♭5, ♭9, 9, sus), dim, chords with no third.
Dynamics:	*pp, mp, mf, f, dim*
Edition:	8 1/2x11 oblong, 18 pages. Rehearsal letters highlighting sections
Guitar part:	chord symbols
Key:	A♭ Ma
Modulations:	none
Mutes:	plunger with pixie in tbn2 solo, cups (tpts)
Orchestration:	baritone voiced high on root, 3, 5, ♭7, 9 of the chord (C, E, F, H), tpt 2 lead over saxes (M, N)
Piano part:	written (two bars in intro, H m. 8, I m. 8 only)
Shout:	last 11 bars (P)
Style:	shuffle
Tempo:	quarter=186 (medium)
Voicings:	saxes: 3-pt, 4-pt close double lead 8vb, 5-pt close and drop2 (E), chords built in stacked thirds (1, 3, 5, 7, 9) from the root up (m. 5, and many spots at letters C, E, F, and H)
	tpts: triadic (all inversions), 3-pt
	tbns: triadic
	br: 3-, 4-, 5-, and 6-part (P), stacked thirds (1, 3, 5, 7, 9) from the root up (K)

Table H.3. "Harlem Airshaft" outline

Chorus		1				2			
Rehearsal Letter		A	B	C	D	E	F	G	H
Form	Intro	A	A	B	A	A	A	B	A
Material	Motives a b c d e	A	A	B	A	C	C	D	C
Texture		contrapuntal---- tpts 3pt, saxes u		saxes 4/5pt		saxes 3/4/5pt (break on first 4 bars of C sections)			
Solo				tbn 2---		tpt 3------------------------------------			

Chorus	3				4				Coda
Rehearsal Letter	I	J	K	L	M	N	O	P	
Form	A	A	B	A	A	A	B	A	3 bars
Material	E	E	F	E	G	G	H	A	b x
Texture	call and response tbns 3pt , saxes u		brass pads		saxes w. tpt lead	tutti ctd	br 3-6pt saxes u		br 3-6pt saxes u
Solo	cl-----------------------------				tpt 3------------ cl----------------------------------				-------

Introductory Notes:

Original recording information, rehearsal notes by Brent Wallarab and Jon Faddis, notes from Wynton Marsalis.

Form and Texture:

The 12-bar introduction is followed by four 32-bar AABA choruses. Each chorus follows the traditional pattern of similar A sections and a contrasting B (bridge) section, with the exception of the last chorus, where the final A section (letter P) features a shout finale. The three-bar coda (mm. 141–43) is a natural extension of the final shout (see table H.3). Although reharmonized, the chord progression remains fairly consistent, while textures, melodic material, and soloists are varied for each chorus.

Melodic, Harmonic, and Rhythmic Materials:

Five motives are presented in the introduction: a (mm. 1–2, br), b (mm. 1–2, sax), c (mm. 5–7, sax), d (mm. 9–10, tbns), e (mm. 11–13, tbns). These motives, as in some opera overtures, are then used to create the piece: a is developed by saxes (letter C), b by trumpets (letters A, B, and D) and then saxes (letters I, J, K, L, M, N, and P), c by saxes (letters A, B, and D), d by trombones (letters I, J, and L), and e by saxes (letters E, F, G, and H).

Ellington wrote many programmatic pieces and described this one as capturing the sounds and smells heard through an airshaft in a Harlem building, including radio, music, food, arguments, and so on. While the above motives might not be pegged to specific items, this might explain the number and variety encountered.

The presentation of material progresses in an additive manner: the saxophone long-toned bridge in the 1st chorus (letter C) foreshadows the first four bars of the A sections in the 2nd chorus (letters E, F, and H). The following four bars of E, F, H present a chromatic motive derived from e. This motive is further expanded in the bridge (letter G). In the third chorus (letters I, J, and L) trombones develop the riff d initially presented in the introduction, answered by the saxophones. The saxophone response becomes foreground material in the last chorus (letters M, and N). A syncopated figure is introduced at the bridge (letter O), and gives rise to the brass finale, with the reeds recapitulating and expanding riff b and the clarinet soloing in the high register.

Technique Highlight:

Writing for the Baritone Sax not on Root Function
Baritone sax and bass trombone are used on the lowest parts of voicings, most frequently in alternation, and occasionally together when a strong low end is desired. They often play the root or the 5th of the chord. In sax solis (see "Cottontail") and 4-part Basie voicings (see "All of Me") the bari doubles the lead one or two octaves below. Here (at letters C, E, F, and H) Ellington exploits the medium and high register of the bari that is assigned often to 9ths, 7ths, and 3rds, in addition to root functions and double lead passages. This allows for closer sax section voicings and for a different timbral combination.

Making Music

See Rehearsal Notes in score. The mp marking at letter M is probably intended to be *p* or subito *pp*, since the *mp* marking appears again at letter N. From the beginning of letter M to the quarter note on beat 4 four measures from the end, there should be an unbroken crescendo *pp* to *ff*. Letter P features the only forte by the brass section, and the highest lead trumpet note D is reached only in the last brass chord (letter P m. 8). Letter O is the only fully concerted passage in the chart, making it a good testing spot for balance and placement of the upbeat (for discussion of placement of the upbeat see "Cute").

Self-Test Question 31

The drummer plays:

  a. sticks throughout
  b. brushes throughout
  c. mallets and switches to sticks
  d. brushes and switches to sticks

For Further Reading

Gridley, Mark. *Jazz Styles: History and Analysis*. 8th ed. Prentice-Hall, 2003, pp.117–119. Listening guide and discussion, with CD.

I

IN A MELLOW TONE

Ellington, Duke 1940

Ellington, Duke 1940

Grade: 5
Duration: 3:19
Instrumentation: 5, 3, 3, 4. Reed 1 plays ss and as, reed 5 plays bari and as. Tpt 3 opt. cornet, tbn 3 opt vtbn.
Publisher: Warner Bros. Publications, Jazz@Lincoln Center series
Recording: Duke Ellington. *The Blanton-Webster Band*, Bluebird (RCA/BMG) 5659-2, 3CDs. Also in *Smithsonian Collection of Classic Jazz*, CD III.

Highest Written Notes:

Tpt 1: B♭ above staff
Tbn 1: D (five ledger lines)
Tbn 2: C (four ledger lines)

Solos:

(written out): pno + bass duet (8 bars), tpt 2 (one chorus), as1 (one chorus minus first 4 bars)

Introductory Notes:

Notes on Playing Ellington, Glossary, The Four Elements of Music, Instrumentation, Original Recording Information, Rehearsal Notes, Notes from Wynton Marsalis.

Form and Texture:

Eight-bar introduction followed by three 32-bar ABAC choruses. In the introduction piano and bass trade "ones." The first chorus is a call-and-response between second tenor and baritone sax answered by trombones. The second chorus (letter E) features second trumpet dialoguing with the saxes. Here the saxes are SAATT, with the bari player on alto.

On the third chorus (letter I) trumpets play for the first time a tutti concerted that launches the alto sax solo. The alto is accompanied in turn by a 2-bar sustained brass background, a 4-part sax sustained background and a final climactic call and response with the full ensemble. Here (letter L), only C material (letter D) in recapitulated, disposing entirely of A and B material. As in "Harlem Airshaft," the final texture is *f* ensemble tutti concerted with a solo woodwind (see table I.1).

For other examples of climactic endings in Ellington's pieces from this period when the recording limit (per side of 78 rpm disc) was three minutes, see "Harlem Airshaft," "C Jam Blues," and "Cottontail."

Melodic, Harmonic, and Rhythmic Materials:

The sax In-A-Mel-low-Tone riff (A) works in tandem with the trombone answer and the harmony. While the riff remains identical in its first three statements, its relation to the harmony changes: the first

At a Glance:

Articulation	• – > ∧
Bass line:	written
Chords:	Ma6, mi, mi7, Dom (♭5, ♯5, ♭9, 9, ♯9,13), dim, dim7
Dynamics:	p, mp, mf, f, cresc, dim
Edition:	8 1/2x11 oblong, 17 pages. Rehearsal letters every eight bars. No measure numbers
Expressive devices:	fall (short), growl, smear (non pitched gliss), trill, wa wa.
Feel:	swing and even eighths
Form:	8-bar intro, three 32-bar ABAC choruses.
Guitar part:	chord symbols
Key:	A♭ Ma
Modulations:	None
Mutes:	plunger (tpt 2 solo)
Orchestration:	SAATT (saxes E, F, G, H), 4-pt tpt 1 lead doubled 8vb by tbn 3 and bari (L), lead exchange (tbn 3 section lead at A m. 5)
Piano part:	written
Shout:	last 8 bars (L)
Style:	swing
Tempo:	quarter=134 (medium)
Voicings:	saxes: 4-pt close ts 2 dbl lead 8vb (E) and t 1 dbl lead 8vb (F, G, H) alternating with 5-pt close in stacked thirds (1–3–5–7–9) from the root up, internal voice clusters surrounded by 4ths and 5ths, 4-pt drop2 with tension substitutions 9/1 and 13/5 (K) tpts: 2-pt tbns: 3-pt triadic, two guide tones and one extension br: 4-pt close tbn 3 dbl lead 8vb (I, L), 5-pt spreads (J mm. 5–6)

statement ends on ♭7 of the chord (letter A, m. 1), while the following two (letter A, mm. 3 and 5) end on tonic (A♭) of the chord, in conjunction with the harmonic resolution (letter A, m. 3).

The first two statements of the trombone response (letter A, mm. 1–4) feature a static lead (tbn1) and changing under parts (tbns 2-3) that adapt to the chord progression. They are mostly in triads and in tertian combinations (see "Across the Track Blues").

Note the major 7 dissonance between the A♭ of the saxes and the G of first trombone (letter A mm. 1, 3), that is resolved when the trombone motive lands on the tonic note A♭.

A diminished structure planing chromatically concludes the B section (trombones, letter B mm. 7–8).

Swing eighths change to even eighths (letter F mm. 7–8, letter H m. 8) and letter K (bass), and there is a double time feel in saxes (letter G and letter H, excluding measure 3). The piano plays color flourishes on two pitches (F and C) at the end of the introduction and of section C (letter D, m. 8). There is a break half way through the alto sax solo at letter J mm. 7–8. Phrasing in three over the 4/4 time is present in the trombones (letter A mm. 7–8), and saxes (letter H mm. 1–2).

Technique Highlight:

Main Musical Motive based on Title of Tune
Titles of tunes have sometimes supplied inspiration for the main musical motive (or vice versa), even in purely instrumental tunes: In-A-Mel-low-Tone=G–E♭–F–G–A♭. Other examples are Thelonious Monk's "Ruby My Dear" (G–F–C♭–B♭), and Miles Davis's "So What" (A–G).

Making Music
See Rehearsal Notes and Notes on Playing Ellington in the score. Work out the voicings in the usual way as fermatas, top down, bottom up, and so on (see also "Elvin's Mambo"). Your players might need to get used to the uncommon SAATT orchestration at letter E. Go through each voicing as there are various voicings with clusters in the three internal parts, and 5-pt chords stacked in thirds from the root up. Saxes at letters F, G, and H might need extra rehearsal; repeated notes at letter H might need extra care, especially the ones on palm keys that could have more pitch fluctuation. Make sure the first trombone belts out the high Cs at letter I.

Chord symbols are kept simple throughout to free guitar and bass (piano does not comp in this piece) to create their own improvised parts. Pencil into the score the complete chord symbols, based on the

Table I.1. "In a Mellow Tone" outline

Chorus		1				2			
Rehearsal		A	B	C	D	E	F	G	H
Form	Intro	A	B	A	C	A	B	A	C
Texture	trading "ones"	call and response t2-bari/tbns				4/5-pt saxes	dialogue w.tpt2 dbl time feel		
Solo	pno bass					tpt2 ------------------------			

Chorus	3			
Rehearsal	I	J	K	L
Form	A	B	A	C
Texture	tutti concerted (first 4 bars)	brass J5–6	saxes4/5-pt	climactic tutti concerted call and response w. as1
Solo	as1--			

Table I.2. "In a Mellow Tone" ensemble chords at letter E

Measure	E 1	2	3	4	5	6	7	8
Actual Chord	B♭7 (9, 13)	E♭7 (9)	A♭	E♭7(♭9)	E♭mi 9	A♭7(♯9)	D♭ A♭7 sus	D♭

actual harmonies in the ensemble, so they can be a guide for you as you listen to the comping and the ensemble. Table I.2 shows the "revised" chords that the ensemble is playing at letter E.

Work out the four parts of the chords at letter L by having each group of instruments play their line in unison with their doubling(s), then play all together.

Self-Test Question 32

The powerful last section at letter L is voiced in four parts. One of the following is true:

a. each of the parts is present in the brass, is doubled, and the lead is tripled

b. each of the parts is present in the brass, parts 3 and 4 are doubled, and the lead is tripled

c. each of the parts is present in the brass, is doubled, and the lead is doubled

d. each of the parts is present in the saxes but not in the brass, and the lead is tripled

Lead Sheet

The New Real Book. Vol 3. Sher Music Co., 1995.
  The Real Book. 6th ed. Hal Leonard, 2004.

⟋⟋⟋

IN THE 80's

Mintzer, Bob 1986

Mintzer, Bob 1986

Grade:	5
Duration:	8:25
Instrumentation:	5, 4, 4, 3
Publisher:	Kendor Music
Recording:	Bob Mintzer Big Band. *Camouflage.* DMP C-456, 1986.

Highest Written Notes:

Tpt 1:	E (three ledger lines)
Tpt 2:	D (two ledger lines)
Tbn 1-2:	B (four ledger lines)

Solos:

dms (open), dms and ts2 duet (open, free tonality), piano, bari (32 bars, open), as1 (32 bars, open), ts2 and tpt 4 duet (4 bars, open), dms (open)

Introductory Notes:

At a Glance:

Articulation:	• – > ≥
Bass line:	written, chord symbols on solo section, written line on unison section (m. 183)
Chord Progression:	D mi centered, with many pedals, ♭VII cadential patterns (CMa or Csus4 to Dmi), half step relations (A♭–B♭, then G–A, mm. 18–26), upper chromatic dominants (mm. 221–22), and modal interchange (Imi–I7, mm. 103–04)
Chords:	Ma 6/9, Ma7(9, ♯11), mi7 (6, 9,11), mi7♭5, Dom7 (♭9, 9, ♯9, ♯11, ♯5, 13, sus4, alt, octat,), triads and 7th chords over bass note
Dynamics:	*mp, mf, f, cresc, dim, sub p, sfp*
Edition:	8 1/2x11 vertical, 16 pages. Measure numbers every bar, boxed numbers highlighting sections
Form:	multisectional
Key:	D mi
Modulations:	to C and G minor for the solo section
Mutes:	none
Orchestration:	the 24-bar imitative passage (mm. 183–99) features unison entrances: (1) tenors, bari, tbns, bass, piano, (2) tpts 2-3-4, (3) altos and tenors, in 3-pt counterpoint.
Piano:	written chords, chord symbols, written line (m. 183)
Shout:	mm. 207 and 247 are climactic.
Style:	mambo
Tempo:	half note=120
Voicings:	saxes: uni, 4-pt, 4-pt sw, 5-pt, spreads
	tpts: uni, 2-pt, 3-pt triadic dbl lead 8vb, 4-pt, 4-pt (triad with added pitch), 4-pt sw
	tbns: uni, 2-pt, 4-pt close, 4-pt 4ths, spreads
	brass: 6-pt structures (octatonic, mm. 227–29), 7-pt structures (octatonic, mm. 23–26), 8-pt structures (in 4ths, with third between top two voices, mm. 18–22), couplings in 4ths/5ths (tpts 1-2-3/tbns 1-2-3, mm. 79–90)
	ens: 4-pt sw (unison couplings: tpt 1-2, tpt 3-4, tbn 1-2, tbn 3-4, sax doubling, no bari)

Form and Texture:

The introduction features an open drum and percussion solo. The ensemble enters on cue with tutti chords, a 3-part texture (m. 13), and constant structures (m. 18). An open duet in free tonality between second tenor and drums follows at m. 27. The rhythm section then vamps over the tonic pedal, with the piano soloing, as an introduction to the head at m. 39. Sections are generally eight bars (clearly highlighted by boxed numbers) and present varied repetitions of the material.

At measures 95–102 an unaccompanied tutti concerted ensemble section launches both bari and alto solos. The second solo truncates the last four bars (mm. 163–66) and leads directly to the coda. The coda sign initiates a long section that includes new material, beginning with a three-part counterpoint fugato-like section (m. 183), followed by a climactic section with high unison trumpets accompanied by contrapuntal riffs in the saxes and trombones (m. 207), an ostinato on a D7 chord (mm. 227–30), an unaccompanied ensemble section with sparse/weird solos by trumpet and tenor (mm. 235–38), and an open section for a drums and percussion solo (mm. 239–42). The climactic section (m. 207) is then reprised (m. 247) and the piece is brought to conclusion (see table I.3).

Melodic, Harmonic, and Rhythmic Materials:

The A section melody (mm. 39–46) uses the D minor natural mode harmonized with "So What" voicings, over a D pedal. The expanded repetition (mm. 47–54) is over a C pedal for the first four bars. The final statement (m. 55) closes on D7, a blues inflected I7, also the final chord of the piece (mm. 267–69). The A theme is comprised of a rhythmic motive (mm. 39–40) beginning on 3+, rhythmically displaced to begin on 1+ upon repetition (mm. 41–42).

Table I.3. "In the 80's" outline

Measure	1	3	27	31	39	47	55
Material	introduction			vamp	A	A1	A2
# of bars	open	24	open	16	8	8	8
Texture	drums	dms/tutti	dms/ts2	rhy sect	tutti/pno	--------	---------

Measure	63	71	79	87	91	95 (Segno)	103	Dal Segno
Material	B	B1	B2	B3	C	D	E E F F1	
# of bars	8	8	8	4	8	8	8 8 8	
Texture	tutti					tutti stop time	solos + bkgs	

Measure	167	183	207	227	231 235	239	247 255 267
Material	C Coda	G	H H1	I	H1 J		H H1 I
# of bars	16	24	16 12	4	4 open	open	16 12 3
Texture	pedal	imitation			tutti a cappella	drums	tutti

In section B (m. 63) the phrasing is in four bars, over an A dominant pedal. Section C (m. 91) features a descending D pentatonic minor motive in bass trombone and bass. Section D introduces an unaccompanied tutti concerted ensemble that leads to a modulation to the key of C (m. 103), using unison pitches G and C ("five" and "one"). The C tonality is established melodically by the prominent note C (mm. 103–04, and mm. 135–38), while the harmony uses sus4 and dominant type chords (Csus and C7) that lead to the G minor key area (mm. 119–27).

Section G (m. 183) employs the D minor scale with passing ♭5, and the D octatonic scale and expands the bass motive first introduced at m. 91. The imitative entrances at mm. 183–99 are: (1) tenors, bari, tbns, bass, piano; (2) tpts 2-3-4; (3) altos and tenors, in 3-pt counterpoint. The trumpet melody at m. 107 is also based on D minor pentatonic.

Ensemble figures feature syncopation, displacement, and often a strong fourth beat emphasis. The bass plays 2-bar mambo ostinato figures, and passages concerted with the ensemble.

Technique Highlight:

"So What" Voicings
"So What" voicings derive their name from the title of the Miles Davis tune that first popularized them.

The voicing consists of stacked fourths built from the root up, with a major third on top. The original chord was a D minor 7 with 11th (fifth in the lead), but these voicings have gone on to be employed on other chords such as major 7 (beginning on the 3rd). They appear here in the theme at m. 39, built on the ♭7 of the chord: C–F–B♭–D (root on the lead). "So What" voicings are also used in the trumpets in the introduction (m. 18) over trombones in stacked fourths to produce an 8-part voicing: A♭–D♭–G♭–B–F–B♭–E♭–G.

Making Music
Listen to this and other mambo recordings. Begin building the rhythm section groove at m. 31. Review bass patterns with the "one" on "four." You might want to have players subdivide them verbally in eighth notes. The 2-bar pattern, starting on beat four, is: 12345 123 12345 123 (see figure I.1).

Review the concept of clave (3–2, 2–3, and its variations). The clave here is a "rumba clave" (see m. 243) with the third note syncopated on beat four "and." It might help to have the ensemble clap the clave while the rhythm section plays, to gain ease with it (see figure I.2).

Though not included in the score, this chart calls for an additional percussion player (congas, cowbell,

Figure I.1 Mambo bass pattern

3-2 clave

2-3 clave

rumba clave

Figure I.2 Clave patterns

timbales, etc.) in addition to the drummer. The player can look over the drummer's part for kicks and ensemble parts. In addition to a strong percussion section, which is spotlighted in the two open sections at m. 1 and m. 241, you need a strong tenor player who can play "out" in the duet with the drummer (m. 27), and then solos by the alto and bari.

Rehearse the imitative passage at m. 183 one line at a time and then as is. Articulations and dynamics are well marked throughout the arrangement. Notice the many *subito p*, crescendos, and decrescendos, and make sure the ensemble as a whole follows them, especially the drummer that has, with the brass, the most dynamic power. In addition to all regular cues for anyone who has been resting more than eight bars, you will need to cue the "on cue" sections. When you feel the soloists in the open sections have played enough, count off four bars in "two" (1 . . . 2 . . . 1 . 2 . 1234) (mm. 3, 31, 135, 239). In the sections where the bass and drums drop out (mm. 95, 235) you might need to step in and conduct with a continuous beat pattern (see also "The Happy Song").

Self-Test Question 33
The second and third imitative entrances at m. 190 and m. 198 are:

   a. at the unison
   b. at the fifth
   c. at the octave, then fifth
   d. at the fifth, then octave

INTERMISSION RIFF

Wetzel, Ray 1946

Wetzel, Ray 1946
Grade: 5
Duration: 3:14
Instrumentation: 5, 5, 4, 4
Publisher: Kendor Music
Recording: Stan Kenton Orchestra. *Milestones.* Capitol LP, out of print.
Stan Kenton. *Retrospective.* Capitol, four CDs. Also on *The Best of Stan Kenton.* Capitol Jazz CDP 7243 8 31504 2 7, CD.

Highest Written Notes:
Tpt 1:   G (four ledger lines)
Tpt 2:   E♭ (two ledger lines)
Tpt 3:   D (two ledger lines)
Tbn 1:   F (two ledger lines)

Solos:
piano (4 bars, written), bass (4 bars, written), ts 1 (two choruses), as 1 (two choruses), bass (4 bars, written)

Introductory Notes:
Director's Notes by Bob Curnow

At a Glance:

Articulation:	> ∧ slurs
Bass line:	chord symbols, written solo
Chords:	mi7 (9), Ma6 (9), Ma7 (9, ♯11, 13), Dom (7, ♯9)
Chord progression:	I 6/9, ♭II Ma 6/9, II–9, ♭II7(♯9), I Ma7
Dynamics:	*p, mp, f, ff, fff, cresc*
Edition:	8 1/2x11 oblong, 16 pages. Measure numbers on each bar. Boxed numbers highlighting form
Expressive devices:	portamento, smear (saxes and tbns), shake, fall (tpts), gliss (piano)
Form:	intro (4+4), 10 choruses (12 bar form), coda (2 bars). Additional head chorus (12 bars) optional (not in original version) after chorus 2
Guitar:	chord symbols with rhythm slashes
Key:	D♭ Ma
Modulations:	none
Mutes:	none
Piano part:	chord symbols with rhythm slashes, written solo intro
Shout:	chorus 9 (m. 117)
Style:	bounce
Tempo:	quarter=168
Time feel:	in 4; ritard and hold on intro
Voicings:	saxes: unis, 5-pt spreads tpts: unis, 4-pt (tertian) with lead doubled 8vb 4-pt close (7th chords) tbns: unis, 4-pt spreads

Form and Texture:

The 4-bar piano solo introduction ends on a fermata. The tempo is then set up by a two-hand dominant-tonic note glissando (A♭–D♭, m. 4), leading to a 2-bar riff played twice by the bass. Ten choruses and a 2-bar coda follow.

The main riff (riff a) is played throughout by the trombones. When the trombones switch to a unison figure z (m. 69), saxes play their own variation of the riff (riff b) (mm. 69, 105, and 117, choruses 5, 8, and 9). The main riff and its variation are specific to the trombones (riff a), and the saxes (riff b), emphasizing the "head" arrangement quality of the piece. Trumpets (not including the optional chorus at m. 33) play only two choruses, entering for the first time in chorus 8 (m. 105) with a unison figure of their own. In chorus 9 (the shout, m. 117), they join the saxes in riff b and then split into a climactic call and response at mm. 124–28.

Chorus 10 follows (m. 129), recapitulating chorus 2 (m. 21) with a short two-bar extension. Choruses are 12 bars in length. Writing is sectional. An additional head chorus (not in the original version) is optional after chorus 2 (m. 33) (see table I.4).

Melodic, Harmonic, and Rhythmic Materials:

The piano introduction cycles a dominant structure (1, 3, ♭7) in the left hand, down an octave (C7 to C7) through the complete chromatic scale, while the right hand sequences a four note motive (B♭–A♭–E♭–F) through the whole tone scale (B♭–A♭—G♭–E–D–C) to cadence on a C13 chord on m. 4.

The main chorus is constituted of three 4-bar phrases in an aab pattern. This design and the 12-bar form of the piece are two connections to the blues, though the piece is not a blues. The first two 4-bar riffs are identical (mm. 9 and 16) bars and feature chromatic planing between D♭ 6/9 and D6/9. The concluding four bars (mm. 17–20) feature oblique motion with the top note F sustaining over harmonies descending chromatically (II–9, ♭II7♯9, IMa7).

Theme A (m. 21) displays the same aab phrasing pattern and is played by unison saxes in a legato fashion that contrasts with the staccato riff ongoing in the trombones. The contrasting unison figure in the trombones (choruses 5, 8, and 9) is based on a three-note descending motive z first presented in ascending fashion by the bass (m. 5–8). The sax unison background to the alto sax solo (choruses 6 and 7) is a two-eighth-note motive x outlining a descending fifth, first introduced by the piano at mm. 4–5, and then found in the fourth trombone part in riff a.

Technique Highlight:

Planing

Planing denotes stepwise movement of all parts of a chord in parallel motion to the lead. Planing yields

Table I.4. "Intermission Riff" outline

Chorus	intro	1	2	2a (optional)	3	4
Measure	1	9	21	33	45	57
Saxes			A	A	ts solo	
Trumpets				sustained +z		
Trombones		riff a	riff a	riff a	riff a	riff a
Rhythm	piano x +bass y	comp				

Chorus	5	6	7	8	9 shout	10	coda
Measure	69	81	93	105	117	129	141
Saxes	riff b	as solo + bkg x	riff b	riff b	A		x
Trumpets				C	riff b		
Trombones	z	riff a	riff a	z	riff a	riff a	x
Rhythm	comp						x
							bass solo y

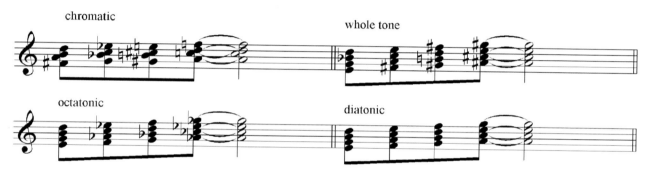

Figure I.3 Planing

exact parallelism when the lead uses chromatic, whole tone, or octatonic scale motion. Planing is diatonic when the voices move stepwise utilizing the scale or mode, without a consistent duplication of the exact intervals of the lead (fig. I.3). In this piece the main riff planes chromatically upward to the second chord (Db 6/9 to D 6/9).

Making Music

Entrust the introduction to the pianist and bass player. The pianist needs to play in tempo at the outset, ritardando only at m. 3, followed by a short hold at m. 4. The bass player will then enter at the tempo first set up by the pianist upon hearing the pianist's glissando into the downbeat of m. 4. If necessary you can count off two bars at the fermata and give the m. 5 downbeat. The rest is straightforward, without tempo changes.

Work out the voicings at mm. 115–28, since it is the only harmonized passage in the trumpets. They are generally 4-part 7th chord inversions, with the fifth trumpet doubling the lead an octave below. This

doubling is especially crucial when the lead needs to get up to Eb, F, G on the last four bars, since it provides support and pitch reference. Notice the relation of the lead to the bass line: Eb =b7, F=b9, G=3.

Self-Test Question 34

In both the head (chorus 2, mm. 21–32), and head out (chorus 10, mm. 129–40):

a. the sax section theme is louder than the trombone riff
b. the sax section theme is louder than the trombone riff, then becomes softer
c. the sax section theme has the same dynamic as the trombone riff
d. the sax section theme is softer than the trombone riff

I'VE GOT YOU UNDER MY SKIN

Porter, Cole 1936

Holman, Bill 1955

Grade:	5.5
Duration:	5:28
Instrumentation:	5, 5, 5, 3 (the original recording has guitar, in addition to piano)
Publisher:	Sierra Music
Recording:	Stan Kenton. *Contemporary Concepts.* Capitol Jazz 7243 5 42310 2 5 CD.

Highest Written Notes:

Tpt 1:	F (three ledger lines)
Tbn 1:	C (four ledger lines)

Solos:
bari (56), trpt 4 (48), ts 2 (28+18), as 2 (6 improvised, 52 written melody with chord changes), tpt 3 (24 written)

Introductory Notes:
Director's Notes, General Performance Comments by Bob Curnow

Form and Texture:
The form of the original tune is 56 measures: A (16), A1 (16), B (16), C/A2 (8). No introduction. In the first chorus (of six), Holman extends the A section with short drum solos in mm. 4–5 and mm. 10–13, repeating the process for A1 (m. 22), and extends the C section by 4 measures, resulting in the following form: A (13), A1 (13), B (16), C (12) (see table I.5).

The solo choruses follow the original 56-bar form except for chorus six, where one bar is added to section C (m. 349, 9 bars total). While the form for the solos repeats regularly, the ensemble frequently states foreground concerted passages that launch solos or interact with them. This results in solos of varied length: bari (56), tpt 4 (48), ts 2 (44), as 2 (52), tpt 3 (24) (see table I.6).

There is an interlude (m. 239, 6 bars), and a coda (m. 358, 9 bars).

At a Glance:

Articulation:	• – > ∧ slurs
Bass line:	written and chord symbols
Chords:	Ma (6, 9), Ma7, mi7 (9, 11), min7 (♭5), Dom 7 (9, ♭9, 9, ♯11, ♯5, 13, sus), dim7
Chord progression:	mostly diatonic to the key, with passing diminished chords, secondary dominants (V/ii), upper chromatic dominants (to ii and V/ii), subdominant minor (iv).
Dynamics:	*p, mp, mf, f, ff, fp, cresc, dim*
Edition:	8 1/2x11 oblong, 33 pages. Boxed numbers highlighting sections
Expressive devices:	drop (all)
Form:	AA1BC (56 bars) with extensions, interludes, and coda. See Form and Texture
Key:	E♭ Ma
Modulations:	none
Mutes:	cups (tpts)
Piano part:	chord symbols
Shout:	mm. 341–48 (chorus 6) are climactic
Style:	swing ("cool')
Tempo:	quarter=280
Voicings:	saxes: unis, 2-pt, 5-pt tpts: unis, 2-pt, triads, 4-pt close (double lead 8vb), 5-pt close, tbns: unis, 2-pt, 3-pt, 4-pt, 5-pt spreads brass: block voicings

The opening A section features concerted 5-part voicings (mm. 1–13) followed by saxes and brass in contrapuntal unison lines (mm. 14–21) with the bass laying out. Section A1 (mm. 22–42) repeats the same alternation of textures. Sections B and C (mm. 43–70) also feature contrapuntal unison lines culminating in a tutti concerted passage (mm. 69–70) that launches the bari solo.

Table I.5. "I've Got You Under My Skin," choruses 1 and 2

Chorus	1				2			
Measure	1	22	43	59	71			
Material	head				solo			
Form	A	A	B	C	A	A	B	C
Number of bars	13+8 13+8 8+8 12 drum solos (2+4 bars) added in A sections				16	16	16	8 form evened out →
Total number of bars	70				56			

Table I.6. "I've Got You Under My Skin," solo choruses of various lengths

Chorus	2				3				4			
Measure	71				127				183			
Material	A	A	B	C	A	A	B	C	A	A	B	C
Number of bars	16	16	16	8	16	16	16	8	16	16	16	8
Ensemble foreground					8				4 (1st A) 8 (B)			
Solo	Baritone (56)→ written				Trumpet 4 (48) → improvised				Tenor 2 (44) → written			

Chorus	Interlude	5				6			
Measure	239	245				301			
Material		A	A	B	C	A	A	B	C
Number of bars	2+ 4 stop time	16	16	16	8	16	16	16	8
Ensemble foreground	one bar stop time figure	4 (1st A)				16 (1st A) 8 (last 8 of B), 8 (C)			
Solo	Alto 2 pick-up (2) and stop time (4) improvised (6)→	Alto 2 (52)→ written				Trumpet 3 (24) → written			

The rest of the piece features migration of unison motives among and within sections, creating long lines of changing instrumental color alternating with concerted tutti passages. The last chorus builds toward the climax (mm. 341–48), before the last C section (m. 349) and coda (m. 358).

Melodic, Harmonic, and Rhythmic Materials:

The original melody is manipulated rhythmically and melodically. In addition, various motives are extracted from the original tune and developed. Two of them appear prominently: x (F–A♭–B♭, trumpets, m. 43), and y (C–C♯–D, trombones, m. 43, later transposed and inverted). They appear individually (x mm. 87, 159, 358; y mm. 62, 95, 127, 199, 269), and combined (mm. 43, 159, mm. 363–66 in rhythmic augmentation).

The form of the original melody lends itself to various analyses, as many phrases are reused and developed in a through composed manner, making it restrictive to name the sections in only one way. While A and A1 are clear-cut, what follows can be viewed in different ways, as Porter's melodic and harmonic materials are inescapably linked to his lyrics.

Technique Highlight:

Ensemble and Solo Statements Overlap
Soloists frequently "spill over" their improvisations into the beginning of the next soloist's chorus, or start their improvisations before or after the beginning (or "top") of the form.

Similarly here the ensemble states foreground concerted passages that launch solos or interact with them (see above discussion). This interaction and give and take between soloist and ensemble is also at the basis of the *concerto* style in classical music.

Making Music

Read the Director's Notes and Performance Comments in the score. See also comments for "Just Friends," as the tempos and some of the approaches to ensemble figures might be similar.

The drummer needs to understand where to fill, play time, and lead the ensemble. Dynamics change rapidly, for example from *f* to *pp* over the course of six bars (m. 358) and in the decrescendo from full ensemble to solo section (mm. 68–71). There are also many *f* and *ff* passages that emerge suddenly from *p* sections (mm. 126, 214, and 240). Because of the numerous solos it is useful to study the form carefully so the many juxtapositions of combo/solo sections with full ensemble and their dynamic peaks and valleys are rendered.

Self-Test Question 35
The piece ends on a:

a. Major 7 chord with 9th and 13th
b. Major 7 chord with 9th and 13th and no 3rd
c. Minor 6 chord with 9th and 11th
d. Major 7 chord with ♯11

J

JUST FRIENDS

Davies, Raymond, John Klenner, and Sam M. Lewis 1931

Holman, Bill 1987

Grade:	5.
Duration:	5:51
Instrumentation:	5, 4, 4, 4
Publisher:	Sierra Music
Recording:	*The Bill Holman Band.* JVC 6004-2 CD.

Highest Written Notes:

Tpt 1:	E (three ledger lines)
Tbn 1:	C (four ledger lines)

Solos:
piano (one chorus), open section for solos (one chorus)

Introductory Notes:
Director's Notes and General Performance Comments by Bob Curnow

Form and Texture:
The piano solos with the rhythm section in the introduction and first chorus. Choruses 2–7 are basically unison ensemble (with the exception of mm. 124–27 and mm. 167–68) and rhythm section comping. Chorus 2 is a reworked "head" and the rest are "written improvisation." Chorus 8 (m. 225) is open for solos on the form. The first four bars are an ensemble kicker in four part counterpoint. The four unison lines are: (1) AATT saxes; (2) trumpets; (3) trombones 1-3; (4) bari sax and trombone 4 (on the recording the trumpets sustain a high E). Choruses 9 and 10 (mm. 257 and 291) are climactic and feature tutti concerted and two and three part imitative textures. Chorus 9 adds two measures to its B section (m. 273–74). Chorus 10

Table J.1 "Just Friends": chord progression in original and arrangement

Section	A							
Original	CMa7		C-7	F7		GMa7	B♭-7	E♭7
Holman	CMa7			F7		GMa7		E♭7
Roman Numeral	IVMa7		iv-7	♭VII7		IMa7	ii of subV7/V	subV7/V

Section	B							
Original	A-7	D7	B-7	E-7	A7		A-7 D7	D-7 G7
Holman	A-7	D7	B-7	G6	A9	E-7 A7	A-7 E♭7	D7 D♭7
Roman Numeral	ii-7	V7	iii-7	I6	V7/V	vi and V7/V	ii-7, upper chrom. dominants to C major	

At a Glance:

Articulation:	• – > ∧ slurs
Bass line:	chord symbols, written conclusion (3 bars)
Chords:	Ma 6 (9), Ma7 (9, #11), mi7 (9, 11), Dom 7 (♭9, 9, #9, #11, #5, ♭13, 13)
Chord progression:	the chord progression from the original tune is used, with some variations.
Dynamics:	*mf, f, ff, fff, cresc, dim*
Edition:	8 1/2x11 oblong, 22 pages. Measure numbers every bar, boxed numbers highlighting sections
Expressive devices:	portamento (all), shake (brass)
Form:	intro (8) ten ABAB1 choruses (32 bars, with some extensions in choruses 9 and 10), coda (10)
Guitar part:	chord symbols and line with the ensemble
Key:	G Ma
Modulations:	none
Mutes:	none
Piano part:	chord symbols, written conclusion (3 bars)
Shout:	last A and coda are climactic
Style:	bop
Tempo:	half=116
Voicings:	saxes: unis, 2-pt, 4-pt (dbl lead 8vb), 5-pt tpts: unis, 2-pt, 3-pt (triads with lead doubled 8vb), 4-pt close tbns: unis, 2-pt, 3-pt, 4-pt close, 4-pt spreads ens: block voicings and cascade effect (unison to 4-pt)

extends its B1 section by 16 bars (mm. 323–38). A coda follows at m. 339, with a fermata on m. 345, and a three bar drum solo and final ensemble chord.

Melodic, Harmonic, and Rhythmic Materials:
The melodic material is through composed, with the tune presented in the second chorus (m. 33), and im-

mediately varied (the second A at m. 49 is reduced to a single rhythmicized B♭ pitch). The concluding B section (mm. 57–64) and the following unison ensemble choruses use motivic development, displacement, sequences, passing notes, and chromatic and diatonic approaches. The "arranger's" choruses 9 and 10 (m. 257–end) feature phrases that are repeated (mm. 257–58, mm. 275–76, mm. 307–08, mm. 339–40), others that are varied (mm. 260–64, mm. 278–82), and developed (m. 273 expands into mm. 283–86, and the quintuplet at m. 257 is extended through mm. 319–35). Among the prominent motives reiterated and developed are: falling 5th (m. 93), chromaticism (m. 129), and ascending 8ve (m. 193). The chord progression is a variation on the original. The first two sections can be seen in table J.1.

The original progression is followed closely through the first eight choruses. While the original chords are still clearly recognizable, reharmonizations are present in choruses 9 and 10. The extension of the last B1 section (m. 315) repeats the cadential V7 of V to V7 (A7 D7) pattern, landing on an E♭ pedal (m. 342–45) over which the ensemble sustains a G triad and the pianist is asked to "fill as if last chord" (on G), creating a humorous mock sense of resolution (tonic chord over its ♭6 scale degree). This is resolved in the final chord G (=I Ma 9 #11) after the short drum solo.

In addition to the use of quarter note quintuplets, three-over-four polyrhythmic passages are present (m. 101, m. 283, and m. 315).

Technique Highlight

Written Solo Improvisation Line
Writing a unison line for the ensemble that has the quality, direction, and developmental characteristics of an improvised solo comes from playing and/or listening to jazz improvisers, specifically single line instrumentalist/vocalists. Many of the techniques used by improvisers, such as rhythmic displacement, motivic development, approach notes, and so on, can be incorporated in a written solo. A written improvisation can also be harmonized as a *soli*. The line here is in a fast bebop style.

Making Music
Read the Director's Notes and Performance Comments in the score. Seven of the ten choruses are a fast unison jazz line. It needs to be worked up gradually so it can be played cleanly, in good time,

and with the articulation called for. The rest of the chart contains many repeated full ensemble rhythmic figures. Focusing on the first 16 bars of chorus 9 will help with the subsequent repetitions/variations.

If encountering challenges, reduce problem passages to the most basic elements: have the ensemble clap, then play rhythms on one pitch in slow tempo and then gradually speed up. Play chords as fermatas and then in tempo. Most voicing are 4-part close and block. Play each of the imitations at m. 291 individually, and then as a whole. Mark in the score with progressive numbers all choruses. Assign the writing of a solo variation on a given tune.

Self-Test Question 36
A *Cascade Effect* is the movement of a line from unison to harmony, generally through progressive splitting of parts. At m. 305 trombones play a:

a. cascade from 2 to 4-parts
b. cascade from unison to 4-parts
c. reverse cascade from 4 parts to unison
d. none of the above

Lead Sheet:
The New Real Book. Vol 3. Sher Music Co., 1995.

K

KATY

Nestico, Sammy 1977

Nestico, Sammy 1977
Grade: 3.5
Duration: 3:30
Instrumentation: 5, 4, 4, 4
Publisher: Kendor Music
Dedication: Katherine (Count Basie's wife)
Recording: A *Portrait of Sammy* at www.sammynesticomusic.com.

Highest Written Notes:
Tpt 1:   G (top of staff)
Tbn 1:   F (two ledger lines)

Solos:
(written) tpt 2 (opt flug) (mm. 22–30, 50–55), piano obbligato in octaves (mm. 1–14, 33–34, 47–50), obbligato and chords (mm. 15–37, 51–55), and obbligato with chord symbols comping and improvisation around the melody (mm. 38–46)

Notes:
Contrapuntal writing over spreads, nice feature for tpt 2 and piano, chord changes and much melodic material are different in A2 and A3, providing a through composed feel that contributes to the drive toward the modulation at the end.

Introductory Notes:
To the Director, About the Writer

Form and Texture:
Intro, AABA with reprise from the B and final A modulating to the subdominant A♭.

Textures are varied, with contrapuntal activity and sustained backgrounds. The melody in the introduction is outlined in its entirety by piano with specific segments doubled by saxes and trumpets. The first A (m. 7) features the melody in the trumpets with the first alto joining in at mm. 8–9. The piano plays a counter line in octaves, while a second counter line emerges gradually in the saxes and trombones. In the second A (m. 15) the piano counter line migrates to the saxes. The B section (m. 23) features a trumpet solo (optional flugelhorn) with sustained background by the saxes. Piano solo follows on the reprise of B (m. 39), while the ensemble and the trumpet solo share the final section (mm. 47–55) (see table K.1).

Table K.1. "Katy" outline

Measure	1	7	15	23	31	39	47
Material	Intro	A	A1	B	A2	B1	A3
Number of bars	6	8	8	8	8	8	9
Key	E♭						A♭

At a Glance:

Articulation:	– > slurs, slight attack (bari, mm. 35, 51)
Bass line:	written
Chords:	Ma6, Ma7, mi7 (Ma7, 9, 11), Dom7 (♭9, 9, ♯11, ♭5, ♯5, 13, sus4), dim7, slash chords, triads over bass
Chord progresssion:	II–V, secondary dominants (V/II), substitute dominants (subV/III, subV/IV, subV/VI), modal interchange (♭IIIMa7, ♭VI Ma7 and their dominants and substitute dominants)
Dynamics:	*pp, p, mf, f, fz, cresc, dim*
Edition:	8 1/2x11 vertical, 4 pages. Measure numbers every bar, boxed numbers highlighting sections
Expressive devices:	connecting gliss (bari m. 7–22), gliss up (saxes m. 25), gliss down (tpt 2 mm. 51–55)
Form:	intro (6), A A1 B A2 (32), B (8), A3 (9). A1 features a different texture, A2 and A3 feature different changes, and A3 is in the subdominant key
Guitar:	chord symbols (arpeggiated), written single line
Key:	E♭ Ma
Linear devices:	counter line (mm. 7–14, saxes mm. 15–22), wedge (tpts and tbn 3-4, bari, mm. 10, 18)
Modulations:	progressive tonality (ends in A♭ Ma)
Mutes:	none
Orchestration:	bari on roots throughout (with some cp lines), and tbn 4 on roots throughout (with occasional 5ths)
Piano:	written obbligato in octaves (mm. 7–14, mm. 47–50), written chords w. single line passages, written single line and chord symbols on solo (mm. 38–46)
Style:	contemporary ballad (straight 8ths)
Tempo:	quarter=76 with rubato
Voicings:	saxes: 5-pt spreads
	tpts: triadic, 2-pt, 3-pt
	tbns: 3-pt, 4-pt, spreads

Melodic, Harmonic, and Rhythmic Materials:

The introduction begins by outlining the parallel minor mode (Eb minor, m. 1), and then four notes from the key of E♭ (E♭, F, A♭, B♭), over the dominant pedal (mm. 2–5). The A section melody is composed of a sequence of 2-bar motives comprised of six ascending eighth notes and a descending resolution, and of a counter line also in 2-bar phrases. Section B features a 2-bar motive in a descending chromatic sequence (mm. 23–30).

The harmony draws from E♭ major with II–Vs, secondary dominants (V/II), substitute dominants (subV/III, subV/IV, subV/VI), and from the parallel minor (♭IIIMa7, ♭VI Ma7 and their dominants and substitute dominants). The third A (mm. 31–38) is varied both melodically and harmonically, and features an entirely new set of changes that reappear also (transposed to the subdominant) in the final A section (mm. 47–54).

Technique Highlight:

Chords Borrowed from the Parallel Minor
See "Ballad for Benny" for a discussion of chords borrowed from the parallel minor. Here the usage of the parallel key E♭ minor is seen at the outset in the piano arpeggio in m. 1.

G♭ Ma7 (=♭IIIMa7), and Bma7 (=♭VI Ma7) are then tonicized by their dominants and substitute dominants at mm. 10–12 steering the A section to the minor key area.

Making Music

While the tempo and ranges should not offer challenges, presenting clearly all the lines and counter lines might need attention. Mark all moving lines, primary, secondary, and tertiary, often short segments that migrate through the orchestration. As an exercise for tuning in to lines and doublings have the ensemble play only lines containing eighths, eighth-note triplets, or quarter notes (and pause when longer values are encountered). Do the same with values a half note or longer.

The pianist needs to play clean single lines in octaves; other that in the intro where it is intended, the pedal should be used sparingly. The drummer plays sticks. Trumpet 2 can play with harmon mute the last solo at mm. 50–55. The first measure is rubato, followed by tempo on the downbeat of m. 2.

Self-Test Question 37
The final chord at m. 55 features a:

    a. 9–8 suspension
    b. 2–3 suspension
    c. 4–3 suspension
    d. leading tone resolution

KING PORTER '94

Morton, Jelly Roll 1902 or 1905

Brookmeyer, Bob 1994
Grade: 6
Duration: 7:00
Instrumentation: 5, 5, 4, 5 (bari on b.cl throughout. Rhythm section: vibraphone, synth 1 and 2 ("el.pno sound with chorus, bell/el. pno. sound"), bass, drums
Publisher: Advance Music
Recording: Bob Brookmeyer. *Waltzing with Zoe.* Challenge CD

Fred Sturm. *Changes Over Time: The Evolution of Jazz Arranging* (book and CD), Advance Music.

Highest Written Notes:
Tpt 1:   D (two ledger lines)
Tpt 2:   D (two ledger lines)
Tbn 1:   C (four ledger lines)
Tbn 2:   A (three ledger lines)

Solos:
none. Extensive "soloistic fills" for drums beginning at m. 42.

Soli:
rhythm section (mm. 150–60)

Notes:
see expanded rhythm section requirements above

Introductory Notes:
None

Form and Texture:
This work is through composed and can be grouped in five main sections that share a similar two-part organization with a first part featuring a static pedal, and the second part exhibiting modulating harmonies. A rhythm section vamp precedes some of these sections. A tonal return occurs at m. 150 where the original A♭ pedal and vamp from m. 25 return. The main climax occurs at m. 195. Textures range from unison lines to 2–3–4–5–8 part counterpoint, 12-tone vertical structures, and concerted passages (see table K.2).

Melodic, Harmonic, and Rhythmic Materials:
Some of the main motives are extrapolated from the original Jelly Roll Morton piece and provide

Table K.2. "King Porter '94" outline

Form	intro	vamp	I, 1	2	II, 1	2	vamp
Measure	1–24	25	42	74	91	123	150
Harmony/ tonal center	chrom.	A♭-------	----------	modul.	C--------	modul.	A♭ return

III, 1	2	IV, 1	2	vamp	V, 1	2	coda	--------
171	185	203	227	255	271	295	325	339
chrom.---	------- climax (m. 195)	C ------	modul.	A--------	---------	modul.	---------	A

At a Glance:

Articulation:	– • > ≥ ∧ , dot over tenuto, sf, slurs
Bass line:	written
Chords:	intervallic structures (Ma/m 3rd tricord and Ma/m 3rd dominant structure), triads, Ma6/9, mi (Ma 7), mi7 (9,11), mi7(♭5), Dom (♭5, #9, #11, sus)
Chord progression:	modal and intervallic construction, occasional functional tonality
Dynamics:	p, mp, mf, f, ff, cresc, dim
Edition:	8 1/2x11 oblong, 32 pages. Measure numbers every bar. Double barlines for articulation of form.
Expressive devices:	no vib, half in stand
Form:	through composed
Key:	progressive tonality A♭ to A modal centers
Modes:	C-nat, C- harm, C-dor, C blues, mixo, aeol, alt, oct 0–1–2, pentatonic major and minor
Modulations:	through modal centers and symmetric scales
Mutes:	none
Piano and synth parts:	written
Shout:	none (climax at m. 195)
Style:	contemporary
Tempo:	half note= 92
Time feel:	swing, loose time feel, active/soloistic drum part, pedal point
Voicings:	unison, intervallic structures, triads, quartal, quintal, constant structures, 12-tone pyramid, couplings (Ma/m 6ths)

structural unity: the four-note motive spanning a minor third (m. 10), the dotted quarter-eighth note ascending major second (m. 20), the descending minor pentachord (m. 219), among others. Much melodic material is based on modal scales or fragments interacting in chain fashion, initiating tonal shifts between stable tonal areas underpinned by pedals.

The harmony features pedal points(bass and inverted), ostinatos (open fifths, triads), and transitional sections based on chromatic constant structures, chord structures moving on octatonic and whole tone scales and in minor third intervals, sometimes exhibiting functional chord progression characteristics. Progressive tonality is used, with the piece ending a half step above the original tonality (A instead of A♭).

Rhythmic features include canonical entrances at various time lags (mm. 219), cross rhythms (3/4 over 4/4, m. 10–18), (3/8 over 4/4, m. 11, m. 26, m. 125, m. 175) and extensive quarter and eighth note anticipations.

Technique Highlight:

Pyramid

The build-up of a chord through progressive sustaining entries. The wide base and the triangular faces meeting in a common apex that make up a pyramidal shape can find a parallel in music in the longer sustaining tones in the lower register, and the joining of the other tones into a single chord at the end of the process (see Figure K.1).

Here (mm. 195–97) the pyramid comprises all 12 tones of the chromatic scale (C–D–E–F–#–G–F–A♭–B♭–A–E♭–C#–B) and is built on a limited number of intervals (minor 7th, minor 9th, minor 3rd, ♭5th). For other examples of pyramids see "Ding, Dong, Ding," "What's New?" "Wind Machine" and "A View from the Side" (inverted pyramid).

Making Music

Careful score study will help assimilate the intricacies of this chart. Ranges, textures, and novel sonorities make this chart challenging for a less than advanced band. Take apart contrapuntal and layered passages

Figure K.1 Pyramid

and rehearse individually, and then balance the whole (intro, m. 195, m. 203, and m. 218). Create warm-ups on specific intervallic sonorities such as the Ma/mi 3rd (from the bottom=mi6, mi3) in m. 1. Listen to the recording for overall shape and role of the rhythm section. All dynamics, articulations, and phrasing are thoroughly marked.

Self-Test Question 38
The bass line at mm. 123–38 spells out a:

    a. whole tone scale
    b. dorian scale
    c. blues scale
    d. octatonic scale

For Further Reading
Sturm, Fred. *Changes Over Time: The Evolution of Jazz Arranging.* Advance Music, with accompanying CD recording, 1995. Contains detailed analysis, recording, and comments by Bob Brookmeyer on this piece, in addition to analyses of arrangements of *King Porter Stomp* by other composers.

KO-KO

Ellington, Duke 1943

Ellington, Duke 1943

Grade:	4–5
Duration:	2:40
Instrumentation:	5, 3, 3, 4. (Reed 3 plays ts and cl, tpt3 opt. cornet, tbn3 opt vtbn)
Publisher:	Warner Bros. Publications, Jazz@Lincoln Center series
Recording:	Duke Ellington.*The Blanton-Webster Band.* Bluebird (RCA/BMG) 5659-2. Also in the *Smithsonian Collection of Classic Jazz*, CD III.

Highest Written Notes:

Tpt 1:	C above staff
Tbn 1:	A♭ (three ledger lines)
Tbn 2:	D♭ (five ledger lines) on solo

Solos:
(written out): pno and bass duet (8 bars), tpt 2 (one chorus), as1 (one chorus minus first 4 bars)

At a Glance:

Articulation	• –
Bass line:	written
Chords:	mi6, mi7 (11), Dom (♭9, 9, #9, 13), dim, dim7
Chord progression:	i–iv–V minor blues
Dynamics:	*mp, mf, f, ff, fp, cresc*
Edition:	8 1/2x11 oblong, 14 pages. Rehearsal letters every twelve bars. No measure numbers
Expressive devices:	½ open (tpts), ya ya (tbn2)
Form:	8-bar intro, seven 12-bar choruses, coda (8+4)
Guitar part:	chord symbols
Key:	E♭ minor
Modulations:	None
Mutes:	plunger + o (=closed and open) (brass), plunger with mute (tbn 2, solo)
Orchestration:	clarinet lead (letters E F G). Independent ts 2 part written later for Ben Webster (see rehearsal notes in score). Bari sax plays very low (written middle C, intro and coda), and very high (palm keys on most passages, to achieve 4-pt close harmony with the saxes). 5-pt and 6-pt voicings featuring brass, clarinet lead, and as 2 (letter G)
Piano part:	written comping and flourishes
Shout:	letter G (7th chorus)
Style:	swing, jungle groove
Tempo:	quarter=160 (medium)
Time feel:	swing and even eighths
Voicings	saxes: triads, 4-pt close with independent ts 2 tpts: triads, 3-pt close tbns: triads, 3-pt close

Introductory Notes:
Notes on Playing Ellington, Glossary, The Four Elements of Music, Instrumentation, Original Recording Information, Rehearsal Notes, Comments from Wynton Marsalis.

Form and Texture:
Seven E♭ minor blues choruses flanked by an introduction (8 bars) and a coda (8+4 bars). Almost a study in call-and-response textures: all seven choruses feature call-and-response, with the fifth chorus featuring two responses. Two solos add to the texture: second trombone (choruses 2–3), and piano (chorus 4). In the first five choruses the call is always a solo instrument or a section in unison, responses are in harmony. This changes in chorus six where the call is in harmony, presented as a series of canons at a half note lag, and the response is the bass's solo line. This prepares the final shout (chorus seven), also displaying a harmonized call and a unison response from ATB saxes.

The introduction and coda feature the baritone sax on a tonic pedal and the trombones and bass outlining a i–iv–V7–i progression. Phrases are two bars in length throughout, with the exception of choruses 1 and 7 (in measures 9 and 10 of the form phrases are one bar length), and the entire chorus 4 (one-bar phrasing) (see table K.3).

Melodic, Harmonic, and Rhythmic Materials:
The upbeat motive of three short notes and one long (no, not that one from Beethoven's 5th symphony), is pervasive. From its first appearance in the floor tom

and the baritone sax, it generates every call in the piece, including chorus 7 (letter G), where the first two notes are elided.

More complex harmony is superimposed over the straightforward minor blues progression: chromatic triads descending to their goal (trombones, intro), four-part close chord inversions connected by passing diminished chords (saxes, chorus 1), and canons creating a three octave tonic triad block chord and 4- and 5-part chords (chorus 6). Both whole tone scales are featured in the piano solo flourishes in chorus 4. They are started off by whole tone clusters (did Thelonious Monk listen to these?).

In addition to many syncopated figures (brass, choruses 2–4), three over four figures can be found in the intro, chorus 5, and coda.

Technique Highlight:

Passing Diminished Chords
Diminished chords can be used to connect the chord tones of a melodic line. They are particularly useful on static chords to provide a sense of harmonic motion. In major and minor they are extracted from scales with an added chromatic between the 5th and 6th degrees, commonly referred to as "Be Bop" scales. The chord tones are 1–3–5–6 or 1–♭3–5–6, and the remaining notes are the diminished chord. Figure K.2 shows the scales in the key of C major and C minor, followed by an example of harmonization with passing diminished chords in C minor.

Ellington uses them to harmonize the four saxes at letter A mm. 1–4, and then transposed up a fourth in mm. 5–8. Disregard the tenor line that was added

Table K.3. "Ko-Ko" outline

Letter			A	B	C
Chorus	intro		1	2	3
Number of bars	8		12	12	12
Call	bari pedal		tbn 3	saxes	saxes
Response	tbns		saxes	brass	brass
Solo				tbn 2	

Letter	D	E	F	G	H
Chorus	4	5	6	7 shout	coda (as intro)
Number of bars	12	12	12	12	8+4
Call	saxes	tpts	ens in canon	brass, as 2 and cl	bari pedal and tbns + tutti finale
Response	tpts	saxes and trombones	bass	as, ts, bari	
Solo	piano				

Figure K.2 Be-bop scales and their harmonization with passing diminished chords

later. The key is E♭ minor: voicings containing only chord tones (E♭–G♭–B♭–C) alternate with voicings containing the diminished chord (D–F–A♭–B). In the second voicing (m. 1) D♭ substitutes B (lead alto) to give more tension to the high point of the motive. Dizzy Gillespie used passing diminished chords in the introduction of his tune "Be Bop."

Making Music

A detailed analysis by David Berger and Wynton Marsalis can be found in the score, with additional rehearsal comments. Though certain accents and dynamics are deliberately not notated in the score because they are common practice, after reading the commentary and listening to the recording you might decide how much you want to transfer into the score and have transferred into the parts. The piano part,

played by Ellington, with sparse chords and the occasional flourish of coloristic runs, recalls a similar approach found in other compositions of the period such as "Caravan," "Harlem Airshaft," "In a Mellow Tone," and "Main Stem," where he might play just an introduction or a short passage and then lay out and listen, conduct from the piano, or in front of the band.

Self-Test Question 39

In "Across the Track Blues" Ellington harmonized the three trombones mostly in second inversion and three-part structures. Here in mm. 1–8 the trombones are harmonized:

    a. predominantly in first inversion
    b. predominantly in root position
    c. predominantly in structures other than triads
    d. predominantly in first and second inversion

L

LIL' DARLIN'

Hefti, Neal 1958

Hefti, Neal 1958

Grade:	4
Duration:	3:00
Instrumentation:	5, 4, 4, 4 (opt. aux. perc)
Publisher:	Warner Brothers
Recording:	Count Basie. *The Atomic Basie*. Blue Note Records CD 28635, 1959.

Highest Written Notes:

Tpt 1:	F (fifth line)
Tbn 1:	E♭ (two ledger lines)

Solos:
tpt 4 feature (written out, also cued in tpt 1, 16 bars, highest note G on top of the staff, harmon mute). Tpt 4 has no ensemble parts.

Solo Section:
none

Introductory Notes:
none

Form and Texture:
AABA (16 bars for each section), framed by an intro (4 bars) and a coda (9 bars). It features a form within a form: each A section is neatly divided into a mini song form aaba1 and aaba2 (4 bars for each section, mm.

At a Glance:

Articulation:	– > ≥ slurs
Bass:	written.
Chord progression:	see Melodic and Harmonic Materials
Chords:	Ma6, Ma7, mi6, mi7, mi7 (♭5), Dom (♭9, 9, ♯11, ♭5, +5, 13)
Dynamics:	*pp, p, cresc, dim*
Edition:	8 1/2x11 oblong. 7 pages. Measure numbers every bar. Rehearsal letters every eight bars.
Expressive devices:	subtone (saxes mm. 23–40). Arco on final chord (bass)
Form:	intro (4), AABA (16 measures for each section), coda (9)
Guitar:	chord symbols
Key:	F Ma
Modulations:	none
Mutes:	bucket mutes (br) harmon mute (tpt 4)
Orchestration:	triple lead throughout on melody (as 1, tpt 1, tbn 1) in unison and octaves. Lead exchange: tbn 2 leads section (mm. 5–12 and 17–19, except 1st beat of mm. 5, 9, 17). Bari and tbn 4 play roots throughout (with the occasional PT and LN)
Piano:	written
Shout:	none
Style:	slow swing
Tempo:	quarter=80–88. Rallentando (mm. 49–51)
Time feel:	in "2"and in "4"
Voice leading:	oblique motion under sustaining lead (mm. 7–8, 11–12, 15–16, 18–19)
Voicings:	sax: 4-pt and 5-pt spreads tpts: triadic (tertian), 3-pt close tbns: 4-pt close and spreads. Root is sometimes doubled in first octave (mm. 5–6)

5–24). The B section (letter C) features fourth trumpet in harmon mute accompanied by saxes in 5-part spreads. The A section reprises *dal segno*, followed by the coda (m. 45) that repeats the last four bars of A twice, cadencing on two fermata chords (m. 51) and a final chord (after a signature ascending octave leap in the piano).

Melodic, Harmonic, and Rhythmic Materials:
Form, melody, and harmony are closely bound together: the intro sets up a dominant pedal in the key of F, but veers deceptively to G9 (V of V, m. 5). The harmony oscillates between tonicizing G (through its ii–V, mm. 7–8), and F (with its V7sus and V7, mm. 6 and 10) while the b phrase (m. 13) emphasizes the subdominants B♭ Major and B♭ minor. The tonic chord is reached only in m. 23. This is also where the melody closes on the pitch F (scale degree 1).

The main riff (mm. 5–8) outlines scale degrees 6–3–9–1 in F and closes on A (scale degree 3) twice (mm. 7 and 11), then G (scale degree 2, m. 19) in tandem with the harmony's delayed resolution. On the b and a1 phrases (mm. 16 and 20) ♭3 and ♭7 are emphasized, giving a blues flavor to the tune. Table L.1 shows the chord progression for the first 16 bars, beginning with the introduction (the tune begins at m. 5):

Technique Highlight:

Spread Voicings
Spread voicings or "spreads" are voicings built from the root up. In addition to the root they generally include the 3rd and 7th of the chord and other pitches depending on the number of parts. Spreads are tradi-

Figure L.1

Table L.1. "Lil'Darlin'" chord progression mm. 1–16

Measure	1–2	3	4	5 tune begins			6	
Harmony	C7sus	D♭7	C7(9,13)	G9	D-7	D♭7	G-7/C	C7
Roman Numeral	V7sus	upper chr	V7	V7/V	vi	subV/V	V7sus	V7
Key	F							

Measure	7	8	9	10		11	
Harmony	A-7	D7	G9	G-7/C	C7	F7 (13)	
Roman numeral	ii	V7	I9	V7sus	V7	I7	
Key	G			F			

Measure	12	13		14		15		16	
Harmony	F+7	B♭	B♭6	F6/C	F7	B♭	B♭-7	A-7(♭5)	D7
Roman numeral	V7/IV	IV	iv	I/5	V7/IV	IV	iv	ii	V7
Key								G	

tionally encounterd at slow or medium slow tempos, where they provide support to the melody. They are less practical at faster tempos. Doublings, dissonances, voicing, and orchestration are variables found in spreads and determine their sound (see figure L.1).

This arrangement is an example of harmonization of a tune with spreads (the A section melody), and of spreads used as sustained harmonic accompaniment for a solo part (the B section).

Making Music

At this slow tempo there is ample opportunity to experiment with the placement of the upbeat (see discussion in "Cute"). Listen to placement of the upbeat and articulation in the recording(s) to determine if the rhythm depicted in figure L.2 is a more accurate rendition of the main motive.

It is ironic that initially the tune was played much faster, until this most apt of tempos was settled upon.

Don't let players shy away from the moving underlines (m. 8, 12, and 16): the changing harmonies need to be full and clear. Run just the unison/octave triple lead (tpt 1, as 1, tbn 1) so everyone can hear what they need to match and blend with. Do the same with bari and bass trombone since they play in unison throughout, a relatively uncommon occurrence, since they generally split the low end responsibilities. They mainly play roots and the occasional passing tone and lower neighbor.

Remind the 2nd trombone that they are playing the top voice in their section most of the time. Drums are on brushes throughout. Brass is in bucket mutes or open, soft. Piano in the introduction needs to produce a chime effect (ping!), non-arpeggiated. Guitar enters with an arpeggio before the first measure of the tune (mm. 4 and 8) from the bottom up so the top note of the arpeggio coincides with the next downbeat. On the *Atomic Basie* recording, the intro is played by the piano right hand alone, without the accompaniment or pedal. The rhythm section chord symbols are simplified: add all tensions in the score so you can match what you hear.

Add written fermatas at m. 51, beats 2+ and 4+ then conduct rallentando (m. 49, into 1st beat of m. 51), give two downbeats (2, 2+), hold, and cut off. Repeat, softer for 4, 4+, hold, dim, cut off, wait for two Cs (piano), give last chord.

It is easy to wallow in a piece like this that is pretty (written for Hefti's daughter), seemingly straightforward, and without apparent challenges, but there is much work to be done to render it fully.

Self-Test Question 40

In mm. 7–8 the sustaining parts in the saxes and brass are:

   a. as 1, ts 1, tpt 1, tbn 1, tbn 2, tbn 3
   b. as 1, ts 1, tpt 1, tpt 2, tbn 1, tbn 2
   c. as 1, ts 1, tpt 1, tbn 1, tbn 2
   d. as 1, ts 1, bari, tpt 1, tbn 1, tbn 2

Figure L.2

M

MAIN STEM

Ellington, Duke 1942

Ellington, Duke 1942
Grade: 5
Duration: 2:47
Instrumentation: 5, 3, 3, 4 (reed 3 on clarinet; tpt3 plays opt cornet, tbn 3 plays opt valve)
Publisher: Warner Bros. Publications, Jazz@Lincoln Center series
Recording: Duke Ellington. *The Blanton-Webster Band.* RCA Bluebird: 5659-2, 3CD set.
                     Also on *Big Band Jazz*, Vol IV. The Smithsonian Collection of Recordings, RD 030-4, 1987. CD.

Highest Written Notes:
Tpt 1:   in staff
Tpt 2:   C♯ (two ledger lines) solo
Tpt 3:   B (one ledger line) solo
Tbn 1:   B (four ledger lines) solo
Tbn 2:   A (three ledger lines) solo

Solos:
(written) tpt 3 (12), as 2 (12), tpt 3 (12), tpt 2 (12), cl (12), tbn 2 (12), ts (15), tbn 1 (15)

Introductory Notes:
Notes on Playing Ellington, Glossary, Original Recording Information, Rehearsal Notes by David Berger, notes from Wynton Marsalis.

Form and Texture:
Large ABA ternary with the A section comprising seven 12-bar blues choruses in D major, followed by a six-bar modulation (letter G), the B section comprising two 18-bar choruses in the subdominant (letters H and I), a return to the first chorus head (letter J) in the home key, and an 8-bar coda (letter K). The A section features call and response patterns in two-bar phrases between sections, soloists, and various combinations of instruments. The modulation and B

At a Glance:

Articulation:	– > slurs. Other accents not notated (listen to recording)
Bass:	written, with additional chord symbols
Chords:	Ma triad, Ma6, Ma7 (9), mi 6, mi7 (9), Dom 7 (♭9, 9, ♯9, ♯11, ♯5, 13), dim
Chord progression:	Ma blues changes and expanded Ma blues changes (V/♭III, V/V, ♭iii ♪, ♭II7) on part B
Edition:	8 1/2x11 oblong, 24 pages. Rehearsal letters every chorus
Expressive devices:	0 + (open/closed), (tpts), bend, ½ valve (tpt 3), portamento, gliss (reeds), bend, slide (tbn 1).
Form:	12-bar blues (7 choruses), modulation (6), 18-bar blues (2 choruses), 12-bar blues (1 chorus), coda (8)
Guitar:	chord symbols
Key:	D Ma
Meter:	4/4
Modulations:	GMa
Mutes:	plunger with pixie mute (tpts), plunger with mute (tbn 2, solo)
Orchestration:	4-pt close with bari lead (saxes, letter E)
Piano:	written chords
Style:	swing
Tempo:	quarter=208
Time feel:	in 4
Voicings:	reeds: uni, 4-pt close, 5-pt open
	tpts: uni, triads, 3-pt close
	tbns: uni, triads (close and open), 3-pt close and open
	brass: 5-pt (stacked thirds from root up), 6-pt

sections feature concerted tutti ensemble and solos by tenor and trombone.

Melodic, Harmonic, and Rhythmic Materials:
There are two main riffs: x (tbns, mm. 1–2), and y (tpts, mm. 2–3). The first emphasizes upbeats ("and of one" and "and of four") and the second downbeats. This characteristic rhythmic placement is maintained as they are both developed throughout the piece. Riff y outlines the tonic triad with both major and minor third (D–F–F♯–A, mm. 2–3). It is reworked at letter A to emphasize scale degrees 2–5–1–♭7 (=E–A–D–C), returns in the original form (letter D), is developed further (letter E), and combines the original and the developed motive found at letter E in the final chorus (letter J). The anticipation on the end of "four" extracted from riff x is used at letter C (trombones), D (trombones, preceded by a dotted quarter), E (saxes), H (m. 4, ensemble).

The chord progression at letters H and I interpolates two-bar harmonies to expand the 12-bar blues into an 18-bar form: subdominant minor (c minor, letter H mm. 7–8), ♭iii diminished (B♭°, letter H mm. 11–12), and ♭II7 upper chromatic dominant (A♭7, letter H mm. 15–16). The V7 sus chord (D7 sus) at letter H m. 14 combines the A minor 9 harmony with the D bass, giving continuity to the third trombone line that descends chromatically from C to G (letter H mm. 7–18).

While letters H and I feature the expanded 18-bar form, the ensemble articulates a 12-bar form (starting at letter H m. 7) with "end of three to one" stop times, preceded by what sounds as an introduction preparing the solo entrance (mm. 1–4, _p_ to _f_), and a two-bar solo pickup for the tenor and trombone soloists (letters H and I, mm. 5–6). This 18-bar form is derived from the blues through interpolation and prolongation, and is articulated texturally as ensemble (4), solo break (2), and solo chorus (12).

Technique Highlight:

Riff
See discussion of riff in "Basically Blues." Here the initial riffs are two and undergo development (see discussion above).

Making Music
Read the Notes on Playing Ellington and Rehearsal Notes by David Berger and Wynton Marsalis in the score, listen to the recording.

Self-Test Question 41
The modulation at letter G mm. 3–6 utilizes a:

  a. series of chromatic chords
  b. cycle 5 chain of dominants
  c. I–VI–II–V progression
  d. dominant pedal

MILES MOOD

Berg, Shelton 2001

Berg, Shelton 2001	
Grade:	3
Duration:	4:00
Instrumentation:	5, 4, 4, 4 (opt. fl, hn in F, tuba, vibes)
Publisher:	Kendor Music
Recording:	recording (no solo section) available on www. sheetmusicplus.com.

Highest Written Notes:

Tpt 1:	G (on top of staff)
Tbn 1:	F (two ledger lines)

Solos:
any (chord changes cued in all parts)

Solo section:
open (mm. 44–75)

Soli:
saxes (mm. 101–08)

Introductory Notes:
Director's notes. Composer's profile.

Form and Texture:
The 16-measure intro begins with trombones in harmony and drums playing a solo with brushes. The rest of the rhythm section is added upon repeat, followed by a woodwind pyramid. The head (m. 10) is in AABA form, with the tune presented by trumpets in unison (first two A sections) and saxes (B section and

At a Glance:

Articulation:	• – > ∧ slurs
Bass line:	written
Chords:	Ma 6, Ma7 (9, ♯11, 13), mi7 (9, 11), Dom7 (9, ♯11, 13), triads over bass note
Chord progression:	modal, alternating Imi dor (Cmi) with ♭VII Ma7 (B♭Ma7)
Chord scales:	dorian, Ma (no 4th), lyd, lyd ♭7
Dynamics:	*p, mp, mf, f, sfz, cresc, dim*
Edition:	8 1/2x11 oblong. 16 pages. Measure numbers every bar, boxed numbers highlighting sections
Expressive devices:	gliss-short (saxes m. 33), scoop (saxes m. 22), trill (fl m. 4)
Form:	AABA (3 choruses) with intro, interlude, and coda
Guitar:	written single line and chords, chord symbols
Key:	C dorian
Modulations:	progressive tonality (ends in B♭ Ma)
Mutes:	harmon (tpts 3-4, last measure only)
Piano:	written chords with additional chord symbols
Style:	swing
Tempo:	quarter=176 (medium-up)
Voicings:	sax: uni, 4-pt, 5-pt close (built on root), 5-pt in 4ths w. added internal note, sw (5-pt in 4ths w. major third between top two voices. tpts: uni, 2-pt, 3-pt, triads w. lead dbled 8vb, 4-pt tbns: uni, 4-pt close, spreads

last A), accompanied by contrapuntal material. The pyramid returns in truncated form (first two notes are elided) at m. 42. The solo section (one chorus) is for any instrument, with backgrounds on cue. The pyramid over the ostinato returns reorchestrated (m. 77), and builds toward the arranger's chorus/climax (m. 85) with imitative and call-and-response textures. A sax soli passage (m. 101) and final tutti hocket gesture (m. 104) wraps up the section. The final A section is then recapitulated (m. 109) and the material is extended into a 10-bar coda (m. 117) (see table M.1).

Melodic, Harmonic, and Rhythmic Materials:
The main melody is in the dorian mode, with the A section material comprising two 4-bar quasi-identical phrases, and the B section featuring contrasting material.

A tribute to Miles Davis's "Kind of Blue" modal style, this chart contains the voicing used in the tune "So What" (see related discussion in "In the 80's") in the piano part and the saxes. The A sections are in C dorian, and the B section is in B♭ major (♭VIIMa7 rather than the dorian minor mode a half step above the tonic as in "So What"). The layered intro (mm. 2–9) and interlude (mm. 77–84) are built on D♭ major (♭II) that resolves to the C minor of the A section, a variation of the more frequently encountered dominant pedal. Similarly the coda veers to BMa (♭II of the final key of B♭ Ma, mm. 122–26).

The pyramids in the introduction and interlude are layered over the ostinato trombones and rhythm section, and feature a three-over-four dotted quarter cross rhythm. For a discussion of pyramids see "King Porter '94." The hocket at mm. 104–07 produces (after the first beat) a compound rhythm made up of quarter notes (fig. M.1). For a discussion of hocket see "Don't Git Sassy."

Technique Highlight:

Ostinato
The word means "obstinate" and indicates a short pattern (melodic, harmonic, or rhythmic), that re-

Figure M.1 Hocket

Table M.1 "Miles Mood" outline

Chorus	intro	1				extension
Measure	2*	10	18	26	34	42
Form		A	A	B	A	
# of measures	16	32				2
Texture	pyramid over ostinato	tpts uni------ saxes---------- sax/tbn bkg br bkg				pyramid
Solo						

* pickup marked as measure 1

Chorus	2 solo section	interlude	3 arranger's chorus/climax	recap	coda
Measure	44	77	85	109	117
Form	A A B A		A A B	A	
# of measures	32	16	24	8	10
Texture	bkg on cue	pyramid/ ostinato	imit. sax soli hocket	saxes br	
Solo	any instrument				

peats persistently. Here the three chords in the trombones (intro and interlude) repeat four times, while the other instruments are introduced. Ostinatos, like pedals, tend to build tension that asks for release, often in the form of straight time with walking bass, as is the case here.

Making Music

Read the To the Director comments. Listen to the recording and to the Miles Davis "Kind of Blue" recording for the general mood and style. You might want to memorize the entrances for the introduction and interlude so you can cue the instruments or groups of instruments.

The drummer needs to make the most of the intro solo and be able to build in the interlude, play good time, ensemble figures, and fill in the appropriate places. Lead the ritardando at m. 124–26 by giving the important beats | 2 3 4 | 3 | 1 | and add a decrescendo with the left hand where marked. Look at the drummer, who plays with the trombones.

Self-Test Question 42

In the introduction (mm. 1–5) the entrances are as follows:

a. 1. tbns/drums, 2. tuba/pno/bass, 3. hn/saxes/flute/guit/vibe
b. 1. tbns/drums, 2. guit/pno/bass, 3. hn/saxes/flute/tuba
c. 1. tbns/drums, 2. bari/pno/bass, 3. hn/saxes/flute/guit
d. 1. tbns/drums, 2. tuba/bari/bass, 3. pno/hn/saxes/flute/guit

---

A MINOR EXCURSION

Caffey, David 1987

Caffey, David 1987	
Grade:	4.5
Duration:	7:50
Instrumentation:	5, 4, 4, 4 (tpt 3 doubles on flugelhorn on last chorus)
Publisher:	Kendor Music
Recording:	California State University Jazz Ensemble, 1997 CD, available through the CSU library, call number MJ CSLA AMI C 97.

Highest Written Notes:

Tpt 1:	E♭ (three ledger lines)
Tpt 2:	C (two ledger lines)
Tbn 1:	B (four ledger lines)

At a Glance:

Articulation:	• – > ∧ accent over dot, slurs
Bass line:	chord symbols and written passages, chord symbols on solo sections
Chords:	Ma, mi7 (9, 11), mi7(♭5), Dom (♭5, ♯5, ♭9, 9, ♯9, ♯11, ♭13, 13, sus, sus ♭9), slash cords (mi7 over its 9th), dominant structures over pedal (mm. 75–76), dim7
Chord progression:	minor blues
Dynamics:	*p, mp, mf, f, ff, fp, sfzmp, cresc, dim*
Edition:	8 1/2x11 vertical, 14 pages. Measure numbers every bar, boxed numbers highlighting sections (every 12 bars)
Expressive devices:	bend (saxes m. 53), doit (br m. 175), long gliss (m. 125), portamento (m. 101) scoop (m. 101), shake (br m. 113)
Form:	4-bar intro, 21 choruses of blues (last chorus is 11 bars)
Guitar:	chord symbols with frequent rhythm slashes and some written parts (mm. 1–4, 112–22, 149–60, 181–87)
Key:	G mi
Modulations:	none
Mutes:	none
Orchestration:	writing across sections (m. 17), reorchestration on recap (chorus 21)
Piano:	chord symbols with frequent rhythm slashes and some written parts (mm.1–4, 112–22, 149–72, 181–87)
Shout:	mm. 173–88 (ch 19)
Style:	shuffle with strong backbeat (chorus 3, 9, 19)
Tempo:	quarter=144
Voicings:	saxes: 2-pt (mm. 2–3, 185–86), 5-pt spreads with occasional 4-parts (mm. 25–40), sw (mm. 201, 203, 205)
	tpts: 4-pt close (mm. 29–37, alternating with unison) with ust (II, ♭V, ♭VI), and 4ths (mm. 38–40)
	tbns: spreads, chr constant structures (+4,4 over pedal mm. 73–76)
	br: 5-pt sw (mm. 201, 203, 205)

Solos:
pno (5 choruses), ts1 (5 choruses), unaccompanied unison and duet section for the ensemble

Introductory Notes:
none

Form and Texture:
A 4-bar introduction heralds 21 choruses of 12-bar minor blues. The head is comprised of three statements of the 12-bar blues: the first section (m. 5) is in unison, the second (m. 17) features a "band within a band" nonet with the five winds drawn one from each of the available instrumental types (as, ts, bari, tpt, tbn), and the third (m. 29) contrasts melodically and is texturally tutti concerted.

Five choruses of piano solo and five of first tenor are linked by a restatement of chorus 3 (m. 77).

The backgrounds to the tenor solo (choruses 13 and 14) lead to a rhythm section groove (chorus 15). An unaccompanied section follows with unison tenor saxes and trombones, with guitar at the octave (chorus 16), joined by a second unison line in altos, trumpets, and piano (chorus 17), harmonized passages against unison trumpets and alto saxes (chorus 18), leading to a tutti shout variation of chorus 3 shortened to eight bars (chorus 19), linked with the intro expanded to eight bars, rescored, and played 8va by the trumpets (mm. 173–88). Measures 181–87 are the climax.

The recapitulation of the first two statements of the blues head, the first with added bari sax and third trombone, the second reorchestrated for double quintet (five saxes and five brass) follows at m. 189. The second of the two is cut short on the last bar and is 11 measures long (see table M.2).

Melodic, Harmonic, and Rhythmic Materials:

Both A and B melodies are based on the G minor pentatonic with added ♭5 (see "Basically Blues"), and on the G natural minor scale, with the natural 7th added as a chromatic approach.

The material of the first three choruses is organized in an AAB pattern ("stollen, stollen, abgesang," for Bach chorale lovers) or "statement, restatement, conclusion" as in the classic arrangement of blues lyrics. This pattern is mirrored in the melodies and is underlined by the fact that the two A sections do not resolve to the tonic g minor, only reached at the end of the B part (m. 39). This leaves the first two choruses harmonically open (V7sus ♭9 and ♭VII7 respectively at mm. 16 and 27) increasing the drive to the tonic cadence.

The harmonic progression features minor blues changes with extensive reharmonizations in bars 9–12 of the blues form. The tenor solo choruses (m. 89) and chorus 18 (m. 161) are reharmonized with secondary dominants, upper chromatic dominants, passing diminished chords, and the harmonic rhythm is doubled (two chords per measure).

Technique Highlight:

Imitative Writing
Imitative fugue like of "fugato" passages often involve groups of instruments or sections in unison entering with similar material at different time lags and intervals evolving into a layered or concerted texture. Often the rhythm section lays out, or the bass, piano and guitar join in playing the actual line(s) while the drums lays out. These kinds of passages create a novel texture, in contrast with concerted ones that frequently precede or follow them.

Here unaccompanied unison tenor saxes and trombones, with guitar at the octave play the first line and continue in counterpoint as they are joined by a second unison line in altos, trumpets, and piano. For another example of unaccompanied imitative writing see "In the 80's."

Making Music

Mark all choruses with a progressive number. Having a clear picture of the overall form (including solos), pacing, and ensemble balance will make this chart sound varied and focused. Have the rhythm section play the main set of chords and the reharmonizations so all can become familiar with them.

In rehearsal the drummer might play simple time for the unaccompanied section. The drummer needs to supply power under the tutti concerted ensemble passages, play combo sections, strong back beat, provide tasteful fills, lay out, and reenter with the ensemble (cue needed at m. 170). Third trumpet goes to flugelhorn for last chorus (m. 201).

Table M.2 "A Minor Excursion" outline

Chorus		1	2	3	4 5 6 7 8	9
Form	Intro	A	A	B		B
# of bars	4	12→				
Texture	tutti	uni	combo ens nonet		sax bkg------ tbn bkg	ens
Solo				pno---	

Chorus	10 11 12 13 14	15	16 17
Form	A		
# of bars	12→		
Texture	combo tutti antiph riffs	rhy. sect. groove	tenors/tbns----------------------------- add tpts/pno/guit
Solo	ts1-------------------------------		soli unis duet unaccompanied------------------------

Chorus	18	19 (shout)	20	21
Form	B	B + intro material	A	A
# of bars	12	12 + 8	12	11
Texture		tutti	uni	tutti
Solo	--------------------------------	rhythm section return		

Self-Test Question 43
The introduction (m. 3) and the retransition section (m. 181) feature a:

a. subdominat pedal
b. dominant pedal
c. one features a dominant and the other a sub-dominant pedal
d. none of the above

MISS FINE

Nelson, Oliver 1963

Nelson, Oliver 1963

Grade: 4
Duration: 4:09
Instrumentation: 5, 4, 4, 4. Ts 1 doubles on fl (32 bars)
Publisher: Sierra Music
Recording: Oliver Nelson. *Jazz Masters 48.* Verve 314 527 654-2, CD, 1995.

Highest Written Notes:

Tpt 1: C (two ledger lines)
Tbn 1-2: B♭ (four ledger lines)
Fl: B♭ (five ledger lines)

Solos:
tpt 2 (32 bars plus 6 bars on coda)

Notes:
Fl doubling (ts 1) highly recommended though not essential (part is doubled in tpt 1, tpt 4, and bari). No piano on original recording: the first head is accompanied by marimba playing dyads and then guitar plays for the rest of the chart. The marimba part is written out for piano and guitar in the score. Tpt 2 in the score has two solos: on the recording they are performed by two different players.

Introductory Notes:
Director's notes and General Performance Comments by Bob Curnow

At a Glance:

Articulation:	– • > ∧ slurs
Bass line:	written and chord symbols
Chords:	dyads, Ma6, Ma7 (9), mi7 (9, 11), mi7 (♭5), Dom (♭5, ♭9, 9, ♯9, ♯11, ♭13, 13, sus, alt, oct), dim7
Chord progression:	I–IV–V in B♭ (preceded by their II–Vs) in the first chorus, then centered around B♭ with secondary dominants (V/II,V/IV,V/V), and iii–vi–ii–V–I preceded by chromatic planing (iv→♭VII7). Ends on a I7 blues chord
Dynamics:	p, mp, mf, f, ff, cresc, dim
Edition:	8 1/2x11 oblong, 15 pages. Measure numbers every bar, with boxed numbers highlighting sections
Expressive devices:	bend, short and long spill, no vib, shake
Form:	2-bar intro, three 32-bar (16+16) choruses, 12-bar shout, 6-bar recapitulation, 8-bar coda
Guitar part:	written chords, melody line, chord symbols
Key:	B♭ Ma
Modulations:	none
Mutes:	none
Orchestration:	sectional and tutti
Piano part:	written and chord symbols
Shout:	mm. 99–116
Style:	easy swing
Tempo:	quarter= 120
Time feel:	bass in 2 (ch 1), in 4 (ch 2–3 to end) drums in 2 (first 16), in 4 (2nd 16 to end)
Voicings:	saxes: unison, drop 2+4 (on shout) tpts: unison, triads, fourths, 4-part close tbns: spreads, clus, unison, 2-pt, 3-pt, 4-pt, fourths, fifths

Form and Texture:

After a 2-bar bass introduction the saxes present the 16-bar head in unison (altos and first tenor, later joined by second tenor and bari), with brass providing concerted, harmonized punctuations. The varied repeat of the head (m. 19) features unison saxes accompanied by short chordal punctuations by trombones and a trumpet section answer that merges into a foreground brass statement at the close of the section. The solo section (one chorus, m. 35) is for trumpet with saxophone and trombone backgrounds. The third chorus (m. 67) is scored for concerted ensemble with second trumpet (after a few bars rest from its solo) and third and fourth trombones joining in to highlight selected passages (mm. 70, 81) or provide counterpoint (mm. 92, 94).

The texture is fully concerted at mm. 83–89. The 12-bar shout (mm. 99–110) features a brass/sax call and response and a trumpet unison line (mm. 107–10). A brief recapitulation of the main motive is tossed around the sections (tbns 3–4/bari, tenors and altos, tutti brass) at mm.111–16, extended by an 8-bar coda with trumpet solo over sustained saxes, and final tutti chord.

Melodic, Harmonic, and Rhythmic Materials:

The one-bar riff at mm. 2–3 is at the root of the main melody, organized in four bar phrases. The motive is transposed to fit the I–IV–V progression. A brass extension of the motive on downbeat quarter notes (1–2–3–4+) closes the head on the tonic (m. 32). The third chorus (mm. 67–96) is an "arranger's chorus," a balanced, flowing, well-paced melodic invention harmonized for concerted ensemble. It features economical motivic development, sequences, and the prominence of the blues scale (♭3, ♭5, ♭7 blue notes).

The shout features a minor third interval (G–B♭–G) repeated in the brass, answered by chromatic and blues-scale saxophone lines. The unison trumpet section that concludes the shout is a sequence down a whole step (mm. 107–10). A six-bar fragmented recapitulation follows (m. 111), with the two last eighth notes (m. 116, upbeat of 4) picked up by the saxes and reiterated over six bars to provide a background for a short trumpet solo over a dominant pedal. A drum fill and a final chord conclude the piece.

The first 16 bars use major second dyads (guitar and piano) over bass. They outline C–11 and FMa (♯11) (mm. 3–5), a cadential pattern that resolves to the tonic B♭ (m. 6). As the melody, they are transposed to fit the subdominant and dominant harmonies (mm. 11 and 15). The harmonic progression is varied on the repeat (m. 19) and closes on I (m. 32) rather than on V7 as at m. 17. The solo and ensemble section feature a similar progression.

Voicings include clusters (tbns, m. 19), "so what" (saxes, m. 51), 4-part close (saxes, m. 67, and tpts m. 71). Fourths add ring to the beginning of the shout (tpts, m. 99) and fifths add resonance under the climactic unison trumpet passage at m. 107.

Technique Highlight:

Placement of the Upbeat
See comments for "Cute." Though tempo here is easy, not slow, attention to the placement of the upbeat will add to the swing feel.

Making Music

Read Director's notes and General Performance Comments by Bob Curnow.

Depending on your ensemble, you can: let the bass player initiate the piece and the saxes enter on their own, help the sax lead in by giving beats 3 and 4 of m. 2, count off two bars for the bass lead in, or any combination of the above. The goal is to accomplish a clean start at the right tempo, dynamics, and feel. Tempo is particularly important in this piece, which needs to unfold at just the right pace (see comments for "Lil' Darlin'").

Notice that the first *f* occurs on m. 32, just for one bar, to launch the trumpet solo. The next *f* will only appear at m. 95 to launch the powerful shout. Keep the dynamic lid on for the whole tutti section (mm. 66–94), as many of the crescendos return to the original *mp*. Don't let the volume get out of hand, this passage has an intimate quality. The shout will benefit.

Measures 66–94 could be played initially in unison as a study in melodic line development as found in improvisation, and then as is with its harmony. The trumpet solo at mm. 117–24 should be intense and carry the energy of the shout and recapitulation through to the final chord.

Cue mm. 3, 50, 58, 66, 70, to help players who have been resting for a while.

Self-Test Question 44

On the recording at mm. 19–30 the drummer plays:

a. two beat with brushes
b. four beat with brushes
c. four beat with sticks and rimshot on 2 and 4
d. four beat with sticks and rimshot on 4

MOANIN'

Mingus, Charles 1976

Johnson, Sy 1997

Grade:	4
Duration:	8:59
Instrumentation:	5, 3, 2, tuba (opt. tbn 3 to replace tuba), 3
Publisher:	Hal Leonard
Recording:	Mingus Big Band 93. *Nostalgia in Times Square.* Dreyfus FDM 36559-2. CD, 1993.

Highest Written Notes:

Tpts 1:	C (two ledger lines)
Tbns 1-2:	E♭ (five ledger lines) on tutti unison m. 109. On rest of chart: tbn 1=B♭ (four ledger lines)

Solos:
bari (ostinato), as 1, ts 1, ts 2, tpt 1, tpt 2, tbn 1, tuba (short solos and collective improvisation).

Solo section:
bari solo. Other solos possible. Bari, tpt, and tbn solo on recording, with the bari also improvising an unaccompanied introduction before the beginning of the chart.

Introductory Notes:
None

Form and Texture:
The basic form is a 16-bar A section comprised of two contrasting 8-bar parts. There are eight 16-bar choruses in the main section (mm. 1–128), with chorus 7 (m. 97) being the B section or contrasting

At a Glance:

Articulation:	• – > ∧ slurs
Bass line:	written (first 8 bars), then chord symbols
Chord progression:	minor turnaround and Fmi harmony
Chords:	mi (7, Ma7, 9), Ma6 (7, 9), mi7♭5, Dom7 (♭9, 9, ♯9, 13)
Dynamics:	*mp, mf, f, ff, cresc, dim*
Edition:	8 1/2x11 oblong, 22 pages. Measure numbers every bar, boxed numbers highlighting sections
Form:	A (16 bars) (4 choruses), AABA (16 each), solo section (AABA), A (4 choruses), AAB
Key:	F mi
Modulations:	none
Mutes:	plunger (tpts)
Orchestration:	extended lower range with tuba. 3 part sonorities such as tbn uni lead, low uni tpts, uni saxes (m. 81). Unison couplings and voicings across sections.
Piano:	chord symbols
Shout:	no shout but mm. 97–112 are climactic
Style:	swing
Tempo:	quarter=216
Voicings:	saxes: uni, 3-pt, 3-pt voicings in 4ths, 4-pt tpts: uni, 2-pt, triads tbns/ tuba: uni, 2-pt, 3-pt, 3-pt voicings in 4ths

part (mm. 97–112). This can be interpreted also as an introductory AAAA (mm. 1–64) and a 64-bar AABA song form (mm. 65–128). The solo section at m. 129 also follows the AABA 64-bar plan. After the solos the repeat is from the beginning (da capo), to chorus 7 that serves as the ending with an additional fermata featuring collective improvisation (m. 112). Much of the texture is layered ostinato riffs with collective improvisation passages. For layered ostinato see "Fables of Faubus" for riffs see "Basically Blues."

Table M.3 "Moanin'" main section mm. 1–128

Measure	1			17				33				49			
Chorus	1			2				3				4			
Motive	a	b	c	a	b	c	d	a	b	d	e	a	b	d	e
Solo	bari ostinato→											as 1	ts 2	tbn 1	tuba

Measure	65					81					97	109	113	
Chorus	5					6					7	climax	8	
Motive	a	b	d	e	f	a	b	d	e	g	g	h	a	tutti
Solo	as 1, ts 1+2, tpt 2, 1+2 tbn 1, tuba					as 1, ts 1+2, tpts 1+2 tbn 1, tuba							as 1, ts 2, bari, tpt 2, tbn 1, tuba	

Melodic, Harmonic, and Rhythmic Materials:

The eight main motives range from one bar to eight bars in length, and are presented in an additive fashion throughout the main section: a (mm. 1–4), b (mm. 9–16), c (mm. 13–16), d (mm. 17–20), e (mm. 34–36), f (mm. 65–68), g (mm. 81–84), h (mm. 97–100), culminating with the fortissimo tutti unison at m.109 (see table M.3).

The ♭5 (B natural) blue note is featured prominently, often harmonized against the 4th scale degree B♭. The first part of the A section harmony is a four bar repeated minor turnaround i–♭VI–ii-7 (♭5) V7, with the upper chromatic dominant (D♭) to the V chord. The second part features the tonic chord over a descending bass line outlining the F minor natural scale and ending on the dominant. The B "bridge" section alternates iv (B♭mi 7) and ♭II (G♭) at m. 97, duplicating the major 3rd relation (F D♭) of the A section harmony. B♭mi 7 is later tonicized with a II–V (Cmi7 F7) when it appears in the solo section at m.145.

Technique Highlight:

Collective Improvisation

Collective improvisation is found in New Orleans jazz, where typically the "front line" instruments (trumpet or cornet, clarinet, and trombone) improvise simultaneously, creating a collective sound where none of the individual solos dominates the texture. This technique was later adopted in jazz from the 1950s and beyond by musicians such as Charles Mingus, The Art Ensemble of Chicago, Weather Report, World Saxophone Quartet, and many others. It came to include also rhythm section players and sometimes unaccompanied sections in free tempo.

Here the collective improvisation begins at m. 41 with the alto, tenor, trombone, and tuba over the bari ostinato, bass and drums. Written sections alternate with collective improvisation passages (mm. 57, 73, 89) leading to the tutti concerted culmination at m. 109.

Making Music

Listen to the Mingus Big Band recording and also to the original one by Mingus. In the first, solo section backgrounds are slightly different and there is an added figure during the trombone solo's B section. On the recording solos are for bari, trumpet, and trombone. While many of the motives are shared by more than one instrument, the bari part has an individual ostinato line that repeats for most of the chart. As your bari player gains familiarity they can begin varying it slightly while maintaining the feel and drive of the original.

Given the predominance of linear material, you might want to focus on the articulation and feel of each of the motives. Players need to be made aware that the collective improvisation passages beginning at m. 41 are part of a texture that grows in activity, range, and intensity to m. 96. Pacing is important, as well as for the soloists to work from within the ensemble, without dominating.

Self-Test Question 45

As the motives are presented in an additive fashion, the first 5-part texture is encountered at m.

a. 57
b. 65
c. 81
d. never

Lead Sheet

Homzy, Andrew, ed. *Charles Mingus: More Than a Fake Book.* Jazz Workshop/Hal Leonard, 1991, p. 64.

MOTEN SWING

Moten, Buster and Bennie 1933

Wilkins, Ernie 1959
Grade: 3.5
Duration: 3:22
Instrumentation: 5, 4, 4, 4
Publisher: Sierra Music
Recording: Count Basie. *Breakfast Dance and Barbecue*. Roulette Records. CD, 1959.

Highest Written Notes:
Tpt 1:   Eb (two ledger lines)
Tbn1:   C (four ledger lines)

Solos:
piano (32), ts 1 (16), tpt 3 (16)

Soli:
brass (mm. 31–40), saxes (mm. 49–56 and mm. 99–106)

Introductory Notes:
Director's Notes and General Performance Comments by Bob Curnow

Form and Texture:
After four bars of unaccompanied piano intro, the rhythm section joins the piano solo. The ensemble adds punctuations, melodic fragments, and sustained backgrounds on the B section of the AABA song form (m. 15), and the piano wraps up the solo on the final A section of the first chorus (m. 23). The statement of the head (2nd chorus) is by brass soli (AA, mm. 31, 31a), tutti (B, m. 41), and sax soli (A, m. 49). The third chorus (m. 57) features a tenor solo with backgrounds by the trombones (AA) and the saxes (BA). The fourth chorus (m. 83) presents a concerted tutti (A), a call-and-response (A), a sax soli (B), and a double riff last A (saxes and brass). The two-riff texture continues through two more A sections (m. 115) climaxing on a concerted tutti on the last two bars of the piece.

At a Glance:

Articulation:	• > ∧
Bass line:	written, with additional chord symbols, and chord symbols
Chord progression:	II–V, passing diminished chords, secondary dominants (V/II, V/V), I–vi–ii–V turnaround
Chords:	Ma6, Ma7, mi7 (9, 11), mi7b5, Dom7 (b9, 9, #11, #5), dim7
Dynamics:	*ppp, pp, p, mp, mf, f, ff,* cresc, dim
Edition:	8 1/2x11 oblong, 14 pages. Measure numbers every bar, boxed numbers highlighting sections
Form:	intro (4) AABA (4 choruses), AA
Guitar:	chord symbols
Key:	Ab Ma
Modulations:	none
Mutes:	hat, plunger (tpts and tbns)
Piano:	written introduction, then chord symbols
Shout:	last chorus is climactic (mm. 123–30)
Style:	easy swing
Tempo:	quarter =112
Voicings:	saxes: 4-pt close dbl lead 8vb (as1 doubled by ts1 or bari), 4-pt close over roots, 5-pt spreads
	tpts: 3-pt, triads with lead doubled 8vb, 4-pt close, 4-pt clus, 4-pt 4ths
	tbns: uni, 4-pt close
	ens: block voicings

The dynamic range is extensive, from *ppp* to *ff*, featuring sudden contrasts, sharp diminuendos, and careful pacing.

Melodic, Harmonic, and Rhythmic Materials:
The melodic material is riff oriented, and is characterized by economy of material. The main motive (m. 31) uses only three notes Ab, Bb, and B (scale degrees

Figure M.2

1, 2, ♭3) for the first few bars and dips to the note F at the conclusion of the section (m. 36). It employs only two rhythmic units (a quarter note and two eighths), both played on the beat until m. 36.

The material of the B section draws from the first six notes of the C major scale. The riffs in chorus 3 (m. 57, trombones), and in the last three A sections (m. 107) emphasize the leading tone and the tonic (brass), while the saxophone riff emphasizes the tonic, ♭3 and 6 degrees. Both A and B section riffs begin on the tonic note (A♭ or C).

The piece is in A♭ major, with the B section in C Major (Major III rather than the diatonic iii C minor), creating a more adventurous contrasting key relationship.

Concerted tutti are generally in block voicings (brass, mm. 107–to the end), and in 4-part Basie voicings (mm. 90–91, mm. 129–30).

Technique Highlight:

Dynamics
Dynamics control the degree of loudness and softness in music. Sometimes they are implied by performance practice, other times they are clearly marked by composers. Either way, they are a necessary component, and can clarify character, texture, and form of the music. The dynamics found here are of two types: sudden and gradual. Sudden dynamic changes are highly contrasting, as the *ff pp* at mm. 14–16, the reverse *pp ff* at mm. 85–87, and the *ff p* at mm. 102–3. Gradual dynamics are encountered in many passages such as mm. 41–48. Sometimes they encompass a wide dynamic range (*ff pp*) in only one (mm. 85, 87), or two bars (mm. 90–91).

Making Music
Read Director's Notes and General Performance Comments by Bob Curnow. Review discussion of 4-part Basie voicings in "All of Me," of riffs in "Basically Blues," of placement of the upbeat in "Cute," and of Basie style rhythm section playing in "All of Me." All are relevant to this chart.

Once the above concepts and the overall harmony and form are clear, focus on dynamics. Review discussion above. With such a wide dynamic range to strive for, you might want to exaggerate them even more (as an exercise). After the initial exhilaration two challenges might become apparent: extreme loudness brings potential for intonation problems, and extreme softness for loss of tone. For the first, proceed gradually while having players monitor themselves, for the second make sure that good breath support helps keep throats open at the softest of dynamics.

Mastering the classic exercise for wind players and singers in figure M.2 will help with breath support: on a middle register note play from pp to fff and the reverse, striving for the steadiest increase and decrease of sound. If you wish, count mentally to 7 and back to 1 really slowly. A gradual, controlled, and smooth decrease will tell you if you are on the right track. This is not a quick fix type of exercise, but something to be practiced over a long period of time.

Not only are there sudden, dramatic dynamic changes, but also quick ones within the duration of a measure. The rhythm section is key in accomplishing all of these, since it would be fruitless to try to have the whole band play as a whisper (m. 31, 83, 107) without the appropriate comping. The drummer sometimes supports the *ff* ensemble "out of the blue" with no preparation (m. 15), other times fills and sets up a section (mm. 89–90, mm. 121–22).

Notice the rhythm section *mp* in m. 15, beat 2. Amplified bass and guitar need to control their volume through knobs or pedals.

Self-Test Question 46
Brass mutes, in addition to timbral changes, contribute to the shaping of the overall dynamics of a piece. In this arrangement the sequence of muting and unmuting is:

a. open, hat, open, plunger, open
b. open, hat, plunger, open, harmon
c. open, hat, open, harmon, plunger
d. open, hat, open, cup, open

N

NO LOOKING BACK

Niehaus, Lennie 1999

Niehaus, Lennie 1999
Grade:	3
Duration:	4:10
Instrumentation:	5, 4, 4, 4
Publisher:	Kendor Music

Highest Written Notes:
Tpt 1:	C (two ledger lines)
Tbn 1:	G (three ledger lines)

Solos:
as 1 feature

Soli:
saxes (mm. 39–56)

Introductory Notes:
Director's notes. Composer's profile.

Form and Texture:
The overall form is a ABA1 ternary design with the A being an AABA 32-bar ballad, the middle part a cut time sax soli with brass punctuations, and A1 a reworking of the last eight bars of the ballad followed by a short coda. The eight-bar intro is divided into four measures without the rhythm section, followed by four measures where the alto solo and rhythm section join in. The alto improvises mm. 5–8 and eases into the main melody at m. 9. It delivers the melody throughout the ballad, with the exception of mm. 23–30 where brass and then the sax section take over. Unison saxes and trombone spread voicings accompany (m. 9, 2nd time).

The sax soli in cut time at m. 39 is interspersed by brass punctuations that lead to a tutti concerted re-

At a Glance:

Articulation:	– > ∧ slurs
Bass line:	chord symbols
Chord progression:	II–V, passing diminished chords, secondary dominants (V/II, V/V), substitute dominants (sub V of IV, sub V of vi), I–vi–ii–V turnaround, chords borrowed from minor (♭IIMa7, ♭VIMa7, ♭VII7)
Chords:	Ma6, Ma7 (9), mi7 (9, 11), Dom7 (♭9, 9, ♯9, ♯11, ♯5, 13), dim7
Dynamics:	*p, mp, mf, f, ff, cresc, dim*
Edition:	8 1/2x11 oblong, 10 pages. Measure numbers every bar, boxed numbers highlighting sections
Form:	intro (8) AABA (32), C (8), C (10), A (8), coda (6)
Guitar:	chord symbols
Key:	B♭ Ma
Modulations:	to CMa, progressive tonality
Mutes:	none
Piano:	chord symbols
Style:	ballad; cut time swing
Tempo:	quarter =69
Voicings:	saxes: 4-pt, 4-pt close double lead 8vb (on soli), 5-pt open tpts: 2-pt, 3-pt, 4-pt close tbns: 4-pt spreads with independent lead ens: block voicings

Table N.1. "No Looking Back" outline

Measure	1	9	39		57	65
Form	intro	AABA1	C	C	A1	Coda
Number of bars	8	32+4	8	8+2	8	6
Key	B♭		E♭		C	

Table N.2 "No Looking Back": first eight measures of the A section

Chord	Bb Ma7 G7	Cmi7 F7 F#°	Gmi Gmi/F	Emi7 (b5) Eb mi7 Ab 7
Roman Numeral	I V7/ii	ii V7 #v˚	vi	#iv sub ii V/vi

Chord	Dmi7 Gmi7	Ab 7 Eb mi6/Gb	Bb/F Bb°/F	Cmi7/F F13
Roman Numeral	iii vi	bVII7 iv/b3	I/5 i°/5	ii/5 V7

capitulation of the ballad at m. 57. The alto picks up the melody at m. 61, and a short coda (m. 65) with a cadenza for the soloist (m. 69) and final chord wraps up the piece (see table N.1).

Melodic, Harmonic, and Rhythmic Materials:

The melody is based on a motive featuring a quarter note triplet followed by a dotted quarter and eighth. The melodic contour makes use of a lower neighbor (2nd note) and an ascending leap of a 6th. The motive is sequenced and varied. The unison sax background line in the second A section (mm. 9–17) is woven into the trombone harmony, sharing many of its pitches with trombones 1–3.

The soli section (m. 39) is in the subdominant Eb, as is the bridge of the ballad (m. 19), ii–V, passing diminished chords, secondary dominants (V/ii, V/V), substitute dominants (subV of IV, subV of vi), I–vi–ii–V turnaround, and chords borrowed from the parallel minor (bIIMa7, bVIMa7, bVII7) are used. The first eight measures of the A section are shown in table N.2.

Modulations are accomplished through ii V (Fmi7 Bb7 to Eb, m. 18; Cmi7 F7 to Bb, m. 26) V (Bb9 to Eb, m. 38), and ii–V–V7/iii cadential patterns (Dmi7–G7–B9 to Cma7, mm. 55–57). The key progression is Bb, Eb (m. 39), ending in C (m. 57).

Technique Highlight

Spread Voicings
See discussion of spreads in "Lil' Darlin.'" In this arrangement spreads are used throughout the intro and main melody (mm. 1–38) and provide a full harmonic background in long values (mainly half notes) to the slow moving ballad and alto solo tune.

Making Music

Read To the Director comments. Add chord symbols to the introduction (mm. 1–4) so you can match what you hear. To achieve a clear texture and support the alto soloist work out line dominance and overall balance: ensemble is prominent at mm. 1–4, alto takes over (f vs mf dynamics in ensemble, m. 5), trumpets come to the fore (m. 18), and recede to background (m. 19), come to the fore again (m. 23) and recede as saxes take over (m. 26, beat 3). Reserve tutti ff to underline the alto reentry at m. 31, articulate the end of the ballad at mm. 37–38, and for the climactic ensemble statement when the ballad melody returns at mm. 57–60.

The sax soli might be slowed down for rehearsal. The tempo does not change between the ballad and cut time sections (quarter=half), so only a switch between a 4 and a 2 pattern is needed at m. 39 and the reverse at m. 57.

Self-Test Question 47

The sax section soli at mm. 39–56 is harmonized with:

a. 4-part voicings with lead doubled 8vb, and the occasional 5-part voicing
b. 4-part voicings with lead doubled 8vb, and the occasional 3-part voicing
c. 5-part voicings throughout
d. 4-part voicings with lead doubled 8vb throughout

NOSTALGIA IN TIMES SQUARE

Mingus, Charles 1976

Cuber, Ronnie 1998
Grade:	5
Duration:	6:40
Instrumentation:	5, 3, 3, 3
Publisher:	Hal Leonard
Recording:	Mingus Big Band 93. *Nostalgia in Times Square.* Dreyfus FDM 36559-2. CD, 1993.

Highest Written Notes:

Tpt 1-2-3:   F (three ledger lines)

Tbn 1-2-3:   A (three ledger lines)

Solos:

tpt 2 and/or ts 1 (3 choruses), 12-bar section open for solos with chord changes for all. On the recording there is a narration over the introduction, and the solos are tpt, bari, piano, and bass.

Introductory Notes:

None

At a Glance:

Articulation:	• – ∧ slurs
Bass line:	written, with additional chord symbols, and chord symbols
Chord progression:	blues using a I7–♭VII7 vamp, a deceptive II-7–V7 of ♭II, and a descending sequence of II–Vs ending on IV-7–♭VII7–I7.
Chords:	mi7 (9), Dom7 (9, #9, 13)
Dynamics:	*mf, f, ff*
Edition:	8 1/2x11 oblong, 11 pages. Measure numbers every bar, boxed numbers highlighting sections
Form:	intro (8), 12-bar blues head with solo sections, coda (7)
Key:	E♭Ma
Modulations:	none
Mutes:	none
Piano:	written, with additional chord symbols, and chord symbols
Style:	swing
Tempo:	quarter =160
Time feel:	in 2, in 4, stop time
Voicings:	saxes: 2-pt (M2, mi3 intervals) bari on roots and 5ths, 2-pt (4th intervals) on backgrounds, 4-pt and 5-pt tertian and quartal spreads tpts: uni, 3-pt tbns: uni, 3-pt (3–♭7–#9), triads, spreads

Figure N.1

Form and Texture:

The 8-bar intro begins with a rhythm section vamp, with trombones and bari joining in at m. 5. The 12-bar blues head (m. 9) is played twice. The first statement is by saxes over the bari and trombone ostinato, with the trumpets presenting the last four bars of the melody in unison (mm. 16–20) while the first alto plays a counter line (mm. 17–18). The restatement by trumpets and saxes (m. 21) is intensified by a unison canon at a half note lag by the trombones.

The first solo chorus (m. 33) is accompanied by a march style quarter note figure in the saxes and trombones. Further solo choruses, backgrounds on cue, and a solo open section follow, with swing style accompaniment. A da capo brings back the intro and the two statements of the melody, followed by a coda (mm. 82–88) that repeats the last four bars of the head twice.

Melodic, Harmonic, and Rhythmic Materials:

The ostinato (m. 1) is one measure in length and is a I7–♭VII7 (E♭7–D♭7) cadential pattern.

The same voicing (1, 3, ♭7, #9, used by many including guitarist Jimi Hendrix) is utilized for the two chords (see figure N.1).

The first eight bars of the tune are based on the E♭ minor pentatonic scale (see figure N.2).

The last four bars (mm. 17–20) utilize E♭ major and blue notes ♭3 and ♭5 in a line descending to the tonic: B♭–A–A♭–G–G♭–F–E♭.

This is one of the infrequent blues progressions that do not feature the IV chord on measure five of the form (m. 13). The subdominant chord A♭ is replaced by G♭mi7 and C♭7, a deceptive II-7–V7 of

Figure N.2 E♭ minor pentatonic

♭II (EMa). The last four bars of the form outline a sequence of II–Vs descending in whole steps and ending on a IV-7–♭VII7–I7 cadence (A♭mi7–D♭7–E♭7).

Voicings are mostly in root position (m. 5 and mm. 17–19), with the bari on the root.

Technique Highlight:

Ostinato
See discussion in "Miles Mood." Here it is found in the form of a one bar vamp. Vamps, while similar to ostinatos, imply an ad libitum repetition (hence the expression "vamp until ready"). This usage can be heard in the recording where the open vamp supports the vocal narration, the end of which is a cue for the main tune to start.

With the tune underway, as is the case with most pedals and ostinatos, they are released by a walking bass and "time" passage (mm. 17–18) leading to a concerted conclusion of the main melody (m. 19). A second ostinato accompanies the first solo chorus at m. 33. The same chords are utilized, now in an on-the-beat staccato quarter note rhythm.

Making Music

Review discussion of other Mingus charts such as "Fables of Faubus," "Ecclusiastics," and "Moanin'."

Like those tunes, this originated as a combo piece, and the arrangement here retains the basic intro-head-solos-head-coda format. The ostinato drives much of the piece, so it would benefit to render it as on the recording with energy and good placement of the upbeat chords. This applies both to the rhythm section and the bari and trombones when they pick it up at m. 5. The whole step voicings (mm. 9 and 13) might need attention. The chromatic alto line (mm. 17–18) needs to be heard.

Self-Test Question 48

The melody presented by the alto and tenor saxes at mm. 9–16 features:

    a. 3-part harmony in major 2nds and minor 3rds
    b. 2-part harmony in 4ths and minor 3rds
    c. 2-part harmony in major 2nds and minor 3rds
    d. 4-part harmony, triadic

Lead Sheet

The Real Book. 6th ed. Hal Leonard, 2004.

Homzy, Andrew, ed. *Charles Mingus: More Than a Fake Book.* Jazz Workshop/Hal Leonard, 1991, p. 84.

O

OCLUPACA

Ellington, Duke 1968

Ellington, Duke 1968

Grade:	4
Duration:	4:20
Instrumentation:	5, 4, 3, 3 (as 2 doubles on cl, tbn 3 opt. bass tbn)
Publisher:	Warner Bros. Publications, Jazz@Lincoln Center series
Recording:	Duke Ellington. *Latin American Suite.* Fantasy OJCCD-469-2, CD.

Highest Written Notes:

Tpt 1:	B♭ (one ledger line)
Tbn 1:	F (two ledger lines)

Solos:
(written) ts 2 (two choruses), pno has a soloistic part

Introductory Notes:
Note on Playing Ellington, glossary, original recording information, rehearsal notes by David Berger, notes from Wynton Marsalis.

Form and Texture:
ABA ternary form framed by a vamp and a 10-bar coda.

The A section comprises seven 12-bar blues choruses in F minor , followed by two choruses in the relative major A♭, and a return to two choruses of the F minor head. Ellington uses a similar form for "Main Stem." The *misterioso* quality is set forth by

At a Glance:

Articulation:	– > slurs. Other accents not notated (listen to recording)
Bass:	written, with additional chord symbols
Chords:	Ma6, mi triad, mi triad (add 9), mi (Ma 7), mi7 (9), Dom 7 (♭9, 9 ♯9)
Chord progression:	minor blues (i–iv–V7), major blues (I–IV7–V7)
Edition:	8 1/2x11 oblong, 23 pages. Rehearsal letters every chorus
Expressive devices:	grace notes, gliss (pno), smear, bend (ts 2)
Form:	vamp (open), 12-bar minor blues (11 choruses, choruses 8–9 are in the relative major), coda (10)
Key:	F mi
Meter:	4/4
Modulations:	A♭ Ma
Mutes:	straight, harmon (tpts)
Piano:	written
Style:	Latin, swing, shuffle
Tempo:	quarter=128
Voicings:	reeds: uni, 4-pt close (double lead 8vb), 4-pt spreads tpts: uni, triads (double lead 8vb), 3-pt close tbns: uni, triads, 3-pt close saxes and tpts: 4-pt block (bari doubles as1 8vb)

the woodwind unison line (choruses 2–5), the piano texture with its repeated high Cs (four octaves above middle C), and by the soft rhythm section groove. Brass punctuates in chorus 3 (letter C, mm. 9–10), trumpets play a dotted quarter-eighth note figure in response to the woodwinds (chorus 5, in straight mutes), and trombones initiate a call-and-response with the piano (chorus 6).

Chorus 7 (letter G) brings a dramatic change of mood. Changes include dynamics from *p* to *f*, Latin beat to swing, saxes from unison to harmony, a long-toned melody featuring a sinuous, meandering contour to a short, rhythmic riff (with a static lead on the tonic note F, letter G, mm. 1–8), and call-and-response to concerted texture. This chorus also serves as an introduction to the contrasting B part of the ternary form, featuring a shuffle beat, and full ensemble (choruses 8 and 9, letters H and I). For the final two choruses (10 and 11, letters J and K) the texture reverts to that of the second chorus, with unison saxes and high tessitura piano, the head is repeated, and a coda on the tonic concludes (letter L) (see table O.1).

Melodic, Harmonic, and Rhythmic Materials:
The four-chorus unison sax melody (letters B, C, D, and E) uses the full resources of the minor key combining the various variants of the 6th and 7th scale degrees: ♭6, Ma6, ♭7, Ma7, in addition to the blues ♭5 and, in one instance, the ♭2 scale degrees (letter D mm. 9–10).

Different minor mode segments alternate or intertwine: harmonic minor (B mm. 9–12), jazz melodic minor (C mm. 1–3), dorian (B m. 4), natural minor (D m. 5), phrygian (D m. 9). The development of this unison line is remarkable from an intervallic

Table O.1. "Oclupaca" outline

Letter			A	B	C	D	E
Chorus	vamp		1	2	3	4	5
Instrum.	bass and drums		add pno	woodwind melody --------------------------------			
						brass	tpts
Solo							
Key	F minor						

Letter	F	G	H	I	J	K	L
Chorus	6	7	8	9	10	11	coda
Instrum.	tbns	saxes +tpts	tutti----------		woodwind melody----------		
Solo	pno		tenor 2--------				
Key			A♭		F minor		

and rhythmic standpoint: the first chorus (letter B) explores the half step possibilities with a chromatic approach from above or below, culminating in a minor 9th interval (D♭–C) at letter B m. 10. This flourishing gesture at the end of the chorus introduces also a descending major second and major sixth interval (letter B m. 10). This basic shape is adopted for the next chorus as a minor second, minor sixth variant (letter B m. 12), then inverted and expanded to a minor 7th (letter C mm. 2–4). The third chorus (letter D) introduces the tonic triad arpeggio (D m. 1), and reaches the highest pitch F at letter D m. 8. The fourth chorus (letter E) adopts the melodic contour of a minor tenth (C–E♭, letter D m. 10) found in the final gesture of the preceding chorus as the basis for its main motive (also spanning a minor 10th=B–D; letter E m. 1), and then expands it to the widest interval (C–F=an eleventh, letter E m. 5) as a culmination of the whole melody.

The chain technique that links motives found at the end of a chorus to the next and the systematic intervallic expansion from a half step to an eleventh works in tandem with the intensification of the rhythm: the initial motives of each chorus progress from a two-note motive (letter B, mm. 1–8), to a three-note motive (letter C), and a five-note motive (letter E), while the concluding flourishes of each chorus expand from seven (letter B, mm. 9–10), to thirteen (letter D, m. 8–11), to fourteen notes (letter E, mm. 9–11). This escalation does not take place on the return of the F minor section (letters J and K), where the letter B melody is repeated verbatim rather than allowed to develop, and the concluding pitch E (major 7th of the chord) is held over the tonic minor ostinato (letter L).

For piano fills and coloristic effects in the high register see also "Caravan." "Oclupaca" is part of Ellington's *Latin American Suite* and is "Acapulco"

spelled backward. Other programmatic works by Ellington inspired by travel are the "New Orleans Suite," "Far East Suite," "Tokyo," and "Togo Brava Suite." For another example of a retrograde title see "Airegin."

Technique Highlight:

Vamp
A simple chord progression, often one or two chords, played ad libitum until a soloist or the melody begins. Vamps are also found at the end of a piece where they allow for a fade out, sometimes with one or more soloists improvising while the rhythm section grooves, gradually winding down the intensity of the music. Vamps, while similar to ostinatos, imply an ad libitum repetition (hence the expression "vamp until ready"). See also "Nostalgia in Times Square."

Here the vamp is at m. 1 and is for bass and drums. It is ad libitum or "open," and establishes the groove and feel. The entrance of the piano follows on cue at letter A.

Making Music
Read Note on Playing Ellington, Rehearsal Notes by David Berger, and Notes from Wynton Marsalis in the score.

Self-Test Question 49
The trombones at letter F, mm. 1–8 play a riff with a voicing containing a dissonant half step followed by a triad. As the harmonies change the:

a. dissonant voicing changes and the triad remains the same
b. triad changes and the dissonant voicing remains the same
c. both change
d. both remain the same

P–Q–R

PROVING GROUND

Niehaus, Lennie 1997

Niehaus, Lennie 1997
Grade: 2.5
Duration: 3:00
Instrumentation: 5, 4, 4, 4. (can be played with 3, 2, 1, 3)
Publisher: Kendor Music

Highest Written Notes:
Tpt 1:   G (top of staff)
Tbn 1:   F (two ledger lines)

Solos:
tpt 2 (mm. 55–72)

Soli:
saxes (mm. 32–40, 88–96)

Introductory Notes:
Director's notes. Composer's profile.

Form and Texture:
The 8-measure introduction alternates a one measure tutti concerted figure with piano solo answers. The main head in AABA form follows at m. 9. The tune is presented by a trumpet and the two altos in unison, with the trombones and the rest of the saxes adding a counterline at m. 17. The B section tune (m. 25) is presented by the brass in octaves, accompanied by sax spreads. An 8-bar sax soli follows, beginning with the pick up at m. 32, leading to a tutti concerted section (m. 41), and the repeat of the intro as an interlude (m. 49).

A trumpet solo (16 bars) follows at m. 57, leading to a tutti concerted variation of the B section (m. 73), an imitative passage for saxes (m. 81), an exact reprise of the sax soli (m. 89), and of the section found at m. 41 (m. 97). A final 8-bar passage brings the piece to a close (see table P.1).

Melodic, Harmonic, and Rhythmic Materials:
The main melodic material is spun out from two basic rhythmic motives. While the phrasing generally fol-

At a Glance:

Articulation:	– > ∧ slurs
Bass line:	written
Chord progression:	II–V, passing diminished chords, secondary dominants (V/II, V/III, V/IV, V/V), ♯IV-7(♭5)
Chords:	Ma6, Ma7, mi7 (9, 11), mi7♭5, Dom7 (♭9, 9, ♯11, ♭5, ♯5, 13, sus4), dim7
Edition:	8 1/2x11 oblong, 14 pages. Measure numbers every bar, boxed numbers highlighting sections
Form:	AABA with additional sections
Guitar:	chord symbols, written pedal
Key:	E♭Ma
Modulations:	none
Mutes:	none
Orchestration:	tpt and as unison melody
Piano:	written
Shout:	no, but mm. 105–11 are climactic
Style:	swing
Tempo:	quarter=152 (moderate)
Voicings:	saxes: 2-pt (mm. 17–24), triadic, 4-pt close with bari on root with some 9/1 tension substitutions (mm. 1–6, mm. 25–32, mm. 41–47), 4-pt close with bari doubling lead or 2nd alto 8vb, occasional 5-pt (mm. 33–40) tpts: 2-pt, triadic, 3-pt (when tpt 2 is not playing, mm. 53–54, 73–76) 4-pt close, 4ths tbn 1: roots (mm. 1–6, 41–54, 73–80), counterline (mm. 17–24), melody mm. 25–30). Tbns 2-3-4: triadic, spreads, 4ths (on the tonic chord, mm. 6, 31, 47, 54)

Table P.1 "Proving Ground" outline

Chorus		1				41	49
Measure	1	9	25	33		41	49
Form	Intro	A	A	B	A	C	interlude (as intro)
# of measures	8	8	8	8	8	8	8
Instrum.	tutti	uni tpt+altos ----------brass 8ves sax soli				tutti	
		tbns/saxes sax spreads					
Solo							

Chorus	2			3			
Measure	57	73	81	89	97	105	
Form	A	A	B	A	A	C	A
# of measures	8	8	8	8	8	8	
Instrum.		uni	tutti	saxes imit.	soli	tutti	sectional imit.
		bkg					tutti
Solo	tpt 2-------						

Table P.2 One bar rhythmic motives

Section:	A							B						C						
Measure:	9	10	11	12	13	14	15	16	25	26	27	28	29	30	31	41	42	43	44	45	46	47
Motive:	a	b	a	c	a	b	a	d	a	e	f	e	f	f	g	a	h	a'	c	i	b	g

lows the classic antecedent/consequent 4-bar pattern (mm. 9–12/mm. 13–16), unity is provided through a mix of repetition and development of the one-bar rhythmic motives shown table P.2.

In the final eight bars motives a and b are used in a rising sequence (three times) followed by motive g (mm. 105–11). By contrast, the introduction features one main rhythmic motive (repeated three times, mm. 1–5), followed by a conclusion (m. 6).

The modulation to the subdominant A♭ (mm. 23–25) for the bridge is very brief, veering quickly back to the key of E♭ (see table P.3).

The tonic chord is avoided in the A sections, and is reached instead at the end of the intro (m. 6), of the B (m. 32), and of the C (m. 47) sections.

Harmonies are designed to be complete with reduced instrumentation (3, 2, 1), generally resulting in 4-part close voicings, often over the root.

Technique Highlight:

Spread Voicings

For a discussion of spread voicings or "spreads" see "Lil' Darlin'." In this arrangement spreads are used in the intro and B section (mm. 25, 73). While often found at slower tempos, they still provide a full harmonic background to the rest of the ensemble.

Making Music

Read Director's Notes in the score that discusses balance and overall dynamics. This is a straightforward chart. Let the rhythm section lead the switches between full ensemble and combo sections (ex: intro /m. 9; m. 49/m. 57), and vice versa (ex: m. 33/m. 41; m. 65/m. 73).

The drummer's fills need to be geared toward setting up the transitions to a softer dynamic (mm. 7–8), or louder (mm. 40, 72). Notice that 2nd trombone plays lead most of the time, while 1st trombone is

Table P.3 Modulation to subdominant

	Bridge						
Measure:	23	24	25	26	27	28	29
Chord:	B♭-7	E♭7	A♭	D7	G-7	C7	F-7 B♭7
Function:	II-7	V7	I	V/III	III-7	V/II	II-7 V7
Key:	(IV)A♭ :-----------			(I) E♭ : ------------------------------			

often on roots, something that might take a little adjusting for your lead bone.

Though m. 107 is marked *ff*, leave a little room for dynamic growth as the sequence rises to m. 111, to be followed by a dramatic subito *p* for the final chord.

Self-Test Question 50

The imitative entries in the saxophones at m. 80 start at:

a. a half bar lag and join at m. 84

b. a one bar lag and join at m. 88

c. a one bar lag then continue at a half bar lag and join at m. 85

d. a one bar lag and join at m. 84

S

SAVANNAH IN HAVANA

Lopez, Victor 1995

Lopez, Victor 1995
Grade:	2.5
Duration:	4:01
Instrumentation:	5, 4, 4, 4 (effectively 5, 3, 3, 4, plus 3 hand held percussionists, see Notes)
Dedication:	Savannah Grace Smith
Publisher:	Educational Program Publications EPP Festival Series

Highest Written Notes:
Tpt 1:	F (fifth line)
Tbn 1:	D (one ledger line)

Solos:

(written out): tpt 1, ts 1

Soli:

piano and bass (mm. 77–84, 103–10)

Solo Section:

(mm. 53–76): any player can solo since there are no written backgrounds and the three-chord progression is quite simple.

Notes:

Bari, tpt 4, and tbn 4 play hand held percussion (guiro, cowbell, claves) throughout.

Introductory Notes:

None

At a Glance:

Articulation	• – > ∧ ≥ slurs
Bass:	written
Chords:	Dom (9, ♯9, 13)
Chord progression:	I–IV–V and I–♭VII–I
Dynamics:	*mf, f, ff, cresc*
Edition:	8 1/2x11 oblong, 15 pages. Measure numbers every eight bars.
Expressive devices:	trill
Form:	intro (16), AABA (32), interlude (4), CDE solo section (24), soli (8), 2-bar tutti, A (8), B (8), soli (8), coda (5)
Guitar:	chord symbols and written line and chords in coda
Key:	E♭ Ma
Meter:	4/4
Modulations:	None
Mutes:	None
Piano:	written
Style:	Latin groove
Tempo:	quarter=138 (medium)
Voice Leading:	oblique motion in main I–IV piano pattern (mm. 1–4): right hand sustains a voicing in fourths, while the left hand plays a tritone descending by half step
Voicings:	sax: uni, 3-/4-pt
	tpts: uni, 2-pt, 3-pt in thirds and 4ths
	tbns: uni, 3-pt

Figure S.1 Piano and bass cha cha pattern

Form and Texture:

A 16-bar introduction is followed by a 32-bar AABA chorus (m. 17) featuring first alto and first trumpet in unison, a trombone background, and an antiphonal section (saxes and trumpets) where the trombones join the rhythm section in a "motor" salsa figure (mm. 33–48). A 4-bar piano rhythmic pattern launches the solos (mm. 49–52).

The solo section (mm. 53–76) features a different form than the head (24 rather than 32 bars) and the chord progression employs the same chord types in rearranged harmonic rhythm (see discussion below). A piano and bass soli accompanied by percussion prepares the return of the head material in reverse order (A2, B). A second soli (m. 103) leads to the coda (m. 111) (see table S.1).

Melodic, Harmonic, and Rhythmic Materials:

The main melodies are based on the E♭ mixolydian mode, with an added F♯ chromatic approach (saxes mm. 8–15). The melodic/harmonic relation (D♭/E♭ at m.17 and G♭/A♭ at m.19 =♭7 of the chord, then A♭=1 at m. 23, at the conclusion of the eight bars) creates a tension-release pattern. This is reversed in the B section, where all sax and trumpet phrases end on 1, with the last phrase ending on the ♭7 (m. 40). The main A melody is in four-bar phrases.

There are three main chords: E♭9, Fm11♭9/A♭, and Gm11♭9/B♭. Though the last two are spelled as inversions, the whole progression can be thought of as a I–IV–V (E♭9–A♭13–B♭13) with all the chords of

dominant quality, as in the blues. For a discussion of inversions see "The Happy Song." The two rhythm section soli (m. 77 and m. 103) and the coda (m. 111) feature a I–♭VII cadential pattern (E♭–D♭).

There are two rhythm section two-bar patterns: cha cha (piano, mm. 1–2) and bass (mm. 5–6). A standard pattern in the key of F is shown in figure S.1.

They adjust to the changing harmonies and work with claves, guiro, and cowbell. The piano pattern is taken up by the trombones (m. 33), and saxes (m. 41). Piano and bass join in a new two-bar soli montuno pattern (m. 77 and m. 103).

Other two-bar rhythmic motives found in the saxes (mm. 8–9) and brass (mm. 13–14), reoccur later (mm. 33–38 and mm. 85–87), and in the coda (mm. 111–12). The coda recalls and summarizes various previously heard materials (m. 111=m. 13, m. 112=m. 8, m. 113=m. 77). Modal interchange in the unison unaccompanied line (mm. 112) tinges of E♭ minor pentatonic the E♭ major tonality. Also, the D♭9 (♭VII) (m. 114) brings to full fruition the ♭VII–I cadence outlined in the two soli sections (I–♭VII–chromatic planing–I) at m. 77 and 103.

Technique Highlight:

Clave

Clave is a two-bar rhythmic pattern at the basis of Cuban and other Afro-Latin music.

It provides the foundation for the rhythms, patterns, melodies, and improvisations of the ensemble, that relies on the downbeats provided by the clave for orienta-

Table S.1 "Savannah in Havana" outline

Measure	1	9	17	25	33	41
Form	intro		A	A1	B	A2
Instrum.	layered. saxes, br pno, bass, perc		as 1/tpt 1unis.----------	tbn unis.	saxes/tpts tbn "motor"	tpts saxes/tbns

Measure	49	53	61	69	77	85	87	95	103	111
Form	interlude	C	D	E	F		A2	B	F	Coda
Instrum.	piano+hi hat	solo section			soli tutti +perc			soli tutti +perc		tutti
Solo	piano	t 1, tpt 1duet			piano/bass soli			piano/bass soli		

tion in a synchopated rhythmic environment. Clave is found in 3–2 and 2–3 patterns. There is also a variant called Rumba clave, where beat 4 of the 3 side is played on the "and" of 4. See "In the 80's" for examples.

Once established which fits the music, the pattern does not change if the number of measures in the form is even.

In this chart the clave (2–3) is spelled out in mm. 5–6 in the claves part (claves are two identical strikers made of resonant wood, that produce a high pitched "tick," used to play the clave pattern). For other Latin style pieces see "Elvin's Mambo," "In the 80's," and other charts listed in the "style" index.

Making Music

Clave is central to Latin style music. A way of having everyone learn the clave is to have all clap the 2:3 clave (mm. 5–6) and then add the drum set (close hi-hat on 2 and 4), percussion (claves, cowbell, guiro), piano, and bass. As mentioned in the Notes bari, trumpet 4, and trombone 4 play hand-held percussion (guiro, cowbell, claves) throughout. After running the tune with the full ensemble, you might want to rehearse the rhythm section and percussion separately, building the rhythmic layers one by one as in a jigsaw puzzle. Everyone needs to keep their parts simple to avoid "overfilling" that interferes with the groove. Fill only where marked.

A layering hierarchy is at work in the winds too: trombones are really part of the rhythm section throughout, saxes are more independent but join the trombones with an embellished variation of their figure (mm. 41–48 and mm. 87–94), and trumpets have the main tune. Building from the clave up to the trumpets can help keep the texture clear.

Chords in fourths are good spots for tuning and balance (trumpets, m.13), (tutti, mm. 110–11). Though understood, adding a *p* marking to the sforzandos (trombones, mm. 33–37; tutti, mm. 113–14) might be a reminder of the resulting sfzp crescendo on the trombone long notes.

As in many other charts there are ways of toying with the materials to fit the needs of a particular ensemble or occasion. Here possibilities range from featuring an open percussion section before beginning the chart at bar 1, to opening up the soli section at m. 77 for percussion, rhythm section, or individual or collective solos.

Self-Test Question 51

Many Latin bass patterns utilize root, 5th, and 8ve and additional tones. Here the two chords at mm. 5–8 use:

a. root, 5th, 8ve, and 9th
b. root, 5th, ♭7th, 8ve on the first chord, and 9th on the second chord
c. root, 5th, and ♭7th
d. root, 3rd, 5th, 8ve

For Further Reading

Mauleon, Rebeca. *Salsa Guidebook for Piano and Ensemble*. Petaluma, CA: Sher Music, 1993.

SHINY STOCKINGS

Foster, Frank 1955

Foster, Frank 1955

Grade:	4
Duration:	5:06
Instrumentation:	5, 4, 4, 4
Publisher:	Walrus Music
Recording:	Count Basie. *April in Paris*. Verve, 1956, CD Also on *Big Band Jazz*, Vol 3. The Smithsonian Collection of Recordings, RD 030-4, 1987, CD.

Highest Written Notes:

Tpt 1:	D (two ledger lines)
Tbn 1:	B♭ (four ledger lines)

Solos:

tpt 4 (32), piano (16)

Notes:

No full score available, only condensed. The piece is discussed here because of its inclusion in the multiple selection list. Articulation in parts is inconsistent: under parts need to be matched to section lead.

Introductory Notes:

None

Form and Texture:

The introduction features the piano on a two-bar unaccompanied vamp, with the rhythm section joining in in the last two measures before the head. The head

At a Glance:

Articulation:	• – > ∧ hat over dot, slurs
Bass line:	written walking bass, chord symbols
Chord progression:	ii–Vs, passing diminished chords (♯iiº), secondary dominants (V/ii), substitute dominants (sub V/iii), temporary tonicization of C major (III)
Chords:	Ma6, Ma7 (9), mi7 (9), mi7♭5, Dom7 (♭9, 9, ♯11, ♯5, 13), dim7
Dynamics:	*mp, mf, f, ff, fff, sfzpp, cresc, dim*
Edition:	9 1/2x13 vertical, 6 pages (conductor's score). Letters on every bar in the introduction, then measure numbers every bar, boxed letters highlighting sections
Form:	intro (7) ABAB1 chorus (32), sax section interlude (8), ABAB1 chorus, piano interlude (16), two ABAB1 choruses, coda (8)
Guitar:	written introduction, chord symbols
Key:	A♭ Ma
Modulations:	none
Mutes:	cup (tpts and tbns)
Piano:	written introduction, then chord symbols
Shout:	last chorus (letter G)
Style:	swing
Tempo:	quarter =132
Time feel:	"4" and "2"
Voicings:	saxes: 4-pt close dbl lead 8vb in bari (letter B), 4-pt close with independent bari on roots and fifths (letter C), 5-pt spreads (mm.

49–56), 4- and 5-pt close and open (letter D)
tpts: 3-pt (tertial and quartal) with lead doubled 8vb, 4-pt close
tbns: 4-pt close and open

(letter A, m. 1) is in A, B, A, B1 form (32 bars), and is presented by concerted brass in cup mutes. The interlude (letter B, m. 33) features the saxes over a pedal on beats 2 and 4. Saxes then provide an ostinato background to the trumpet solo on the second chorus (letter C). The trumpet solo continues for another 16 bars at letter D, with concerted tutti background. A 16-bar piano solo follows at letter E.

The third chorus at letter F is for tutti ensemble and leads to the shout. The fourth and final chorus (letter G) is a tutti concerted shout that uses two-bar figures (first 8 bars), developing and sequencing the closing phrase from the second ending of the head (mm. 29–30). A bass line cliché ending introduces the coda (m. 145), followed by a saxophone concluding phrase, and is repeated (m. 147) before a final tutti conclusion.

Melodic, Harmonic, and Rhythmic Materials:
The tune is comprised of two main elements: a four-bar phrase a (mm. 1–4), and a contrasting two-bar phrase b (mm. 9–10). The first phrase is sequenced down a step (mm. 5–8), the second is sequenced up twice in whole steps (mm. 11–12 and mm. 13–14). While phrase a highlights and embellishes a fixed pitch (C the first time, B♭ the second), phrase b outlines an ascending minor 7th arpeggio that moves through the harmonies leading to the temporary tonicization of C major (mm. 13–15). On the second ending the last sequence is replaced by a descending line based on the rhythm of phrase a, closing firmly in the tonic A♭ (mm. 29–30).

The bass line cliché ending is on scale degrees 3–4–♭5–5–6–7–8, as shown in figure S.2.

The chord progression uses ii–Vs, upper chromatic dominants and chromatic planing minor seventh

Figure S.2 Bass line cliché ending

Table S.2 "Shiny Stockings" outline

Letter		A	B	C	D
Chorus	intro	1	interlude	2	
Material	vamp	ens	saxes+tbns	saxes ostinato+riff	ens
# of bars	7	32	8	32	
Solo	piano			tpt	

Letter	E	F	G	m. 145
Chorus		3	4 shout	coda
Material		brass	tutti	saxes, rhy sect, tutti
# of bars	16	32	32	8
Solo	piano			

chords. Voicing are mostly 4-part close. Brass at letter A is in block voicing with the top three trombones doubling the trumpets at the lower octave.

Technique Highlight:

Vamp

For a discussion of vamp see "Oclupaca." Here a vamp is played by the piano at the very beginning, followed by a classic left hand bass line cue that leads to the ensemble entrance.

In the score the vamp is seven measures long, while on the recording it is nine, underscoring its ad libitum quality.

Making Music

As outlined in Notes, only a condensed score is available. Full scores generally contain much of the information needed, though remain a good starting, if incomplete tool from which to begin to make music. Condensed scores are like trying to play Chopin on a 24-key piano keyboard. So much is missing. To study harmonies, voicings, dynamics, mutes, changes of feel, and rhythm section parts it will be necessary to make a score from parts. In doing so you will notice that the articulation on parts is inconsistent, so you might want to match under parts to section lead. You will also be able to insert in the score all missing dynamics heard on the recording.

Basie style improvised piano flourishes are a trademark of the style. They are found throughout the head and at letters D and F, between phrases and where gaps or sustained notes occur. The drummer needs to know where to fill and set up the ensemble. For more on Basie-style rhythm section playing and four-part Basie voicings, see "All of Me," for placement of the upbeat, see "Cute." The tune has a set of

lyrics composed by Frank Foster, and many recorded versions with vocals are available for study.

Self-Test Question 52

At letter C the trumpet solo is accompanied by:

a. a 2-bar ostinato followed by a 2-bar riff
b. a 1-bar ostinato followed by a 4-bar riff
c. a 1-bar ostinato followed by a 2-bar riff
d. the rhythm section alone followed by a 1-bar ostinato

Lead Sheet

The Ultimate Jazz Fakebook. Hal Leonard, 1988.

THE STAR-CROSSED LOVERS

Ellington, Duke, and Billy Strayhorn 1957

Ellington, Duke, and Billy Strayhorn

Grade: 4.0
Duration: 4:00
Instrumentation: 5, 3, 3, 3. T 1 doubles on cl
Publisher: Warner Bros. Publications, Jazz@Lincoln Center series
Recording: Duke Ellington and his Orchestra. *Such Sweet Thunder.* Columbia CK65568.

Highest Written Notes:

Tpt 1: F (staff, top line)
Tbn 1: G (three ledger lines)

Solos:

as 1 feature

At a Glance:

Articulation:	– > ∧ slurs
Bass:	written
Chords:	Ma6, Ma7 (9), mi triad, mi7 (9), mi (ma7), mi7 (♭5), Dom 7 (♭9, 9, ♯9, ♯11, ♭5, ♯5, ♭13, 13, sus), chords with no 3rd
Chord progression:	see Melodic, Harmonic, and Rhythmic Materials:
Edition:	8 1/2x11 oblong, 8 pages. Rehearsal letters every section
Expressive devices:	lift, portamento, bend
Form:	intro (4), two choruses A (8), B (8), A (6), coda (4)
Key:	D♭ Ma
Meter:	4/4
Modulations:	none
Mutes:	hat (tpts and tbns)
Piano:	written, plays only on intro and coda
Style:	ballad
Tempo:	ad lib, quarter=52
Time feel:	ad lib piano intro and coda. Swing eighths
Voicings:	sax: uni, 3- and 4-pt, spreads tpts: uni, triadic (tertian), 4-pt close, clus tbns: uni, 2-pt, 3-pt over bass, 4-pt close, in 5ths, spreads, spreads with bari, clus. brass: concerted 5-, 6-, 7-part

Introductory Notes:

Note on playing Ellington, Glossary, Original Recording Information, Rehearsal Notes by David Berger, Notes from Wynton Marsalis.

Form and Texture:

An ad lib piano introduction and coda frame two choruses in ABA (8+8+6) form. The programmatic character of the piece guides some of the musical choices (lead alto sax depicts Juliet and second tenor plays Romeo). The alto solo is accompanied by saxes (letter A), and saxes and brass (letters B and C) in concerted and contrapuntal passages in unison and harmony. The ensemble articulates the end of sections with melodic statements and states the 8-bar melody with 2nd tenor lead at letter D. The alto returns for the second B (letter E) and final A (letter F) sections. The piano chords and arpeggios from the introduction return as the final tonic chord is stated (letter F m. 6).

Melodic, Harmonic, and Rhythmic Materials:

The main A melody is in four-bar phrases (truncated in the shorter A sections), while the B is in two-bar phrases developed from a one-bar motive. A chromatic line (G♭–G–A♭) appears at the outset as the piano left hand bass line. It supplies, in rhythmic diminution, the roots of the first three chords of section A (letter A mm. 1–2 and 5–6), and then develops into a chromatic counterpoint (letter B mm. 7–8 tbns, letter C mm. 1–2 saxes, letter C mm. 4–5 tbns, letter C m. 6 tpt and so on).

This line built on 4-♯4-5 (in the key of D♭) works in tandem with the progression that opens on IV (G♭Ma7) and moves through a whole tone G7 (no third) chord to a I 6/4 chord (letter A mm. 1–2). The tonic D♭ in root position is reached in m. 4, after a ii–V. The chords at letter A are shown in table S.3.

The B section modulates to the subdominant in the last four bars (letter B, mm. 5–8). The return of section A (letters C and F) opens in the tonic and then progresses to IV, inverting the process found in the initial A section. The harmony oscillates between D♭ and G♭ tonal centers. The last A (letter F) closes in the tonic with the root in the alto melody, and overlaps with the piano coda. The coda, like the

Table S.3 Chords at letter A

Measure	1		2		3		4	
Harmony	G♭Ma7 (13)	G9 (no 3rd)	D♭Ma7/A♭	B♭mi7	E♭mi7	A♭7 (♭5)	D♭Ma7	G7
Rom. Num.	IV	subV7/IV	I	vi	ii	V7	I	subV7/IV

Measure	5		6		7		8
Harmony	G♭Ma7 (13)	G9 (no 3rd)	D♭Ma7/A♭	B♭mi7	Gmi7(♭5)	C7 (♭9)	Fmi
Rom. Num.	IV	subV7/IV	I	vi	related ii	V7/iii	iii

intro, ends on a G7 whole tone chord, an ambiguous chord to begin with that can be seen as a substitute dominant of IV in D♭, but also a suspended ♭II in G♭.

Voicings range from spreads (letter A, saxes), to triadic, and 4-part close. In the "Romeo" passage at letter D the couplings in the 4-part close voicings are: (1) ts 2/tbn 1 8vb; (2) as 2/tbn 3 8vb; (3) tpt 3 in hat, no coupling; (4) bari/tbn 2 unison.

Technique Highlight:

Program Music
Program music is instrumental music that seeks to recreate in sound the events, characters, or emotions portrayed in some extramusical source such as a story, a play, or painting. Since the *Four Seasons* by Antonio Vivaldi, program music has been used by composers such as Beethoven, Berlioz, Strauss, Mussorgsky, and Tchaikovsky (in another Romeo and Juliet rendition). The intended program is often made explicit in the title of the piece.

Ellington wrote a wide range of programmatic works including portraits of people ("Portrait of a Lion," "Second Portrait of a Lion," of Ella Fitzgerald, of Louis Armstrong, of Mahalia Jackson, of Sidney Bechet, "Self-portrait of the Bean," "Ray Charles' Place"), of locations ("Harlem Air Shaft," "Harlem Flat Blues," "Echoes of Harlem," "Harmony in Harlem," *New Orleans Suite*, *Far East Suite*, "Tokyo," *Togo Brava Suite*) and inspired by colors ("Transblucency," "Black, Brown, and Beige," "Blue Abandon," "Magenta Haze," "Black and Tan Fantasy"). See also "Caravan" and "Harlem Airshaft."

Making Music
Read Notes on Playing Ellington, Rehearsal Notes by David Berger, and Notes from Wynton Marsalis in the score. Mark chords in score, as there aren't any chord symbols since guitar is not present and piano plays only intro and coda. This is a programmatic piece, so the alto and tenor need to know who they are depicting, and identify with the characters they portray. This piece is part of a larger suite, comparable to a chapter or scene from a larger play, so its placement in a program will need some thought as to what precedes and follows. See also "Such Sweet Thunder," the first movement of the same suite known as the "Shakespearean Suite."

Self-Test Question 53
As discussed above, the use of whole tone chords contributes to the floating quality of the music. Dis-

counting passing tones E♭ and E, the alto melody at mm. 4–5 outlines a:

a. major triad
b. augmented triad
c. diminished triad
d. dominant 7th chord

Lead Sheet
The New Real Book. Vol 2. Sher Music Co., 1991.
The Real Book. 6th ed. Hal Leonard, 2004.

STOLEN MOMENTS

Nelson, Oliver 1961

Nelson, Oliver 1961
Grade:	5
Duration:	5:12
Instrumentation:	5, 4, 4, 3
Publisher:	Sierra Music
Recording:	Oliver Nelson. *The Blues and the Abstract Truth.* Impulse 1961 CD (septet version).

Highest Written Notes:
Tpts 1-2: G (four ledger lines)
Tbns 1-2: B♭ (four ledger lines)

Solos:
tpt 2 (four choruses minor blues, opt. open form), as 1 (four choruses minor blues, opt. open form, and 36 bar interlude and one chorus minor blues)

Soli:
saxes (8 bars)

Introductory Notes:
Director's notes, and performance comments by Bob Curnow

Form and Texture:
After an 8-bar introduction over the tonic pedal, the 16-bar head is played twice (mm. 9, 25). It is in AB form with each part 8 bars long. The A part features

At a Glance:

Articulation:	• – > ∧ slurs
Bass line:	written, chord symbols on solo sections
Chord progression:	constant structures over pedal outlining 1–4–5, chromatic constant structures. Minor blues
Chords:	Ma7(9), mi7 (9, 11), mi7♭5, Dom7 (♭9, 9, ♯11, ♭5, sus4)
Dynamics:	*p, mp, mf, f, ff, fff, cresc, dim*
Edition:	8 1/2x11 oblong 20 pages. Measure numbers every bar, boxed numbers highlighting sections
Form:	composite: A B (8+8), C (12-bar minor blues), D (18)
Key:	C mi
Modulations:	to Dmi and back to Cmi
Mutes:	harmon (tpts, 8 bars)
Orchestration:	four-part paired brass (tpt 1-2, tpt 3-4, tbn 1-2, tbn 3-4). tpt voicings duplicated by tbns 8vb. Voice crossings (tpt 3, tpt 4, tbn 3, ts 2, bari)
Piano:	written and chord symbols
Shout:	mm. 125–36
Style:	swing, bolero
Tempo:	medium
Voicings:	saxes: uni, 4-pt, 5-pt, clus tpts: uni, 2-pt, 3-pt, 3-pt triadic dbl lead 8vb, 3pt w. independent lead, 4-pt constant structures, clus. tbns: uni, 2-pt, 3-pt, 3-pt w. independent lead, 4-pt constant structures, clus. brass: tpt voicings duplicated by tbns 8vb. ens: four-part paired brass (tpt 1-2, tpt 3-4, tbn 1-2, tbn 3-4) with saxes doubling at pitch and ts 2 on additional line.

saxes the first time and tutti on repeat, while the B part on repeat is reorchestrated an octave lower.

Solos follow on a 12-bar minor blues form. There are four solo sections; the first and third (mm. 41, 65) are open and have no backgrounds, the second and fourth (mm. 53, 77) have backgrounds and repeat only once. Trumpet takes the solo on the first two and alto on the second two. The alto sax solo continues through a modulation to Dmi (m. 91) to a repeated 18-bar section with full ensemble sustained backgrounds, to a final chorus of minor blues (m. 113).

A chorus with saxes calling and brass responding follows at m. 125. A modulation leads back to the original key of Cmi (m. 137), and a written repeat of mm. 9–40. A 3-bar coda concludes (mm. 169–71). There are tonic, subdominant, and dominant bass pedals, in addition to the tonic-dominant pedal in the introduction. Textures are mainly sectional and tutti concerted.

Melodic, Harmonic, and Rhythmic Materials:
The introduction establishes the C dorian mode (see figure S.3) with the lead line in the first trumpet and trombone outlining G–A–B♭–A. This line is harmonized with alternating E♭Ma7 and FMa7 constant structures over the tonic-dominant pedal. G♭Ma7 is used as a variant at m. 7.

Part A of the main theme is constructed from a 2-bar motive that is varied and transposed. It outlines the C dorian mode, with the A natural turning to A♭ on the IV chord (m. 13). Part B of the theme features a C minor second inversion triad outlined by the two-pitch pedal (C–E♭, tpt 1 and altos), and G (bass pedal). This triad sandwiches a dominant 7th sus 4 (9, 13) constant structure in the inner parts. The structure ascends and descends chromatically (mm. 17–20). On repeat (m. 33), the bass G pedal is replaced with a chromatic bass and the constant structure outlines a minor triad with added fourth (D–F–G–A, mm. 33–36).

The repeat of the head (m. 25) is harmonized similarly to the introduction with major 7th constant structures over the tonic pedal. For a discussion of constant structures over ostinato bass see "Blues and the Abstract Truth." The 4-part chords are orchestrated with two brasses on each part, pointing to the fact that the piece originated as a four horn chart for trumpet, alto, tenor, and baritone.

Figure S.3 Dorian mode

Figure S.4 Seven-part cluster in final chord

Backgrounds (m. 113), and shout (m. 125), develop the melodic motive from the introduction. The coda repeats the last phrase and ends with two fermata chords.

Technique Highlight:

Clusters
Clusters are voicings predominantly in seconds (see "Airegin," and "Ding, Dong, Ding"). Here 5-part clusters are used in the sax section melody (mm. 9–16) and background (mm. 53–60) and a seven-part cluster outlines the complete C dorian mode in the final chord (m. 171) (see figure S.4).

Making Music

Read Director's notes and performance comments. This is a straight ahead chart in medium swing tempo. The only feel change is in mm. 91–98 to a bolero accompaniment. Solo sections are discussed above. If there is a reason, a different soloist (trombone or rhythm section player) can be featured in the first two sections (mm. 41, 53). Dynamics need to be followed. The introduction chords are played sfp crescendo, with the sections in balance within themselves and among each other. Notice the voicing: trombones double trumpets two octaves below and saxes have a cluster that fills that space and connects the two while providing additional "bite" (see figure S.4).

Voice crossings are generally used to obtain more melodic underparts. Here they occur between tpt 2

Figure S.5 Voicing in introduction

and 3 and tbn 2 and 3 (mm. 2–3) and tenor 2 and bari (mm. 10–11 and mm. 23–24). Players might want to take note of them so they can play with confidence. Cluster tuning might need attention. Play as fermatas from the top down. At the apex of the piece (m. 129) the lead trumpet plays high E, F♯, and Gs: rehearse without the lead so the trumpet 4 part at a lower octave can be listened to.

Self-Test Question 54

The chord progression at mm. 113–24 is a transposition up a step of mm. 65–76. The two are:

a. similar, but two chords are of radically different quality
b. different, with many passing chords added in the second
c. identical, just transposed
d. basically the same, with a ♭IIMa7 added in the first

Lead Sheet

The Real Book. 6th ed. Hal Leonard, 2004.

———

SUCH SWEET THUNDER

Ellington, Duke, and Billy Strayhorn 1957

Ellington, Duke, and Billy Strayhorn 1957

Grade:	5
Duration:	3:22
Instrumentation:	5, 4, 3, 3 (tpt 4 plays opt cornet, tbn 3 plays valve)
Publisher:	Warner Bros. Publications, Jazz@Lincoln Center series
Recording:	Duke Ellington and His Orchestra. *Such Sweet Thunder.* Columbia Legacy CK65568.

Highest Written Notes:

Tpt 1:	F (three ledger lines)
Tbn 1:	A (three ledger lines)

Solos:

(written) tpt 4 (12), tbn 3 (12)

At a Glance:

Articulation:	slurs
Bass:	written, with additional chord symbols
Chords:	Ma triad, Ma6, Ma7 (9), mi7 (9), mi7 (♭5), Dom 7 (♭9, 9, ♯9, ♯11, ♭5, ♯5, ♭13, 13), dim, chords with major and minor 3rd
Chord progression:	minor blues changes over ostinato (with ♭II, ♭VI, ♭VII dominant chords) and major blues changes
Edition:	8 1/2x11 oblong, 10 pages. Rehearsal letters every chorus
Expressive devices:	wa wa (brass)
Form:	12-bar blues (6 choruses), with 4-bar interlude between chorus 4 and 5
Key:	G minor (G Ma in choruses 3 and 4)
Meter:	4/4
Modulations:	none
Mutes:	plunger with mute (tpts 2-4, tbn 2)
Orchestration:	"pep section" trio (two tpts and tbn in plunger mutes)
Piano:	written
Style:	swing and even eighths
Tempo:	quarter=99
Time feel:	in 4
Voicings:	sax: uni, 4- and 5-pt close and open, spreads tpts: 4-pt open tbns: uni, 3-pt close and open ens: 6- and 7-part; pep section (ma, mi, dim triads and incomplete 6th and 7th chords)

Introductory Notes:

Note on Playing Ellington, glossary, original recording information, Rehearsal Notes by David Berger, Notes from Wynton Marsalis.

Form and Texture:

Essentially six choruses of 12-bar blues with a 4-bar interlude between choruses 4 and 5, no introduction or coda. A unison ostinato is the basis for choruses 1, 2, and 6: it is played by saxes, first and third trombones, and bass. Choruses 2 and 6 (letters A and E) feature the plunger muted trio "pep section" (second and fourth trumpets and second trombone in plungers with mute) over the ostinato, and piano "pitched percussion" triplets in the high register.

Choruses 3 and 4 (letters B and C) abandon the ostinato and switch to walking bass, and feature a sax soli (letter B), and a trumpet solo with sustained sax background (letter C). The ostinato returns for a couple of measures before the interlude (letter C mm. 13–16). The interlude is the only tutti concerted passage in the piece. The sax figure in chorus 5 (letter D) is derived from the rhythm of the ostinato (see figure S.6), and is paired with a trombone cantabile solo and bass embellishments at the end of every other measure of the accompaniment. Chorus 6 is identical to chorus 2 except for the piano part being much sparser, helping to diffuse the textural density and bring the piece to a close.

Melodic, Harmonic, and Rhythmic Materials:

The programmatic nature of this piece (based on Shakespeare's *Othello*) determines much of its composition, and melodies, themes, keys, and solos become prime suspects for leads in revealing characters or events. Though in program music the exact sources of inspiration cannot always be pinned down with accuracy, Ellington has given indications of it being inspired by Othello, specifically his seduction of Desdemona. This is the first movement of a twelve-movement "Shakespearean" suite.

If the first two choruses are "Othello," then chorus three could be "Desdemona," since the contrast in

rhythm of ostinato   sax figure

Figure S.6

Figure S.7 G phrygian

character is so remarkable: from ostinato to walking bass, from intense, quasi-vocal trio to lyrical saxes, from minor blues to major blues. In chorus four "Othello" (trumpet solo) seduces "Desdemona" (the saxes), and the interlude joins them in tragedy in a double forte tutti. Chorus five is a mournful meditation on the fateful events (jealousy, murder, suicide), and chorus six is a return (needed also for formal balance) of "Othello" now ending with an unresolved F (=♭7) in the low octave of the piano, a likely link to the next movement.

The "Othello" ostinato is based on G phrygian, with the third B♭ omitted, and a natural A as a chromatic tone in mm. 9–10 (fig. S.7).

The entrance of the trio chords (letter A) completes the mode by delivering the B♭ in the top part (tpt 2, letter A m. 1). The blues form is also clarified, with a degree of modal ambiguity maintained by the G major harmonies (letter A mm. 3 and 12) juxtaposed to G minor ones (letter A mm. 1, 7, and 11), and the B♭/B alternation of the melody.

Letters B and C feature a major blues chord progression. The Bmi7, B♭mi7 planing chords at letter B m. 8 are a reminder of the B/B♭ polarity at the root of this piece, and their likely representation of our two characters (major and minor third, light and dark, good and evil). In the interlude (letter C, mm. 13–14) B and B♭ join in the tutti concerted. The half step clash is strident (tpt 1 and 4, beat 1 m. 13 and 14; tpt 4 and ts 1 beat 2+, m. 14). The programmatic intensity of this passage is further underscored by the extreme ranges (open voicings in the trumpets, baritone down to low B), the density (6 and 7 parts), and the dynamics.

For another movement of this suite and a discussion of program music see "The Star-Crossed Lovers."

Technique Highlight:

Suite
A suite is a work comprised of a series of movements not tightly unified by thematic and key relations. Sometimes a common key or a common program (as here) is the main unifying element. See J. S. Bach's *English* and *French Suites* for baroque era examples. Suites have also been extracted from larger works for programming purposes, among these the *Nutcracker Suite* by Tchaikovsky, *Daphnis and Chloe* by Ravel, and the *Firebird* by Stravinsky.

Making Music
Read Notes on Playing Ellington, Rehearsal Notes by David Berger, and Notes from Wynton Marsalis in the score. Listen to the recording of this movement and to the rest of "Such Sweet Thunder." Review placement of the upbeat discussion in "Cute." Is figure S.8 an accurate rendition of how the ostinato in mm. 1–2 is played?

Self-Test Question 55
The sax soli at letter B is harmonized in:

a. 4-part close voicings, with bari doubling the lead 8va below
b. 4- and 5-part open and closed voicings, without part crossings
c. 4- and 5-part open and closed voicings, with bari and 2nd tenor often crossing parts
d. 5-part open voicings throughout

Figure S.8

T–U

TEMPLE STREET

Wilson, Dale 1994

Wilson, Dale 1994

Grade:	5.5
Duration:	7:40
Instrumentation:	5, 5, 5, 4 (as 1 on ss throughout, tpts double on flugs)
Publisher:	Sierra Music
Recording:	*The North Texas One O'Clock Lab Band* 1993 www.music.unt.edu/jazz/records.html.

Highest Written Notes:

Tpts 1:	F♯ (three ledger lines)
Tbns 1:	B♭ (four ledger lines)

Solos:

pno (16 bars, written or improvised, 5 bars light improvisation), tpt 5 (three 24-bar choruses), pno (open), ts 1 (three 24-bar choruses)

Soli:

ts 1, tpt 5

Introductory Notes:

Director's notes and General Performance Comments by Bob Curnow

Form and Texture:

Ten choruses plus introduction, interlude, and coda. Form is multisectional with varying section lengths and through composed material. The main ABCD sections are defined by their harmonic and melodic content that remains recognizable through its various manipulations. While sections A and B invariably open the chorus, sections C and D alternate with each chorus throughout the piece. The head choruses (first, second, and last) and the shout (chorus 6), include additional closing sections based on A. The interlude (m. 186) is an open unaccompanied piano solo. A three-chorus tenor solo follows (m. 198), and builds to the recapitulation of the second chorus material A, B, and D at the octave (m. 270). D material is repeated at m. 294 concluding

At a Glance:

Articulation:	– > ∧ slurs
Bass line:	written throughout
Chords:	Ma6, Ma7(9, ♯11), mi7 (9, 11), mi7♭5 (11), Dom7 (♭9, 9, ♯9, ♯11, ♭5, sus4), phry, lyd, alt
Chord progression:	functional and non-functional harmony, pedal point, modal passages
Dynamics:	*pp, p, mp, mf, f, ff, cresc, dim*
Edition:	8 1/2x11 oblong, 34 pages. Boxed numbers highlighting sections, no individual measure numbers
Form:	ABCD with variable length sections
Guitar:	chord symbols
Key:	B mi
Modulations:	none
Mutes:	harmon, straight, cup (tpts), cup (tbns), in stand (all)
Orchestration:	SATTB saxes; ss, as, 2 tpts (straight mutes), guitar (mm. 52–55)
Piano:	written and chord symbols
Shout:	mm.160–183
Style:	modal contemporary
Tempo:	quarter=160. Slowly, conducted on last 4
Time feel:	Latin-straight eighths, spacey "ECM broken 8ths," swing (spacey), swing (straight ahead)
Voicings:	saxes: uni, 2-pt, 4-pt, 5-pt tpts: uni, 2pt, 3-pt, 3-pt triadic dbl lead 8vb, 4-pt, 4-pt clus tbns: uni, 2-pt, 4-pt, 4-pt clus, 5-pt

on a fermata, followed by a 4-bar conducted, slow coda (m. 302).

The opening textures build from unaccompanied piano to trio (m. 9), quintet (m. 17), reaching full ensemble on the restatement of the head (m. 52). In addition to unaccompanied and combo passages there are contrapuntal textures (mm. 120–27), unison and harmonized couplings across sections (saxes and trumpets, saxes and trombones), tutti concerted (mm. 168–75), and pedal points (see table T.1).

Melodic, Harmonic, and Rhythmic Materials:
The main trumpet and tenor sax tune (m. 17) uses the jazz melodic minor and natural minor modes in alternation: jazz melodic (mm. 17–22), natural minor (mm. 23–26), jazz melodic (mm. 27–31), natural minor (mm. 32–38), jazz melodic (mm. 39–41), natural minor (mm.48–51) (see figure T.1).

It also alternates unison (mm. 17–22, mm. 35–41) with two-part harmony (mm. 23–34, mm. 48–51). The two-part harmony features variable intervals

mixing parallelism (thirds and sixths) with intervallic tension resolution (for example: major 7, major 7, resolving to minor sixth, mm. 23–24).

In the ensemble repeat the tune is varied at the end of the B section (mm. 68–71).

The motive at mm. 23–26 of the A section is used for the closing of the first head (trumpets 1 and 5, mm. 48–51), and of the second head (trombones and low saxes, followed by trumpets and high saxes, mm. 80–87). The B phrygian mode is featured in the introduction, the interlude (m. 186), and the coda (piano and trumpets, open fifths, m. 303).

The harmony includes chord structures over pedal points, as the chords with no third at m. 17 (third is in the melody), modally derived chords (G lydian, m. 23), polychords(A♭ sus over C triad, mm. 44–45), various tonic minor variants (natural minor and

Figure T.1

Table T.1 "Temple Street" outline

		soli head		ens variation of head			
Chorus		1		2			3
Measure	1 9	17 30 38 46		52 63 72 80			88 96 104
Material	Intro	A B C A1		A B D A2			A B C
# of bars	8+8	8+5 8 8 6		6+5 9 8 8			8 8 8
Texture	pno, rhy	ts 1/tpt 5 ens soli					tpt 5 solo------
Time feel	straight 8ths "ECM broken 8ths" spacey						swing, spacey

			Shout		
Chorus	4	5	6		
Measure	112	136 144 152	160 184	186
Material	A B D	A B C	A B D A3	Interlude
# of bars			8 8 8 2	12 (open)
Texture	(+ ens) ---------	-----------------	ens	pno solo
Time feel	straight spacey ahead	straight ahead		straight 8ths spacey

				head out	
Chorus	7	8	9	10 Coda
Measure	198	222	246	270 294 302
Material	A B C	A B D	A B C	A B D D A1
# of bars	8 8 8	8 8 8	8 8 8	8 8 8 8 4
Texture	ts1solo ------	(+ ens) -------	---------------	
Time feel	straight 8ths spacey	straight ahead		slowly conducted

Table T.2 Harmonic rhythm of the head compressed into 2-bar even harmonic rhythm in the solo section

Chord	Bmi	A♭mi11(♭5)/B	GMa♯11/B	B♭7(♯9)
Duration (bars) in head mm. 17–29	4	2	3	4
Duration (bars) in solo section mm. 88–95	2	2	2	2

harmonic minor clusters, mm. 52–55), and triad with added fourth structures over pedal (D add4 over B and over B♭, mm. 72–74).

The looser harmonic rhythm of the head (mm. 17–29) is compressed into a 2-bar even harmonic rhythm in the solo section (mm. 88–95) (see table T.2).

Pedal points are on the tonic (A sections, beginning), moving to the leading tone (spelled as B♭, end of the A section), alternate tonic and leading tone (D sections), and are on the tonic or on a double tonic-dominant pedal on the shorter A section variations that close the head and shout choruses (m. 46, m. 80, m. 184).

The main rhythmic durations are dotted quarter notes and quarter note triplets treated with anticipations, delayed attacks and syncopation. On the beat concerted passages articulate the end of the B section (mm. 68–71, and mm. 282–85). The D section ostinato displays a strong fourth beat anticipation.

Technique Highlight:

Ostinato: Minimalist
The word means "obstinate" and indicates a short pattern (melodic, harmonic, or rhythmic), that repeats persistently. See "Miles Mood." Minimalism denotes music that uses small intervallic cells (often two notes, as here) steady pulse, repetition, and very slow changes, often creating an hypnotic effect. In the ostinato (mm. 46–51) each of the three saxophones plays a repeating two note interval (Ma2nd, 4th, and 5th) that yield alternatively an interval of a fourth (F♯ B) and of a fifth (F♯ C♯), since one of the parts is always doubled. The resulting compound sonority spells out degrees 1, 2, and 5 (B–C♯–F♯) in B, the tonality played by the rhythm section.

Making Music
Changes of feel occur throughout, and need to be worked out by the rhythm section. They include straight 8ths Latin feel, "ECM broken 8ths," swing: very spacey, swing: straight ahead (see form outline chart, Table 58). Note also the brass mute changes, including Harmon, straight, and cup (tpts), and cup (tbns). Switches to flugelhorns are found at mm. 63, 119, 222.

There are many peaks and valleys as the chart explores the range of dynamics from *p* to *ff*, and develops from loose spacey feel to tight swing. The two main peaks are the shout (m. 160) roughly midway through the chart and the recapitulation of the melody (m. 270). The first follows the trumpet solo (trumpets reach high written E), and the second follows the tenor solo (trumpets reach high written F♯). The solos need to build and lead organically into these sections.

Self-Test Question 56
The chords in the trombones at mm. 52–55 are:

a. 4-part close over the root of the chord
b. 5-part spreads
c. 4-part clusters over the root of the chord
d. 5-part drop 2+4 (2nd and 4th voice form the top drops 8vb)

———— ✧ ————

TENNESSEE WALTZ

Stewart, Redd, and Pee Wee King 1948

Holman, Bill 1995
Grade: 6.5
Duration: 7:56
Instrumentation: 5, 4, 4, 3
Publisher: Sierra Music
Recording: Bill Holman Band. *A View from the Side*. JVC-2050-2.

Highest Written Notes:
Tpt 1:   F (three ledger lines)
Tbn 1:   G (three ledger lines)

At a Glance:

Articulation:	• – > ∧ ≥ slurs
Bass line:	written, chord symbols
Chord progression:	diatonic, secondary dominants (V/ii, V/iii, V/IV) upper chromatic dominants, chords borrowed from the minor (♭I-IMa7, ♭IIIMa7, ♭VIMa7, ♭VI-IMa7), Ma7 chords in cycle 4 and in chromatic sequences
Chords:	triads, triads (add 9), Ma 6 (9), Ma7 (9), mi7 (9, 11), mi7♭5, Dom7 (♭9, 9, sus4)
Dynamics:	p, mp, mf, f, ff, cresc, dim
Edition:	8 1/2x11 oblong 39 pages. Measure numbers every bar, boxed numbers highlighting sections
Form:	strophic with extensions and interludes
Key:	C Ma
Modulations:	E♭ Ma
Mutes:	straight (tbns 1-2-3)
Piano:	written, chord symbols
Shout:	mm. 221–30 and mm. 279–86 are climactic
Style:	jazz waltz
Tempo:	dotted half =63
Time feel:	in "1"
Voicings:	saxes: uni, 4-pt tpts: uni, octaves, triads, 4-pt close tbns: uni, triads, triads w.lead doubled 8vb, 4-pt drop2 brass: 5-/6-pt, tpt triads duplicated by tbns 8vb.

Solos:
as 1, tpt 3, (70), dms (open), bass (6 +32, written)

Introductory Notes:
Director's Notes and General Performance Comments by Bob Curnow

Form and Texture:
The basic form is strophic, with many alterations. An 8-bar introduction is followed by six choruses (the last one truncated), and a coda. In addition, there are various codettas, interludes, and modulating passages. Though the four strophes (A, A', A", A"') share the same key (C major) and the main motive, A" contains textural, melodic, and harmonic contrasts (see bass line) that make it a pseudo B section. While generally a bridge modulates also to a new key, the contrast here creates a sort of AABA form superimposed on the strophic arrangement.

The main tune is comprised of a 10-bar antecedent, and an 8-bar consequent, both with pickups (A, A', A"'), and an 8-bar antecedent and 8-bar consequent (A"). A 4-bar codetta follows (m. 75), bringing the head chorus to a total of 74 bars. The solo section (choruses 2 and 3, mm. 79–148) totals 70 bars, with each strophe 16 bars (8+8) in length, and a 6-bar codetta. An 8-bar piano solo vamp and a 4-part counterpoint passage in the trombones lead to an arranger's chorus (64 bars+ 10-bar extension, mm. 157–230). After an open drum solo and an 8-bar modulating interlude a full chorus in the new key of E♭ major follows (strophes here are 12+8, 10+8, 12+8, 10+8 bars). A bass solo retransitions back to the original key of C major (m. 349), where A and A"' are recapitulated and merge into an 8-bar coda (m. 385).

A wealth of different textures is found throughout: the arranger's chorus (mm. 157–230) features tutti unison, two part counterpoint over harmonized trombones, concerted brass over tonic pedal tone (on middle C) in saxes, and a unison canon (four entrances, saxophones and trumpets in pairs, m. 205) (see table T.3).

Melodic, Harmonic, and Rhythmic Materials:
The tune is based on C pentatonic major, with blue notes added at the consequent phrase's closing (♭7, ♭3, mm. 17–18). While the antecedent is the same (A, A', A"'), the consequent varies, concluding on the second scale degree D (A, A"), or closing on the tonic C (A', A"'). A" begins with the main motive at the octave, followed by a variant of the melody.

In A' and A"' the flat third (E♭) is introduced in the counter line, producing a cross-relation with the E natural (m. 23). The E♭ reappears in the lead line throughout (m. 42, mm. 77–78, mm. 162, mm. 234–40), foreshadowing the modulation to E♭ major (m. 241). After a "false" recapitulation in E♭ major by the bass (mm. 333–48), the head returns in the original key of C major (m. 349).

Paralleling the melody, the harmony changes with the consequent phrase, featuring harmonic variants for

Table T.3 "Tennessee Waltz" outline

Chorus	1	head		2–3	solos
Measure	1	5		79	
Material	intro A A'	A" (pseudo B) A"' codetta		A A' A" A"' codetta	
# of bars	8 10+8 10+8 8+8	10+8 4		8+8 8+8 8+8 8+8 6	
Key	C major				

4 arranger's chorus		drums solo	modulating interlude	5	shout
149		231	233	241	
vamp A A' A" A"' extension				A A' A" A"'	
8 8+8 8+8 8+8 8+8 10		open	8	12+8 10+8 12+8 10+8	
				E♭ major	

317 "false" recap		6	head
		349	
A A"' extension		A A"' coda	
8+8 8+8 +4		10+8 10+8 8	
		C major	

each strophe. The A section closes with a chromatic sequence of major 7 chords in descending minor thirds (B♭Ma7 GMa7; BMa7 A♭Ma7, mm. 19–22), A' displays a sequence of major 7 chords borrowed from the minor in cycle 4 (A♭Ma7–E♭Ma7–B♭Ma7–FMa7, mm. 37–40), A" a chromatic sequence descending to the dominant (A7–A♭7–A♭mi7–Gmi7–G7, mm. 52–56), and A"' a IV–V–I cadence (F–G7–C, mm. 69–71).

Other features include a reverse cascade (3–2–1= three parts to unison, mm. 44–45), unison canon at a quarter beat lag (mm. 169–70), and at one measure lag (mm. 205–16).

Technique Highlight:

Alternate Fingerings: Saxophone
On most wind instruments certain notes can be played with non-standard fingerings. These enable different timbres to be used, and sometimes are employed to produce multiphonics, or altissimo range (notes above the standard range). These "non-standard" techniques are constantly redefined by the virtuosos of each instrument. In this chart the saxophones play a pedal middle C (mm. 184–96) toggling between the "regular" finger-

ing (marked with the o open sign), and the "alternate" fingering (marked with the + closed sign), producing timbral. They are produced using the "long" fingering (an octave below, without using the octave key).

Making Music
Read Director's Notes and General Performance Comments in the score. For ease in playing in waltz time in "one," provide changes to all and warm up on the solo section at mm. 79–94. Develop exercises to practice 2, 4, and 5 over 3 rhythms (clapping, one note, two notes, scales, etc.) (see figure T.2).

Stepping in with active conducting will be needed in passages where the rhythm section drops out (mm. 149, 205). All main cues need to be given as the ensemble and the rhythm section reenter one by one: m. 152 (tbns), m. 156 (ens), m. 169 (dms), m. 173 (bass), m. 189 (piano), m. 217 (tbns + rhythm section), m. 233 (saxes), m. 235 (tbns), m. 237 (tpts).

Understanding the elaborate form of this piece and its details will help its interpretation. There are many humorous passages such as the "teaser" bass solo (mm. 287–90) that foreshadows the more extensive one at

Figure T.2

m. 317, and the "false" recapitulation in E♭ Major by the bass (mm. 333–48). The apex is at m. 276 where the ensemble joins in a tutti concerted, after sections of contrapuntal texture, and the relentless two-note B♭–C motive in the lead line is released.

Self-Test Question 57
The canon at mm. 241–46 between 1st tpt and 1st tbn is:

 a. at the octave below, one bar lag
 b. at the fifth below, two beats lag
 c. at the fourth below, one bar lag
 d. at a fifth plus an octave below, three beats lag

THREE AND ONE

Jones, Thad 1970

Jones, Thad 1970

Grade:	5.5
Duration:	5:50
Instrumentation:	5, 5, 4, 4 (5th tpt player plays solo flug throughout)
Publisher:	Kendor Music
Recording:	Thad Jones/Mel Lewis Orchestra. *The Jazz Orchestra.* Solid State 18048 LP. Out of print. Reissued in *The Complete Solid State Recordings of the Thad Jones/ Mel Lewis Orchestra.* Mosaic Records MD5-151, five CDs, 1994. Out of print. Eastman Jazz Ensemble on CD that accompanies Rayburn Wright's *Inside the Score* text, Kendor Music.

Highest Written Notes:

Tpt 1:	E♭ (three ledger lines)
Tbn 1:	B♭ (four ledger lines)

Feature:
flug, bari, bass

Solos:
bari (opt. changes cued for ts 1, one chorus), flug (one chorus), bass (two choruses)

Soli:
flug, bari, bass (on head), saxes (one chorus)

Introductory Notes:
Brief commentary on the Thad Jones/Mel Lewis orchestra and his music

At a Glance:

Articulation:	• – > ∧ slurs
Bass line:	written melody, written walking bass with chord symbols cued, chord symbols
Chords:	Ma6, Ma7 (9), mi7 (9, 11), Dom (7, 9, #11, #5, ♭13, 13, sus, alt, lydian, octatonic), dim, aug
Chord progression:	secondary dominants, upper chromatic dominants, dominant chains
Dynamics:	*p, mp, mf, f, ff, cresc, dim*
Edition:	8 1/2x11 vertical, 10 pages. Letters every 16 bars. No measure numbers.
Expressive devices:	bend fall, lift, smear, turn, spill (saxes), bend, fall, spill (brass)
Form:	7 and 1/2 choruses ABAB1 (32 bars)
Guitar part:	chord symbols and rhythm slashes
Key:	E♭ Ma
Modulations:	none
Mutes:	none
Orchestration:	soli combination of flugelhorn, baritone sax, and string bass
Piano part:	chord symbols and slashes, occasional written parts
Shout:	chorus 7 (letters I J)
Style:	swing
Tempo:	quarter=160
Time feel:	in 4
Voicings:	saxes: 4-pt, 5-part closed and open (drop2, drop2 and 4) with internal clusters tpts: triads dbl lead 8vb, 4-pt closed and open tbns: 4-pt, spreads ens: 8-pt octatonic chord with additional 9th line (mm. 29–30) Upper structure triads: II, ♭III, ♭VI

Form and Texture:

The piece is in ABAB1 binary form, with the second A (letter B) varying a couple of notes by octave displacement and slight elongation. The B1 section varies its last four bars to emphasize the I7 tonic chord (letter B, mm. 13–14), followed by a dominant pedal and a break that launches the sax soli. The sax soli is one chorus (letters C and D), and the solo section (letters E and F) features bari the first time and flugelhorn with ensemble backgrounds the second time. The bass solo (letters G and H) is repeated.

Chorus 7 (letters I and J) is the tutti shout. A *dal segno* to letter B brings to the recapitulation of the second half of the head. On the last two bars (where the coda sign is) there is a break for a last statement by the soli trio, and a final chord. This is not a coda per se, since it does not add bars to the form. The lack of introduction, coda, or interludes yields a concise seven and a half chorus form.

The soli trio of flugelhorn, bari sax, and bass delivers the main tune and then each of the three instruments takes a solo. For more on small group "band within a band" writing see "Daahoud" and "A Minor Excursion." Other textures are mainly sectional (sax soli) and tutti concerted (shout).

Melodic, Harmonic, and Rhythmic Materials:

The tune is constructed from a handful of motives, carefully varied and developed through sequence, rhythmic displacement, and note interpolation. Though the initial chord progression is quite simple, reharmonizations become very complex as the piece progresses. Lines are harmonized with passing and substitute chords using chromatic and diatonic planing. Voicings are dense and employ verticalizations of modal collections such as in the 8-part octatonic chords at mm. 29–30. Two octatonic scales are used

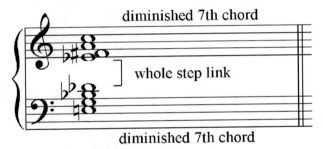

diminished 7th chord

Figure T.3

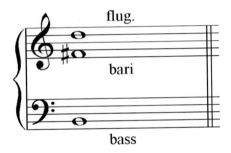

Figure T.4

here: "C" (C–Db–Eb–E–F#–G–A–Bb) and "D" (D–Eb–F–F#–G#–A–B–C). Each note of the lead line is harmonized (from the top down) by two diminished 7th chords linked by a whole step (figure T.3). The flugelhorn plays an additional 9th line beginning on the note Ab.

Among the many rhythmic devices there is an extended three over four in mm. 138–41.

Technique Highlight:

Reharmonization of each Note of
the Melody with a Different Harmony

For a discussion of reharmonization of each note of the melody with a different harmony see "Cherry Juice." In "Three and One" the soli trio instruments are harmonized in triads, beginning at m. 7. The triads are built down from each note of the melody and are in open position, with the bass an octave below (figure T.4). The three parts move in parallel (from the top down they are on the 3rd, 5th, and root of the triad) This technique is also used in the shout (letters I and J), where chord substitutions are spelled out in the guitar part, and their roots written out in the bass line.

Making Music

The trio of flugelhorn, bari sax, and bass needs to blend. The instruments are from different sections and need to hear each other. With the standard seating arrangement bari and bass sit far from each other and it might be challenging for the bass to hear the bari.

Drums are on brushes for the head and the bass solo, sticks on the rest, including the final chord (after the final head played with brushes). No tempo changes throughout. Very last two bars have ritardando: the trio can lead it and the drummer can give the last chord. Conduct if necessary. The sax soli might need a sectional rehearsal. For more on soli see "Cottontail," "Cherry Juice," "Groove Merchant," and "TipToe." The full ensemble in the shout needs to observe the many crescendo and diminuendo passages and operate as a unified group with balanced dynamics.

Self-Test Question 58

In the octatonic chord passage (mm. 29–30) that marks the end of the head and the beginning of the sax soli, the trumpet lead is doubled in:

    a. bari sax, bass, and first tenor
    b. bari sax and bass
    c. first trombone and bass
    d. piano, second tenor, and bari sax

For Further Reading

Wright, Rayburn. *Inside the Score.* Kendor, 1982.

TIPTOE

Jones, Thad 1963

Jones, Thad 1963
Grade: 5
Duration: 6:38
Instrumentation: 5, 4, 4, 4 (as1 on ss through-out, substitute part for alto provided)
Publisher: Kendor Music
Recording: Thad Jones and Mel Lewis. *Consummation.* Blue Note 7243 5 38226 2 0 CD.

Highest Written Notes:
Tpt 1:   F (three ledger lines)
Tbn 1:   Bb (four ledger lines)

Solos:
tpt 1 (1 chorus), dms (1 chorus, w.ensemble), as 2 (1 chorus)

Soli:
tbn section and bass unison (1 chorus)

Introductory Notes:
None

At a Glance:

Articulation:	• – > ∧ slurs
Bass line:	written
Chords:	Ma6, Ma7 (9), mi7 (9), Dom (7, 9, #11, 13, alt, octatonic), dim
Chord progression:	"rhythm" changes
Dynamics:	*pp, mp, mf, f, cresc, dim*
Edition:	8 1/2x11 vertical, 11 pages. Letters every eight bars. No measure numbers.
Expressive devices:	fall, lift, smear (saxes), doit, fall (brass)
Form:	8 choruses of rhythm changes, coda (7 bars)
Guitar part:	chord symbols
Key:	Ab Ma
Modulations:	none
Mutes:	cup
Orchestration:	soprano lead
Piano part:	chord symbols and slashes, occasional written parts
Shout:	chorus 7 (letters Q, R, S)
Style:	swing
Tempo:	quarter=132
Time feel:	in 2 and in 4
Voicings:	saxes: 4 and 5 part variable voicings (close and open) with internal clusters tpts: 2-pt, triads, 4-pt tbns: 3-pt (in 5ths), 4-pt, spreads

Form and Texture:

The form is straightforward: eight choruses of AABA "rhythm" changes in Ab, and a 7-bar coda. No introduction: the head is presented by saxes who continue to accompany the cup muted trumpet solo in the second chorus (letter D). A tutti brass (this is their first entrance) introduces the third chorus (letter G) featuring a trombone section and bass unison soli accompanied by drums. The drums are then featured in a dialogue with the ensemble in chorus four (letter J). Alto 2 solos on choruses 5 and 6 (letters M, O, N, and P) with backgrounds the second time. Chorus 7 (letter Q) is the shout. Da capo of the head leads to a coda over the tonic pedal, ending with the main motive sounded one more time in the final bar. The coda (actual additional measures beyond the recapitulation of the form) starts on the fourth bar after the coda sign (see *Coda* in Glossary).

The texture is mostly concerted (other than the backgrounds to the alto solo), with concerted saxes, concerted trombones and bass, and concerted tutti ensemble sections.

Melodic, Harmonic, and Rhythmic Materials:

The catchy motive, with its marcato articulation, medium-soft dynamics, characteristic intervals, use of space, and rhythmic interest, captures the essence of the tune's title. The A section (letter A, mm. 1–8) melody is built from two rhythmic motives (fig. T.5), developed into eight bars (table T.4).

There is a strict alternation of descent and ascent in the last interval of each of the motives, beginning with the E♭–E♭ descending octave in m. 1, followed by the ascending F–C♭ diminished 5th in m. 2 and so on. The melody uses many double approaches (chromatic note from below, step from above, target note): m. 1, F–D–E♭; m. 4, C–E♭–D♭; mm. 7–8, C–E♭–D♭ (see figure T.6 for an example of double approaches).

"Rhythm" changes denotes the chord progression of the tune "I Got Rhythm" written by George Gershwin in 1930. This chord progression has been used for numerous jazz tunes, and is encountered most frequently in the key of B♭. A set of "rhythm" changes in B♭ for the A and B sections can be found in table T.5.

The "rhythm" changes progression here is in A♭ and is reharmonized quite extensively beginning on chorus four. How so?

In the shout (as in other arrangements, such as his "Cherry Juice" and "Three and One") Jones uses his characteristic reharmonization of each melody note with a harmonic structure, employing tritone substitution, chromatic and diatonic planing, diminished chords, chord substitutions, and interpolations.

Technique Highlight:

Expressive Devices
Expressive Devices are discussed in "Big Dipper." Jones here uses fall, lift, and smear (saxes), doit, and fall (brass).

Making Music

Drummer plays brushes throughout. Note the comping sections for guitar, piano, and for both. The trombone section and bass unison chorus (letters G, H, and I) might need a sectional rehearsal. Piano plays light fills in the pauses in the melodic line (letters A, B, and C): both piano and electric piano are used on the recording (light, with a vibe/glockenspiel type sound patch).

Some dynamics and articulations are implied by the style, and might be determined by section lead players. Unless players are familiar with the style, you might want to add in the score markings derived from score study and from listening to the recording. Among these are natural dynamics implied by melodic contour (letter B mm. 5–6 crescendo and decrescendo with the line; letter J mm. 5–7 crescendo with the ascending line), and articulations (smear, saxes letter E, mm. 2–3). Marcato quarter notes are played as in figure T.7.

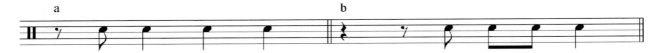

Figure T.5

Table T.4 Eight-bar theme spun out from two rhythmic motives

measure	1	2	3	4	5	6	7	8
motive	a	b	a1 (elided)	b1	a2 a1(varied)	b2 (developed)	b3 (displaced)	a3 (elided)

Figure T.6 Double approaches to C major triad

Table T.5 Set of "rhythm" changes

Measure	1		2		3		4	
A section	B♭	Gmi7	Cmi7	F7	Dmi7	Gmi7	Cmi7	F7
	5		6		7		8	
	B♭	B♭7	E♭	E♭mi	Dmi7	G7	Cmi7	F7
Measure	1		2		3		4	
B section	D7				G7			
	5		6		7		8	
	C7				F7			

Self-Test Question 59

The sustained, full ensemble chord (wind and bass) one measure after the coda sign is harmonized with:

a. an A♭ diminished scale, all 8 pitches
b. an A♭ diminished scale, 7 out of the 8 pitches
c. an A♭ mixolydian scale
d. a D♭ major over A♭ pedal

Figure T.7

⁕

TRIBUTE

Mintzer, Bob 1984

Mintzer, Bob 1984

Grade:	4.5 (5)
Duration:	10:30
Instrumentation:	5, 4, 4, 3 (ts 1-2 on opt fl mm. 96–108)
Publisher:	Kendor Music
Recording:	Bob Mintzer Big Band *Incredible Journey* (DMP 451).

Highest Written Notes:

Tpt 1: E♭ (three ledger lines), G (four ledger lines, m. 84, opt. lower octave, and m. 156 opt. D two ledger lines)

Tbn 1: B (four ledger lines)

Solos:

pno, tpt 3, tbn 1

Solo Section:

mm. 1–32 (pno solo) and mm. 64–95 (tpt 3, pno, tbn 1) can be opened up for further solos

Introductory Notes:

Form and Texture:

AABA song form with additional sections. Chorus 1 is for piano solo with bass and drums accompaniment. The head (chorus 2, m. 33) is presented by saxes with a trombone counterline on the 2nd A section. The B section (m. 42) is tutti concerted, and the last A is for saxes with brass counterline. Brass takes over the melody on the 6-bar extension (mm. 58–65). Choruses 3 and 4 are open for solos, with backgrounds on cue. A through composed 24-bar march style section follows (mm. 96–119), with trombones and bari on a staccato quarter note pulse and a trumpet unison riff.

The shout (mm. 120–35) features a brass and bari concerted riff and a different figure in the rest of the saxes, joining in a tutti concerted at m. 128. The dal segno is to the solo section (m. 64), followed by the recapitulation of the first two A sections (m. 136), a varied B section in three part counterpoint (mm. 145–51) and a recomposed 4-bar final A (mm. 153–56) (see table T.6).

Writing is mostly sectional. Textures include unison trombones against 4- and 5-part saxes (m. 33), tutti (m. 42), counterpoint (2-part mm. 50–63; 3-part mm. 145–51) featuring saxes against brass, independent unison lines (trumpets mm. 53–54, saxes mm. 62–63), and tutti (m. 61).

At a Glance:

Articulation:	• – > ∧ ≥ hat over tenuto, slurs
Bass line:	written (mm. 96–111), and chord symbols
Chords:	Ma7, mi7 (9, 11), Dom7 (♭9, 9, ♯9, ♯11, ♯5, 13, sus4, sus4 with third of chord above the 4th), dim, triads over bass note
Chord progression:	see Harmonic Materials
Chord scales:	alt, oct
Dynamics:	*p, mp, mf, f, ff, sfp, cresc, dim*
Edition:	8 1/2x11 vertical, 9 pages. Measure numbers every bar, boxed numbers highlighting sections
Expressive devices:	fall-short (saxes m. 36, tutti m. 72), ghost (saxes m. 40), gliss-short (saxes m. 48) gliss-long (m. 92), scoop (tpts. m. 48) shake, vibrato.
Feel:	2, 4, march, strong backbeat (mm. 120–35)
Form:	AABA (6 choruses) with codetta extension, through composed march, shout, elided last A in final chorus.
Key:	F Ma
Modulations:	none
Mutes	harmon no stem (tpt 1 m. 96), straight (tpt 2 m. 96)
Orchestration:	bari and tbn 4 dovetail root functions while weaving in and out of unison, doubling the lead 8vb, and playing chord tones or tensions (mm. 41–63).
Piano:	chord symbols with a couple of written measures
Shout:	mm. 120–35
Style:	swing (Basie-style), march (mm. 96–119)
Tempo:	quarter=120 (moderate)
Time feel:	in 2, in 4, strong backbeat, light time on hi-hat
Voicings:	variable voicings
saxes:	4-pt close dbl lead 8vb (mm. 33, 42), 5-pt drop2 with tension substitutions 9/1 13/5 (m. 33)
	tpts: triadic, 3-pt, 4-pt close, 4ths
	tbns: triadic, 4-pt, spreads
	br: 4-/5-/6-pt (m. 42)
	sw (tbns m. 58), ust (♭VI mm. 39, 50, VI m. 125)

Table T.6   "Tribute" outline

Chorus	1 intro	2 head				extension	3–4 solo section			
Measure	1	33				58	64			
Form	AABA	A	A	B	A		A	A	B	A
# of bars	32	32				6	32			
Instrum.	rhy section	saxes		tutti		br/tutti	bkg on cue			
Solo	pno------						tpt3, pno------------			

Chorus	march			shout			5 solo section				6 head out			
Measure	96			120			D.S. to 64				136			
Form	C	D	E	A	A	A	A	A	B	A	A	A	B	A
# of bars	8	8	8	8	8	8	8	8	8	8	8	8	8	4
Instrum.	tpts tutti over tbns+bari			concerted br + bari, saxes cp			bkg on cue				as mm. 33-40	3-pt cp	tutti	
Solo	pno------						tbn 1--------							

Melodic, Harmonic, and Rhythmic Materials:

The A and B sections are built on 2-bar riff phrases that are varied and developed. Both sections use dominant quality chords (F7 and B♭7 respectively) as their tonic chords. The A sections feature cycle five dominant chains with interpolations and tritone substitutions. The shout (mm. 120–35) is a variation of A material, with the I chord now presented as Ma7 rather than dominant 7. While in counterpoint sometimes line tends to predominate over harmony, in the final 3-part counterpoint (tpt4, tbns1 and 4 over light hi-hat time, mm. 145–51) the resulting harmony (a variation of the B section) is quite clear:

B♭7 G7/B | C D♭Ma7 B♭/D | G7 C(♯11)A♭ | F F- |
B♭7 G7/B | F6/C D7(A♭) | GMa7 C7 |

Generally baritone and bass trombone alternate covering the low end of the ensemble. At mm. 41–63 root functions are dovetailed, with the occasional overlap (mm. 49, 61, 64) to articulate end of sections. The two parts also weave in and out of unison, double the lead 8vb (bari), and play chord tones or tensions (see table T.7).

Technique Highlight:

Riff

A riff is a short motive, generally 1 to 4 bars in length that repeats (see "Basically Blues"). This piece uses mostly 2-bar riffs that are varied and developed.

Making Music

This piece is a tribute to the Basie medium swing, riff based style (see "Moten Swing").

As many of Basie's charts it begins with a piano solo accompanied by bass and drums that can be opened up for more choruses. For Basie style rhythm section playing see "All of Me."

Another tip of the hat to Basie is in the dynamics such as the rapid crescendos over a couple of beats (mf to f, mm. 41, 124), and the sudden, highly contrasting dynamic changes as the f mp at mm. 42, 44, 46. All need to be played with drama and accuracy. Measures 120–21 and 122–23 are played on the recording with a mf to f crescendo over the course of the two-bar riff. Add dynamics that are not in the score. For a discussion of dynamics, see "Moten Swing."

Interpretation of markings and placement of the upbeat are determined by performance practice. Generally in jazz the hat (∧) or marcato is played with an accent and shortened depending on the tempo and the context. Note that if one desires a marcato with full value, the notation of hat over tenuto line found at mm. 50–52 can be used. For a discussion of placement of the upbeat see "Cute." A way of notating mm. 33–34 that approximates how they are played can be found in figure T.8.

The staccato quarter note accompaniment in the march is played with a more classical staccato, and should be light, not ponderous, and accented only where marked.

Mixed voicings (4-part double lead to 5-part, triads to 4-part), and unison to 4-part cascades (trumpets, mm. 50–92) are widespread in this piece (for more on cascades see "Young Blood"). Players need to develop an awareness of the shifting function of their lines at any given point.

Figure T.8

Table T.7   Baritone sax and bass trombone functions in "Tribute" mm. 41–63

Measure	41	42	47	48	49	50	58–63
Bari	dbl as2+ on 5th part	dbl lead 8vb	5-part (chord tones)	root --------		dbl lead 8vb interspersed with guide tones	root/ unison
B.Tbn	root (occasional 5ths)-------			chord tones	root	root/ unison	chord tones, tensions/root

Self-Test Question 60
To play the passage at mm. 96–108 as scored, the following trumpet mutes and woodwind doublings are needed:

    a. one harmon mute with stem inserted, one straight mute, two flutes

    b. two harmon mutes, no stem, one straight mute, two flutes, and a clarinet

    c. one harmon mute, one cup mute, two flutes with low B foot

    d. one harmon mute, no stem, one straight mute, two flutes with low B foot

---

TURN AROUND

Harris, Matt 1997

Harris, Matt 1997

Grade:	5
Duration:	4:20
Instrumentation:	5, 4, 4, 4 (tpt 3-4 double on flug, or can be played on tpts with cup mute)
Publisher:	Kendor Music

Highest Written Notes:

Tpt 1:	generally C (two ledger lines), one E♭ (three ledger lines)
Tbn 1:	B♭ (four ledger lines)

Solos:
chords cued in all parts (mm. 64–87)

Introductory Notes:
Director's notes. Composer's profile.

Form and Texture:
Harmonically the form of the main tune is A A1 A2 and is built on three different keys (B♭, D, and G♭) related by major third interval. Each section is eight bars. The head is stated, without introduction, by a unison small group comprised of alto, tenor, and two flugelhorns (m. 1), and restated reorchestrated and with ensemble accompaniment at m. 25. A tutti unison multimeter 7-bar section

At a Glance:

Articulation:	• > ∧ slurs
Bass line:	written and chord symbols
Chord progression:	II–V, passing diminished chords, secondary dominants (V/II, V/III, V/IV, V/V), ♯IV-7(♭5)
Chords:	Ma6, Ma7, mi7 (9, 11), mi7♭5, Dom7 (♭9, 9, ♯11, ♭5, ♯5, 13, sus4), dim7
Edition:	8 1/2x11 oblong, 17 pages. Measure numbers every bar, boxed numbers highlighting sections
Form:	A A1 A2 (8 bars each) with additional sections
Guitar:	written melodic line, chords, chord symbols with top note of voicing, chord symbols
Key:	no key signature. Three key centers (B♭Ma, DMa, G♭Ma)
Modes:	mixolydian, octatonic
Modulations:	progressive tonality beginning in B♭Ma and ending in G♭Ma
Mutes:	opt cup (tpts 3-4)
Orchestration:	two flug, as, ts (mm. 1–24), and flug, tbn, as, ts (mm. 25–48) unison melodies.
Piano:	written melodic line, chords, chord symbols with top note of voicing, chord symbols
Shout:	no, but mm. 105–11 are climactic
Style:	samba
Tempo:	half=112–116
Voicings:	saxes: 2-pt, 3-pt, 4-pt, 5-pt, 5-pt spreads tpts: 2-pt, triads (ust II, ust ♭VI), triads with lead doubled 8vb, voicings in 4ths with lead doubled 8vb, 4-pt seventh chord structures. tbns: voicings in 4ths with lead doubled 8vb, 4-pt tertian structures brass: 4-, 5-, 6-, 7-pt

Figure T.9

follows (mm. 49–55), and an 8-bar tutti chordal passage (mm. 56–63) closes the head presentation.

The solo section (open for solos, mm. 64–87) follows the 24-bar form. The development/shout (mm. 88–130), follows the A A1 A2 B C form of the head restatement (mm. 25–63) with the only deviation being an added 4-bar sustained chord (mm. 119–22) before section C. After a *dal segno* repeat (to m. 25), a 5-bar coda concludes the chart. The coda is 5 bars, and begins at m. 132, one bar after the coda sign (see *Coda* in Glossary).

Melodic, Harmonic, and Rhythmic Materials:
The melodic material springs from the motives presented in the initial eight bars, transposed to adapt to the changing keys, varied, and developed. After the unison passage (mm. 49–55), the concerted section (mm. 56–63) features two contrasting 4-bar phrases, the first descending on G♭ mixolydian, and the second ascending on G♭ major. The shout section (mm. 88–130) develops motives from previous sections and features tutti chord punctuations and extensive drum fills.

The basic chord progression of the A section can be seen in table T.8.

A quick comparison will yield similarities and differences with the A1 and A2 sections. While at the outset the three keys carry the same weight, after the restatement the tonal center shifts toward G♭ with

the unison passage (mm. 49–55) outlining a ii V (A♭-7 [A♭7] D♭7) in G♭, and the chordal section featuring a G♭ pedal (m.60). This is also confirmed later with the dominant of G♭ strongly emphasized (4-bar D♭7, m. 119), and in the coda with a V–I cadence (m. 135), followed by a final G♭ chord featuring all eight pitches of the G♭ octatonic scale.

The unison passage at mm. 49–55 features a meter shift from cut time to 6/8 and a return to cut time. The tempo remains the same. Across this meter shift the phrasing outlines different durations: 5/4 (m. 49 to beat 2, m. 50), 7/4 (to beat 4, m. 52), 3/4 (to beat 4, m. 53), 3/4 (to beat 2+, m. 54), 4/4 (to beat 2+, m. 55) (see figure T.9).

Technique Highlight

Harmonic Motion by Major Thirds
Harmonic motion by major thirds was made famous in jazz by John Coltrane's tri-tonic or cycle major 3 chord progression for his 1959 tune "Giant Steps." The form in "Giant Steps" is 16 measures and the pattern of major thirds is descending, with the thirds preceded by their V or ii V harmonies:

B D7 | G B♭7 | E♭ | Ami7 D7 | G B♭7 | E♭ F♯7 | B | Fmi7 B♭7 |

Figure T.10 Conducting mm. 49–55

Table T.8 Basic chord progression of the A section in "Turn Around"

m. 1	2	3	4		5	6	7	8
B♭ A♭7	G-7 D♭7	C-7 F7	C/E	E♭-7	B♭/D G7	C-7 F7	B♭/D E♭-7	E-7 A7
I ucd or ♭VII7	vi ucd	ii V7	V/V	iv or II Lyd	I V/ii	ii V7	I iv	ii V7
Key: B♭								D:

E♭ | Ami7 D7 | G | C♯mi7 F♯7 | B | Fmi7 B♭7 |
E♭ | C♯mi7 F♯7 |

Using root motion by major thirds instead of the customary descending fifths or half steps was novel at the time. Coltrane used this technique also in other tunes such as "Countdown" and in reharmonizations of standards such as "Body and Soul. "He also experimented with harmonic motion by minor thirds (cycle minor 3) in tunes like "Central Park West." A cycle is a pattern that divides the octave by equal intervals. Six harmonic cycles are possible: semitones (12 notes), whole tones (6 notes), minor 3rds (4 notes), major 3rds (3 notes), fifths (12 notes), and tritone (2 notes).

Making Music
Read the To the Director notes. If you need to, establish the samba groove by warming up the rhythm section on the solo section (m. 64). As samba is felt "in two," your conducting at mm. 49–55 will be as in figure T.10.

If you need to slow the passage down for rehearsal you can use one bar of 4/4, four bars of 3/4, and two of 4/4, no change in tempo.

The pianist moves between single line and chords (at cadence points, mm. 8, 15, then with the ensemble, m. 17), comping (m. 29), and a 4-bar transition with the rhythm section (mm. 127–30). The drummer also wears many hats and needs to navigate playing ensemble figures, grooving on the solo section, building its dialogue with the ensemble (mm. 88–118), wrapping up things with a few final bars of solo groove, and setting up the last chords (mm. 132–36).

Self-Test Question 61
In the restatement of the head (mm. 25–32) the main tune is reorchestrated for:

a. alto, tenor, trumpet, trombone, guitar, piano
b. alto, tenor, flugel, trombone, piano
c. alto, tenor, flugel, trombone, guitar
d. alto, tenor, trumpet, trombone, guitar

V

A VIEW FROM THE SIDE

Holman, Bill 1989

Holman, Bill 1995

Grade: 5
Duration: 7:30
Instrumentation: 5, 4, 4, 3
Publisher: Sierra Music
Recording: Bill Holman Band. A *View From the Side*. JVC-2050-2.

Highest Written Notes:
Tpt 1:   A (four ledger lines)
Tpt 2:   D (two ledger lines)
Tbn 1:   B♭ (four ledger lines)

Solos:
tbn 1 (38), tpt 3, (4+38), tbn 1/tpts duet (8), pno (36), fills (tbns, 5)

Introductory Notes:
Director's Notes by Bob Curnow

Form and Texture:
As with other complex works, the form can only be briefly sketched here. It is a large ternary with three main sections A, B, and C. There are subtle changes in the number of measures: the first A (15 bars, mm. 4–18) concludes with a 2-bar link (mm. 19–20) that does not reappear later, the A1 section is 11 bars (mm. 21–31), the B section is 16 (mm. 32–47), and the C section varies its length depending on its function as head (32 bars, mm. 48–79), interlude (22 bars, mm. 146–67), or piano solo section (36 bars, mm. 222–47). The varied restatement of A (m. 90) rounds off the exposition of the main material, while also initiating the development section (the solos).

Trombone and trumpet solos are 38 bars. These two instruments join in an improvised duet (mm. 206–13) that prepares the ensemble climax (mm. 214–21). The piano solo follows and leads to the recapitulation of the ostinato and A section (15 bars), concluding with a coda (9 bars) (see table V.1).

Melodic, Harmonic, and Rhythmic Materials:
As with the form, melody, harmony, and time feel interact in an intricate balance of repetition and

At a Glance:

Articulation:	• – > ∧ ≥ slurs
Bass line:	written, chord symbols
Chord progression:	ostinato based, tonal areas within chromatic environment
Chords:	Ma7, min (dor), min7, min7 (♭5), Dom7 (♭9, 9, ♯9, ♯11, ♯5, 13, sus4)
Dynamics:	mp, mf, f, ff, cresc, dim
Edition:	8 1/2x11 oblong, 35 pages. Measure numbers every bar, boxed numbers highlighting sections
Form:	large ternary, through composed, with ABC sections
Key:	G center
Modulations:	B section is the most harmonically transient
Mutes:	cup (tpts), straight (tbns)
Piano:	written, chord symbols
Shout:	climax mm. 214–22
Style:	jazz straight 8ths/swing
Tempo:	quarter=116
Time feel:	in 4, double time
Voicings:	saxes: uni, 2-pt fifths (tenors) 4-pt, 5-pt
	tpts: uni, 2-pt fourths, 3-pt triads dbl lead 8vb, 4-pt close
	tbns: uni, 2-pt, 2-pt fifths 3-pt fourths, 3-pt close, 4-pt spreads
	ens: 7-pt chord (complete dorian mode)

development that creates a through composed feel while reintroducing to the listener familiar elements as they return in new guises. For example C is initially presented as a march (m. 48), then in swing (developed, m. 146), and finally as a chord progression for the piano solo (transposed and reworked, m. 222). The solo sections (m. 108, m. 168) maintain the G/A♭ half step relation of A and A1 (with the respective subdominant minor chords Cmi and D♭mi added), while the irregular form of the head (20 and 11 bars) is made more symmetric (8+8) for soloing.

Much melodic and harmonic material is intervallically conceived: the first theme (mm. 4–20) features trichords in fourths that fan out chromatically from the pitch D to yield eleven of the twelve chromatic pitches (D–G–C, C♯–F♯–B, C–F–B♭, E♭–A♭–D♭, . . . A–D).

The resulting collection (C–C♯–D–E♭– . . . F–F♯–G–A♭–A–B♭–B) is capped by the missing pitch E completing the chromatic spectrum (m. 16, lead). This arrival point is enhanced by the inverted pyramid that precedes it, the stop time, and the new concerted texture.

The A section bass ostinato features two elements (x, m. 1 and y, m. 2). Their combination gives rise to different phrase lengths (3, 2, or 1 bars) and motivic combinations (xyy, xy, yyy). The ostinato then follows a regular two bar pattern (xy) for the solo sections and coda (see table V.2).

The ostinato in the saxes (m. 1) is based on a whole tone cell (A–G) also present in the piano part. The three-note motive (A–A–G) interlocks at a one-eighth-note lag (in the order: tenor 1, baritone, tenor 2), producing a kaleidoscopic effect over the bass. It reappears similarly in all A sections. In the C section it overlaps, now rhythmically synchronized, to prepare the transition back to A (m. 80–89). In the cadential chords in the interlude it is expanded to four pairs of whole tone dyads over F pedal (mm. 161–63). In the climax it appears in rhythmic diminution (m. 215–19). In the coda (also expanded to four pairs of whole tone dyads) the time lag between entrances is one measure (mm. 266–74). The intervallically conceived ostinato structures are grounded by the stable (though varied) bass ostinato.

Harmonically, the first theme builds from an undefined (neither major nor minor) modality to a 7-part chord outlining the complete G dorian mode (m. 15). The major/minor identity of the tonic reappears in the solo section changes (G major/minor, m. 108). The half step relation of the trichords in the first theme is echoed in the restatement of the theme in Ab (m. 21) and in the first chord changes that appear in the piece at (m. 32) as they descend chromatically from E♭mi7 (♭5).

Time feels contribute to the clarity of the form. The B and C sections always feature double time feel. The C section is initially presented as a march (m. 48), then in swing (developed, m. 146), and finally as a chord progression for the piano solo (transposed and reworked, m. 222). Double time feel effectively frames the climax played in single time (mm. 206–14).

Technique Highlight:

Ostinato and Inverted Pyramid

The word means "obstinate" and indicates a short pattern (melodic, harmonic, or rhythmic), that repeats persistently. Here there are two ostinatos: the bass line

Table V.1 "A View from the Side" outline

Form	intro	head			
Measure	1	4	21	32	48
Material	ostinato	A link	A1	B	C
# of bars	6	7 8 2	7 4	8 8	8 10 8 6 10
Harmony		Gmi	Abmi	chr.planing Bmi Gmi	BMa⁷ AM⁷/D⁷ BMa⁷ Am⁷/GM F⁷
Feel/style		straight 8ths		swing	march
Time feel	single			double	

Form	head (varied)	trombone solo (38 bars)			interlude
Measure	90	108	124		146
Material	A2	A3	B		C
# of bars	3 7 8	8 8	8 8 6		8 10 4
Harmony	Gmi	GMa Ab Ma/mi CMi Db mi	chr. planing Bmi Gmi Bb7		BMa⁷ AMa⁷ Ab Ma⁷ GMa Gb Ma F
Feel/style	straight 8ths	straight 8ths	swing		
Time feel	single		double		

Form	trumpet solo		tpt/tbn duet	climax
Measure	168	184	206	214
Material	A3	B	A2	
# of bars	8 8	8 8 6	8	8
Harmony	GMa/mi Cmi Ab Ma/mi Db mi	chrom. planing, Bmi Gmi Bma⁷	GMa/mi Cmi	GMa/mi Cmi
Feel/style	straight 8ths	swing	straight 8ths	
Time feel	single	double	single	single

Form	piano solo		intro recap	head out	coda
Measure	222		248	251	266
Material	C		ostinato	A	
# of bars	16 16 4		6	7 8	9
Harmony	DMa CMa Bb Ma DMa CMa BMa F7			Gmi	Gmi
Feel/style	swing		straight 8ths		
Time feel	double		single		

Table V.2 Ostinato length and motivic combinations in "A View from the Side"

Measure	1 4 7 9	11 13 15	16	18 19 20
Ostinato length (in bars)	3 3 3 2 2	2 2 1	stop time	1 1 1
Motivic combination	xyy xyy xyy xy xy	xy xy x (dim.)		y y y

and the one by the saxophones (see above). For further examples of ostinato see "Miles Mood," "Fables of Faubus," "Haitian Fight Song," and "Temple Street."

A pyramid is the build-up of a chord through progressive sustaining entries. For examples of pyramids see "King Porter Stomp" and "What's New?" Here inverted pyramids (built from the highest pitch down) are used (see above).

Making Music

Read Director's Notes. While there aren't any tempo variations, there are numerous shifts in feel (straight 8ths, swing 8ths), time (single and double), and style (march) that need to be rendered with character and through seamless transitions. The ostinato in the winds is always marked *mp*. Its unchanging dynamics contrast with the tune that begins one dynamic level higher (*mf*) and grows into the *f* pyramid. For the climax of the piece a lead trumpet that can deliver the concert D–E–F–G above the staff is needed (mm. 214–19). This motive is stated an octave lower in the preceding bars (m. 206). Measure 273 is repeated nine times on the recording.

Self-Test Question 62
Often with pyramids, if enough instruments are available, each new pitch entrance is doubled so it has more definition. In the inverted pyramid at mm. 12–15 the entrances not doubled are:

a. trumpets 3 and 4
b. trombones 1, 2, and 4
c. trombones 1, 2, 3, and 4
d. none of the above, all entrances are doubled

W–X

WHAT'S NEW?

Haggart, Bob, and Johnny Burke 1939

Holman, Bill 1955

Grade:	5
Duration:	5:38
Instrumentation:	5, 5, 5, 4
Publisher:	Sierra Music
Recording:	Stan Kenton. *Contemporary Concepts*. Capitol Jazz 7243 5 42310 2 5 CD.

Highest Written Notes:

Tpt 1:	F (three ledger lines)
Tpt 2:	D (two ledger lines)
Tbn 1:	C (four ledger lines)

Solos:
ts 1, tpt 4, as 1, tbn 3 (all one chorus except as1 that begins on the second A of the form)

Introductory Notes:
Director's Notes by Bob Curnow

Form and Texture:
Four main textures shape the form: a pyramid on C minor, the recomposed head, solo sections, and interludes. The pyramid opens and closes the piece and is found also in the first A section (m. 22), at the end of the first chorus (m. 50), and at the reca-pitulation of the intro (m. 207). The recomposed tune (chorus 1, and m. 215) features a variable number of measures (A=11 bars, A1=8 bars, B=8 bars, A2=6 bars).

Solo sections are on the standard AABA 32-measure form, with the exception of the alto sax solo section (chorus 4) that begins with the ensemble playing the first eight bars. A four-bar

At a Glance:

Articulation:	• – > ʌ slurs
Bass line:	written walking bass and ob-bligato lines with the en-semble, chord symbols
Chords:	Ma (6, 9), mi7 (9, 11), Dom (7, ♭9, 9, ♯11, ♯5, 13)
Chord progression:	the chord progression from the original tune is used: IMa, II–V of ♭VIMa7, ♭VIMa7, V/V,V, I minor, II–V, IMa and turnarounds
Dynamics:	*pp, p, mp, mf, f, ff, fp, cresc, dim*
Edition:	8 1/2x11 oblong, 25 pages. Mea-sure numbers every bar, boxed numbers highlighting sections
Expressive devices:	none
Form:	modified AABA (32 bars) with interludes; see Form
Guitar part:	chord symbols and rhythm slashes
Key:	C Ma
Modulations:	to FMa and GMa
Mutes:	straight (tpt 1), cup (brass)
Orchestration:	pyramid with spatial and color variations
Piano part:	chord symbols and rhythm slashes
Shout:	last A and coda area climactic
Style:	swing
Tempo:	quarter=178
Voicings:	saxes: unis, 4-pt and 5-pt open, tpts: unis, 2-pt, (4ths, 5ths), 3-pt, 4-pt and 5-pt close, tbns: unis, 2-pt, 3-pt, 4-pt close, 5-pt open, 5-pt spreads brass: block voicings

Table W.1 "What's New?" outline

Chorus	intro	1 head		2	interlude 1	3
Measure	1	17 28 36 44	50	59	91	99
Material		A A B A	codetta	AABA		AABA
# of bars	16	11 8 8 6	9 break	32	8	32
Solo				ts1------		tpt4-----
Key	cmi	F C	cmi	C	modulatory	F
Pyramid	√	√	√			

Chorus	interlude 2	4	5	recap (intro)	head	interlude 3	coda
Measure	131	139	175	207	215	223	233
Material		A A B A	A A B A		A var		
# of bars	8	32 +4	32	8	8	8+2	10
Solo		tutti (8) as1 solo (26)	tbn3----				
Key	modulatory	G	G	G to C	C	C	cmi
Pyramid				√			√

codetta is also added (mm. 171–74). Tenor sax and trombone solos begin on a 2-bar break. The first two interludes are eight measures, the third is ten and leads to the coda. Textures are contrapuntal, concerted, and layered, with substantial unison writing (see table W.1).

Melodic, Harmonic, and Rhythmic Materials:

The melodic material is through composed. The original tune is fragmented, abstracted into motives, and developed throughout, supplying also the material for the backgrounds to the solos.

The arrangement preserves the chord progression of the original tune, where the B section is a subdominant transposition to the A section. Also, the original chord progression features modal interchange with the tonic minor chord (C minor) played on measure five of the form. This is exploited and expanded by the pyramid on C minor that frames the work.

The two modulations (to FMa and GMa) are initiated by the two interludes that precede them. The introduction returns with a "false" recapitulation in the key of G major (m. 207) that shifts quickly to the tonic C major (m. 211), leading to a through composed A section and the final climactic interlude linked to the coda. Dominant to tonic (G to C) movement is emphasized by the brass motive (mm. 221–22), and by the bass trombone (mm. 231–32).

The pyramid (mm. 1–16), while being relatively stable (on the bass trombone pedal) is varied through its internal rhythmic processes, color changes (mutes), and spatial distribution of entrances. It features 3-bar phrases in the brass, with the last phrase extended (3+3+3+3+4), to end on the concerted D♭ Ma7 (♭IIMa7) chord at m. 15. Within this framework the attacks (individual and in pairs) shift their metric positions. The pyramids at the end of chorus one and in the coda display 2-bar phrasing, providing long range metric resolution and stability with their even phrasing.

Saxophones (mm. 4–16) use rhythmic displacement and asymmetrical phrasing (=7, 10, 9, 10, 14 beat phrases), and phasing in 3/8 over a 4/4 meter for the presentation of the first A section tune (mm. 17–27).

Technique Highlight

Pyramid

A pyramid is the build-up of a chord through progressive sustaining entries. For a discussion of pyramid see "King Porter Stomp." For its usage here, see above.

Making Music

Read Director's Notes. Section leaders need to set the articulation and dynamics for the many sectional unison passages and lead trumpet determines the brass and full ensemble tutti.

Players need to be aware of the frequent switches from unison to 4-part harmony so they can balance the chords when they encounter them (ex: m. 28 uni., m. 35 harm., m. 40 uni., m. 221 harm., m. 223 uni., m. 224 harm.).

Conducting might be needed from m. 1 to m. 28 since the bass is not playing and the drums play time without the added definition provided by the hi-hat. The drum part is marked "brushes-no hi-hat" (though on recording hi-hat on beats 2 and 4 is used). It might be useful to write out the compound rhythm of the pyramid entrances to have a concise reduction displaying all attacks. After you determine what is most needed, you might give only some of the cues for entrances, phrases, and "markers" of events (ex: m. 4 saxes, m. 7 pyramid phrasing, m. 10 pyramid phrasing and saxes, m. 15 brass chord, m. 17 "head," m. 22 brass, m. 25 bass tbn, m. 26 bass, m. 28 2nd A section).

If possible, to better savor the arrangement, begin by playing the tune as a combo from the lead sheet.

Self-Test Question 63
In this arrangement comping (accompaniment by either guitar or piano):

a. begins with guitar and ends with piano and is not found on sections with the pyramid
b. begins and ends with guitar and is found on some sections with the pyramid
c. begins and ends with guitar and is not found on sections with the pyramid
d. begins with piano and is found on sections with the pyramid

Lead Sheet
The New Real Book. Sher Music Co., 1988.

WIND MACHINE

Nestico, Sammy 1976

Nestico, Sammy 1976
Grade: 4
Duration: 3:16
Instrumentation: 5, 4, 4, 4 (as 1 doubles on picc, as 2 doubles on fl, last 6 bars)
Publisher: Hal Leonard
Recording: Count Basie and His Orchestra. *On the Road.* Pablo Records OJCCD 854-2 1980.

At a Glance:

Articulation:	• > ∧ slurs
Bass line:	written
Chords:	Ma (6, 9), mi6, mi7 (9, 11), mi (Ma7), Dom (7, ♭9, 9, ♯11, ♯5, 13, oct) passing diminished (♯i, ♯ii)
Chord progression:	diatonic chords connected by passing diminished harmonies, secondary dominants (V/ii, V/V), chords borrowed from minor (iv, ♭VI, ♭VII)
Dynamics:	*p, mp, mf, f, ff, subito mp, fz, cresc, dim*
Edition:	8 1/2x11 oblong, 23 pages. Measure numbers every bar, boxed numbers highlighting sections
Expressive devices:	gliss (saxes), drop, slide (tbns), gliss (all)
Form:	six 32-bar ABAB1 choruses, with codetta (8) after 2nd and 6th chorus, and coda (8)
Guitar part:	chord symbols and rhythm slashes
Key:	C Ma
Modulations:	to E♭Ma and FMa (progressive tonality)
Mutes:	none
Orchestration	two pyramids
Piano part:	written, with additional chord symbols
Shout:	last chorus and coda are climactic
Style:	swing
Tempo:	half=152
Voicings:	saxes: unis, 3-pt, 4-pt close (lead doubled 8vb), 4-pt open, 5-pt spreads tpts: unis, triads (lead doubled 8vb), 4-pt close tbns: unis, 3-pt, 4-pt close, 4-pt drop2, spreads brass: 4-pt block voicings (tbns doubling tpts 8vb), 5-pt ens: slash chords

Highest Written Notes:
Tpt 1:   D (two ledger lines)
Tbn 1-2-3:   Ab (three ledger lines)

Solos:
pno (chords written out, 32), ts 1 (written, 64), dms (4+4+4)

Introductory Notes:
none

Form and Texture:
Six 32-bar ABAB1 choruses. The first chorus is a rhythm section groove with piano solo. The head choruses (second and last) include an 8-bar climactic extension (based on B, mm. 65, 169). Tenor sax solos on chorus 3 and 4, accompanied by trombone backgrounds on the A sections of chorus 4. Chorus 5 (m. 105) features sectional writing with some brass soli passages, leading to a tutti concerted closing (mm. 131–33) and a 4-bar drum solo. The final chorus builds through a first pyramid (mm. 149–52), more 4-bar drum solos punctuated by the ensemble (mm. 165–68), a tutti concerted (mm. 173–76), and a coda with a second pyramid (mm. 177–81), to end on three final fermata chords followed by a 2-eighth-note tutti conclusion.

Melodic, Harmonic, and Rhythmic Materials:
The tune is a fast, eighth-note-based line with chromatic approaches and blue notes. The A section's ascending melodic contour is balanced by a descending one in the first bars of the B section. Both are based on characteristic rhythmic motives (figure W.1) that are sequenced and developed. In the 8-bar extension the B section motive (mm. 65–68) is juxtaposed with a variation of the brass background motive from the second A (mm. 69–71) providing a summary of the

main material at the close of the head.

The A section progression is characterized by an ascending chromatic bass line that connects the first and third scale degrees (Eb–G, mm. 33–37) through passing diminished chords. Similarly the B section chord progression displays a stepwise bass line created by the use of inversions (F–G–Ab–A–Bb–C–Db–D, mm. 45–48).

The first pyramid (mm. 149–52) outlines a C7 (b9 #11 13) chord, while the second (mm. 177–80) cycles through the interval of a fourth (eight pitches: C–F–Bb–Eb–Ab–Db–F#–B) with some of the remaining pitches (E, A, [D], G) found in the FMa9 resolution chord (m. 181).

Rhythmic vitality is provided by pickups, anticipations (eighth and quarter notes), delayed attacks, and cross rhythms (three over four, in both the melody and the background figures).

Technique Highlight

Four-part Close
This technique consists of voicing the chord from the lead down, using available chord tones (1, 3, 5, 6, or 7) without skipping. This yields a close position (less than an octave span) "block" voicing. Substitutions are commonly used to increase the musicality of the under lines. Substituting the root of the chord with the 9th or b9th (known as "nine for one") is common (see figure W.2).

Here block voicings are found in the brass (trombones doubling trumpets an octave lower), juxtaposed with unison and other voicings such as drop2, 5-part, and spreads.

When a part doubling the lead of a 4-part close voicing an octave below is added, it is sometimes referred to as Supersax style, from the group that popularized it (mm. 41–44). For another example

motive section A   motive section B

Figure W.1

CMa⁶   Fmi⁷ 9 for 1   D⁷   FMa⁷

Figure W.2 "Block" voicings

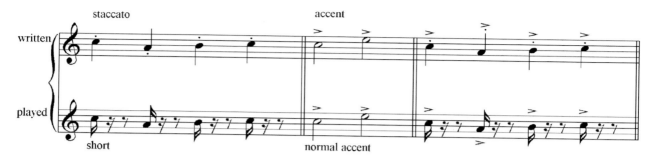

Figure W.3 Basic articulations

see "Cottontail." When all sections play the same voicing (the trombones and top four saxes doubling the trumpet parts an octave below and the bari sax doubling the lead trumpet two octaves below) the technique is referred to as Basie 4-part. For an example see "All of Me."

Making Music

As in other arrangements from the Basie book, this chart begins with a piano solo "out" chorus accompanied by guitar, bass, and drums. This can be opened up if desired. On the recording Basie begins by playing a couple of notes half way through the chorus. Given the medium up tempo some ensemble passages might need to be rehearsed slower. Note the standard articulations such as • > ∧. Basic articulations are listed in figure W.3. Articulations are interpreted relative to the tempo, dynamics, and style of the passage at hand. While accents don't alter durations, notes with marcato in jazz are often shortened, so to assure full duration a tenuto can be added under the marcato articulation.

The bass player is asked to improvise a walking bass only in a few spots (after the root is given on the downbeat). The rest is entirely written out, providing a good model for walking bass line creation. A transcription of Jimmy Forrest's solo is provided for the tenor sax. The last four measures require conducting: m. 181=hold, cut off (drums continues fill-ing), m. 182=hold, cut off (drums continues filling), m. 183=hold (drums continues filling), m. 184=any final gesture that looks like the music (ex: high ictus and drop to low freeze).

Self-Test Question 64

In the pyramid at mm. 149–52 the number of instruments on the six consecutive new pitch entries is:

a. 5, 3, 4, 4, 3, 1
b. 2, 3, 4, 4, 3, 2
c. 5, 3, 3, 4, 3, 1
d. 5, 3, 4, 3, 4, 1

———— ❦ ————

WYRGLY

Schneider, Maria 1989

Schneider, Maria 1989
Grade: 5
Duration: 10:20
Instrumentation: 5, 4, 4, 4 (tpts 3-4 double on flugs for 20 bars)
Publisher: composer
Recording: mariaschneider.com.

Highest Written Notes:

Tpt 1:   E (three ledger lines)
Tbn 1:   B♭ (four ledger lines)

Solos:
ts 1 (16 bars open, 16 + 9 with ensemble), tbn 1 (open +16), guit (8+13+8+8)

Introductory Notes:
none

Form and Texture:
After an open drum solo introduction (eight bars on recording), a 64-bar concerted ensemble section (A, mm. 1–64) follows (tutti with drums, no bass and bass trombone). Bass and bass trombone enter at m. 65 and are joined by saxes, guitar, and piano in a shuffle groove ostinato (B) in half time, while brass and drums continue with a varied rendition of the A material in cut time meter, creating a polymetric feel. The polymeter is resolved with all parts adopting the 4/4 meter (m. 80), and the drums transitioning to shuffle groove (m. 90). A 16-bar three-chord vamp (m. 104) introduces a contrasting section (C) that includes a tenor sax solo (16 bars open, + 16 + 9 with ensemble, mm. 125–58).

A varied return of A material follows over a new 2-bar pattern in half time (m. 159), and the polymeter is again resolved into an open trombone solo over ostinato (m. 168) that continues with ensemble backing (m. 172, 16 bars). A guitar solo follows (m. 188, 8+13+8+8+3). The piece concludes with a recapitulation of the first two C section chords (varied) over B section ostinato (mm. 228–34), and a fade out ad lib (m. 235) (see table W.2).

Melodic, Harmonic, and Rhythmic Materials:
Material A features melodic shape manipulation: the second phrase (mm. 7–9) has the same intervallic shape of the first (mm. 1–4) in retrograde inversion (see table W.3).

In its various reapprearences throughout the piece it is reworked with anticipations, displacements, elongations, phrase extensions, and the interpolation of rests between phrases.

Harmonic structures use parallelism and added chromatics, and progress through various tonal centers (B♭7sus, m. 4; G7 sus, m. 9; F#7sus, m. 14; Cmi11, m. 20 etc.).

At a Glance:

Articulation:	• – > ∧ ≥ slurs
Bass line:	written and chord symbols
Chords:	Ma7 (9, #5, 13), mi7 (9, 11), Dom (7, 9, 13, sus4, sus4 with third of chord above the 4th)
Chord progression:	through composed, with evolving ostinatos
Dynamics:	*ppp, p, mp, mf, f, ff, cresc, dim*
Edition:	8 1/2x11 vertical, 39 pages. Measure numbers on each bar
Form:	through composed
Guitar part:	written and chord symbols
Key:	no key signature. B♭ and various tonal centers
Modulations:	non-functional tonality. Juxtapositions of tonal centers and ostinatos
Mutes:	cups, harmon (tpts), harmon or straight (tbn 1)
Piano part:	written and chord symbols
Shout:	none, though the ensemble passages that conclude the last two solos are climactic (mm. 184–87, and mm. 214–22)
Style:	swing and shuffle
Tempo:	half=approximately 120 (on recording)
Voicings:	saxes: 4-/5-pt closed and open, clus, quartal, const struct. tpts: 4-pt closed and open, clus, quartal, const struct. tbns: 3-pt quartal and const struct, 4-pt over root and inversions ens: dom7 sus4 with major third above fourth

The ostinato pattern (m. 65, tbn 4, bass, piano left hand) begins by spanning a chromatically filled tritone (A♭–D, mm. 65–68), and continues to extend its range in both directions to incorporate all 12 chromatic pitches (F at m. 73 is the last note added). The ostinato travels through various tonal centers such as E (m. 168), to bring the piece to a close in F# (mm. 205–25).

Table W.2 "Wyrgly" outline

Measure		1	65	104	107		
Material	intro	A	A1 and B	C			
Number of bars	open	64	39	16	24+8	16+16+9	
Instruments	drums	ensemble w. drums	tutti polymeter	rhythm section vamp	tutti	ts solo	

Measure	159	168	188	225
Material	A2	B		coda B+C
Number of bars	9	open + 16	8+13+8+8+3 transition	10+1 (fade)
Instruments	tutti varied recap and polymeter	tbn solo	guit solo	tbns, saxes, rhythm

Table W.3 Intervallic manipulation in "Wyrgly"

First phrase					Second phrase				
third up	second down	second up	fourth up	half step up	half step up (link)	fourth down	second down	second up	third down

Rhythmic manipulation is pervasive at the phrase level and also at the form level, with the polymetric sections in cut time over 4/4. There are many three over four passages throughout.

Technique Highlight

Ostinato: Developing
The word means "obstinate" and indicates a short pattern (melodic, harmonic, or rhythmic), that repeats persistently. Frequently ostinatos repeat unvaried, and momentum is created through layering (see "Fables of Faubus"), or vary slightly, rearranging the same pitch content (see "Temple Street" and "A View from the Side"). Here the ostinato develops melodically (range, intervals, and pitch content), and harmonically (reappearing at different pitch levels).

Making Music

Dynamics and articulation shape the concerted section and need to be followed in detail, as they change constantly. They include staccato, tenuto, accent, marcato (see "Wind Machine" for marcato "hat" example), and many crescendos and decrescendos. The ensemble needs to sound as one in terms of durations, dynamic inflections, and ensemble balance.

Drummer needs to stay with the brass as the rest of the ensemble plays in half time swing 8ths (m. 65) and, after a passage of broken time (mm. 80), settles into a shuffle groove (m. 90). The drummer is instrumental in setting up transitions such as the double time feel at m. 158 and supports the ensemble through the various peaks and valleys of the music. The piece builds to the most extensive apex at mm. 206–22, with other build-ups to points of formal articulation (mm. 107, 157, 187). These are in contrast with the quiet section C beginning with the chords at m. 104. Piano fills are used on the long notes at the end of phrases throughout this section.

Self-Test Question 65
In the piano part at m. 113 there is a GMa9 (no 3rd) over C chord (for review of slash chords see "The Happy Song"). The third of the chord (B):

a. is never present
b. is played anyway by the piano player
c. is in the 1st trumpet on the 2nd repeat
d. is in the 1st trumpet on the 3rd repeat and the saxophone line on 2nd and 3rd repeat

Y

YOUNG BLOOD

Mulligan, Gerry 1952

Mulligan, Gerry 1952
Grade:	5
Duration:	3:13
Instrumentation:	5, 5, 5, 3
Publisher:	Sierra Music
Recording:	Stan Kenton Orchestra. *New Concepts*. Capitol.

Highest Written Notes:

Tpt 1:	F (three ledger lines) on last four bars; rest of the chart=C (two ledger lines)
Tpt 2:	F (three ledger lines) on last bar
Tbn 1:	B♭ (four ledger lines)

Solos:
tpt 2, ts 2, as 2 (32 bars each)

Introductory Notes:
None

Form and Texture:
Five choruses of AABA with a codetta at the end of the first chorus (mm. 38–42), an eight-bar interlude between third and fourth chorus and a seven-bar coda (m. 181). The form features modified section lengths in both heads (choruses 1 and 5), and standard 32-bar form for solos (choruses 2–3–4) (see table Y.1).

Table Y.1 "Young Blood" outline

Chorus	1			2	3
Measure	1			43	75
Form	A A′ B A″ codetta			AABA	AABA
# of bars	9 10 8 10 5			32	32
Solo				tpt 2	ts 2
Key	B♭				

Chorus	interlude	4	5	coda
Measure	107	115	147	181
Form		A A B A	A A B A	
# of bars	8	32	8 8 8 10	3+4
Solo		as2		
Key	E♭			

At a Glance:

Articulation:	• – > ∧ slurs
Bass line:	written
Chords:	triads, Ma 6 (9), Ma7 (9), mi (Ma7), mi7 (9, 11), mi7♭5, Dom7 (♭9, 9, sus4), dim 7
Chord progression:	diatonic, secondary dominants (V/ii, V/IV, V/V), upper chromatic dominants, chromatic planing
Dynamics:	*pp, p, mp, mf, f, ff, cresc, dim*
Edition:	8 1/2x11 oblong, 20 pages. Measure numbers every bar, boxed numbers highlighting sections
Form:	AABA (5 choruses) with modified section lengths, interlude (8), and coda (7)
Key:	B♭ Ma
Modulations:	E♭ Ma (progressive tonality)
Mutes:	none
Piano:	chord symbols, a few written passages
Shout:	last chorus (m. 147)
Style:	swing
Tempo:	quarter=200
Time feel:	in 4
Voicings:	saxes: uni, 4-/5-pt and cascade effects
	tpts: uni, triads (lead doubled 8vb), 4ths, 4-pt close
	tbns: uni, triads (open), 3-/4-/5-pt, spreads
	brass: 6-/7-pt

Textures are contrapuntal, with many unison lines. Writing is mostly sectional. There are 2-part passages in contrary motion (mm. 15–17), and 3-part passages in contrary and parallel motion (mm. 33–35). Cascade effects are found in the saxes (2 to 5 parts, mm. 55–56). The coda features a unison canon at a 2-bar lag between saxes and trumpets (mm. 181–184). Harmonized chords are found at the end of phrases or in tutti concerted climactic passages such as chorus 5 (m. 147).

Figure Y.1 Cascade or fan technique

Melodic, Harmonic, and Rhythmic Materials:
The first unison sax section presents two main motivic shapes a (mm. 1–2), and b (m. 3).

Motive a emphasizes the flat third (D♭), while b emphasizes the major third (D natural). These are treated with various elisions, interpolations, anticipations, and extensions throughout the A sections of the head. The bridge (m. 20) develops a new motive c (descending fourth, descending half step) introduced in mm. 17–19 by the saxes. The backgrounds to the solos develop motives from the head (a, mm. 71–81), and b (mm. 81–90).

Chorus 4 introduces three new motives x y z (x in trombones, m. 115; y in trumpets mm. 115–16, z in saxes, m. 123). They are reorchestrated in mm. 139–44 (x in first and second trumpets, y in trumpets 3-4-5, z in trombones). The shout chorus (m. 147) introduces a new repeated note theme and a fanfare-like motive on the new tonic triad (E♭–B♭–G, trumpets, mm. 150–54).

The chord progression uses diatonic and passing diminished chords, in addition to the upper chromatic dominant to the V (♭VI7=G♭7, mm. 15–16). Here the two 4-note patterns superimposed in the saxes and trombones are derived from the octatonic scale: F♯–G–A–B♭ plus E–E♭–D♭–C=F ♯–G–A–B♭–C–D♭–E♭–E (G♭ octatonic). The B section tonicizes the subdominant (E♭) and displays a chromatic ascending and descending bass. The A" section and codetta also use a descending bass connecting the ♭VI7 chord to the I chord (G♭7, FMa7♯5, EMa7♯11, E♭-7, D-7, E-7♭5, E♭-7, D♭7, C-7, B♭, mm. 34–40).

The interlude (m. 107) modulates to the subdominant E♭, and the progression is transposed to that key, with reharmonizations, for the rest of the piece. The final chord (m. 184) is a polychord resolving into a 5–1 unison (B♭–E♭).

The coda uses multimeter, with three measures in 3/4, followed by four in 4/4.

Technique Highlight

Cascade
A cascade effect is the movement of a line from unison to harmony, generally through progressive splitting of parts (figure Y.1). It is found in much choral music. Reverse cascade would denote the opposite process. Examples are found here in the saxes (m. 55), where they cascade from 2 to 5 parts, and the brass (mm. 145–46) fanning out from unison to 4-parts. See also "Body and Soul" and "Just Friends."

Making Music
Other than the trombone background in mm. 20–25, the head material is all in unison until m. 35. Intonation issues, if present, will quickly become obvious. Similarly, dynamics are soft (mostly *pp*, *p*, *mp*) until m. 36, where the ensemble crescendos into the *ff* codetta (mm. 38–40) that sends off the trumpet solo. This is also the point where the various contrapuntal unison strains join into the first tutti concerted. It needs to be played powerfully without the benefit of much preparation (trumpets, which have been playing in the staff up to here, climb to repeated high Cs).

Backgrounds for both solos are quite busy, often with all three sections playing, so they need to be played soft and with the soloist in mind. The interlude (m. 107) is a tutti foreground statement played forte that seals the preceding trumpet solo and introduces the alto solo in the new key: it also needs to be played with vigor. Chorus 5 (m. 147) and the coda are climactic, played *ff*, with many *sfz* crescendo dynamics that need to be brought out. Conduct the three bars of 3/4 (mm. 181): in "one" if chart is played at tempo (quarter=200).

The passages where the unison winds switch suddenly to four-part harmony or vice versa (as in the interlude) might require additional awareness on the part of the players in the areas of tuning and balancing. The same applies to cascading effects (see above). Breaks introduce the solos (mm. 41, 114). There are some part exchanges where the third and fourth trumpets are above the second. Trumpet 5 doubles the lead at the lower octave, plays the lowest part of closed voicings when one trumpet rests, and plays a genuine 5th part in passages such as mm. 176–80.

Self-Test Question 66

A polychord is a chord made up of two or more distinct chords (see "The Happy Song"). The polychord at mm. 184–85 is:

a. E♭6 over D7
b. E♭6 over D9
c. D7 (♯11)
d. not a polychord but a triad over a bass note

Z

ZWEET ZURZDAY

Ellington, Duke 1963

Ellington, Duke 1963

Grade:	4
Duration:	3:55
Instrumentation:	5, 4, 3, 3 (ts1 plays cl)
Publisher:	Warner Bros. Publications, Jazz@Lincoln Center series
Recording:	Duke Ellington. *The Great Paris Concert.* Atlantic Jazz 304-2, 2 CDs.

Highest Written Notes:

Tpt 1:	C (two ledger lines)
Tbn 1:	G (three ledger lines), B♭ (four ledger lines, on solo)
Tbn 2:	C (four ledger lines)

Solos:
(written) piano (24), tbn 1 (8), ts (8)

Soli:
saxes (8), tbn 2-3 and ts (8)

Introductory Notes:
Notes on Playing Ellington, glossary, instrumentation, original recording information, Rehearsal Notes by David Berger, Comments from Wynton Marsalis.

Form and Texture:
Like "Such Sweet Thunder," this piece is part of a multimovement work and is programmatic. It is the third movement of a four-movement work inspired by John Steinbeck's novel *Sweet Thursday.* The form features a 24-bar piano introduction on the A section chords, AABA head, BAA solos (each section is 8 bars), and coda (27 bars, on the A section chords).

The piano part sets the mood, introduces and develops the main motives (intro, letters A and B), and continues to play chords and flourishes around the melody (letters C, D, H, J, K). The main melody is played by clarinet and tenor in octaves (letters C, D, E), and returns in a trio rendition (two trombones in half plungers and tenor sax playing subtone, letter H).

Trumpets are used sparingly and enter for the first time at letter G (the B section) with sustained 4-part close harmonies accompanying the trombone, and then the tenor solo (letter I). These reappear in the concluding bars in the form of a cluster (letter L, m. 2).

Melodic, Harmonic, and Rhythmic Materials:
There are two main motives: x (D–E♭–D–C♯–B, mm. 1–2), and y (D♭–F–G–B♭–D♭–F, letter I m. 8 and J mm. 1–2). Like x, y is presented in the improvised piano introduction in numerous runs on the E♭ chord (letter A, mm. 1, 3), and transposed (D♯–F♯–A–C♯) on the B7 chord. X and y join to create the A section melody (letter C mm. 1–2=x, mm. 6–8=y). This tune is then distilled into a sustained version (letter F, clarinet over four-part saxes), and transformed into a misterioso legato line (letter H: the tune is in the tenor sax, the lowest voice in the triads).

Motive y with its characteristic rhythm is presented by the clarinet in the coda, beginning on the "end of four" at letter I m. 8 (see figure Z.1). The motive is repeated nine times, concluding on a high D♭.

At a Glance:

Articulation:	• – ∧ slurs
Bass:	written
Chords:	Ma triad, Ma6, Ma7 (9), mi triad, mi7 (9), mi (ma7), mi7 (♭5), Dom 7 (♭9, 9, ♯9, ♯11, ♭5, ♯5, 13, sus)
Chord progression:	I ♭VI7 alternation and turnarounds using vi-7–ii-7–♭II7 (A section) i–V7–i and chain of descending chromatic dominants (B section)
Edition:	8 1/2x11 oblong, 16 pages. Rehearsal letters every section
Expressive devices:	subtone (ts), gliss (bari)
Form:	intro (24), AABA (32), B (8), A (8), A (8), coda (27)
Key:	E♭ Ma
Meter:	4/4
Modulations:	none
Mutes:	tight plunger with mute (tpts), half plunger, tight plunger (tbns)
Orchestration:	cl and tenor melody in octaves, two muted tbns and ts in triads, ts low pedal A♭, voice exchanges (tpts 2-4, tbns 1-2, tbns 1-3)
Piano:	written, with additional chord symbols
Style:	Latin, swing
Tempo:	quarter=110
Voicings:	reeds: uni, 2-pt, 4-pt close and open with cl melody tpts: uni, 4-pt close, clus tbns: uni, triad, 3-pt close

Y is then verticalized in the two piano trichords in the coda (letter J, mm. 6–8, letter K mm. 2–3). The first trichord contains three pitches of y (G–B♭–D♭), and the second contains the remaining one (F).

While these trichords recapitulate y in harmonic form, they clash with the B7 harmony (producing Ma7, 9, and ♭13 intervals), while they are consonant with the tonic E♭ chord (producing a blues inflected dominant-quality I7 tonic).

The final bars (letter L mm. 3–9) feature a polytonal combination of the two main chords of the piece: E♭7 (clarinet, trumpets, and trombones), and B7 (altos, bari and bass), over the subdominant pedal A♭ introduced in the tenor sax (letter K, m. 3). This A♭ is the lowest part in the texture since bari and bass play the pitch B a minor third above it (letter L mm. 6–9). This layered harmony resolves to a single E♭ in the bass on the last bar, with the A♭ pedal creating a subdominant (4–1) cadence.

Harmonic relations in thirds are evident in the two main chords (E♭ and B7), and in the mediant key of the bridge (g minor).

Technique Highlight

Clarinet Lead over Saxes

Clarinet lead over saxes creates a unique sound, in contrast with the more frequent alto or soprano lead. The clarinet is in the medium-high ("clarino" and above) register where it projects well and has a clear sound. Ellington used this scoring combination often (see "Across the Track Blues"), generally with the four saxes in 4-part close and the clarinet at variable intervals above, sometimes referred to as "color coupling."

Here (letter F) the clarinet favors the interval of a minor 7th above the first alto in the middle measures of the passage, with more consonant intervals (6ths, 5ths, 3rd) used at the beginning and end. The occasional doubling creates a four- rather than five-part texture. The clarinet continues to lead at letter G over saxes and trumpets.

Making Music

Read notes on playing Ellington, rehearsal notes, and comments at the beginning of the score. The piece switches between even eighth Latin and swing eighth feels, often before the new section (to swing one bar before letter E, to Latin two bars before F, to swing two bars before letter G, etc.), requiring

Figure Z.1

awareness from all players. As with most Ellington pieces from this period, one of the tenor players needs to be a strong clarinet player. Depending on your player, the tenor sax low B♭s (letter K m. 3 to end) might be a bit "honky" especially if the horn has some small leak (this is the lowest note and needs plenty of air support). Sightly less mouthpiece in the mouth (and a bit more lower lip on the reed) for subtone.

Self-Test Question 67

The sustained trumpet cluster at letter L, m. 3–5 is fragmented into individual entrances (mm. 6–8) and reassembled at m. 9. The resulting chord at m. 9 is:

a. exactly the same as the original

b. the same as the original, but trumpet 3 and 4 parts are switched

c. pitch A is added

d. the ♭9th of the chord is added

INDEXES OF MUSICAL FEATURES

Instrumentation

5–4–4–4

"Back Bone"

"Basically Blues"

"Big Dipper"

"Elvin's Mambo"

"Good Bye Pork Pie Hat"

"Happy Song, The"

"Just Friends"

"Katy"

"Moten Swing"

"No Looking Back"

"Proving Ground"

5–4–4–4 with Optional Doubles

"All of Me" — opt. aux. perc

"Child Is Born, A" — opt. a.flts. for a.saxes and flts for t.saxes and bari.

"Full Nelson" — opt. fr.hns 1-2

"Groove Merchant" — as1 plays ss throughout, substitute part for as

"Lil' Darlin'" — opt. aux. perc

"Miles Mood" — opt. fl, hn in F, tuba, vibes

"Savannah in Havana" — bari, tpt 4, and tbn 4 play hand held percussion (guiro, cowbell, claves) throughout.

"Tiptoe" — as1 on ss throughout, substitute part for as

"Turn Around" — tpt 3-4 double on flug, or can be played on tpts with cup mute)

5–4–4–4 with Doubles

"Ballad for Benny" — cl solo, ATTB, 4, 4, 4 (optional fr.hns 1-2)

"Body & Soul" — tpts double on flugs; mallet aux. perc. optional

"Daahoud" — aux perc.

"Don't Git Sassy" — as 1 doubles on ss

"Minor Excursion, A" — tpt 3 doubles on flugelhorn on last chorus

"Miss Fine" — ts 1 doubles on fl (32 bars)

"Wind Machine"   as1 doubles on picc, as 2 doubles on fl (last 6 bars)
"Wyrgly"   tpts 3-4 double on flugs for 20 bars

5–4–4–3
"Black, Brown, & Beautiful"
"Blues and the Abstract Truth"
"In the 80's"
"Stolen Moments"
"Tennessee Waltz"
"View from the Side, A"

5–4–4–3 with Optional Doubles
"Tribute"   ts 1-2 on opt flts

5–4–4–3 with Doubles
"Airegin"   as 1 on ss, fl or picc; ts 1 on ss; ts 2 on ss
"Cherry Juice"   solo flug, ss 1 and ss 2 throughout (opt. as 2 part for ss 2)

The Ellington Band

5–5–3–4
"Caravan"   reed 3 on cl, tbn 3 opt.vtbn

5–4–3–3
"Oclupaca"   as 2 doubles on cl
"Such Sweet Thunder"
"Zweet Zurzday"   reed 3 on cl

5–3–3–4
"Across the Track Blues"   reed 3 on cl
"C Jam Blues"   reed 3 on cl., tpt 2 doubles on vln.
"Cottontail"   reed 3 on cl
"Harlem Airshaft"   reed 3 on cl
"In a Mellow Tone"   reed 1 on ss and as, reed 5 on bari and as.
"Ko-Ko"   reed 3 on ts and cl, tpt 3 opt. cnt, tbn 3 opt vtbn
"Main Stem"   reed 3 on cl, tpt 3 opt cnt, tbn 3 opt vtbn

5–3–3–3
"Star-Crossed Lovers, The"   reed 3 on cl, tbn 3 opt vtbn

The Mingus Band

5–3–3–3
"Duke Ellington's Sound of Love"   as 1 to cl and ts 1-2 to flts on background at mm. 46–53
"Ecclusiastics"   tuba or btbn as third low brass
"Fables of Faubus"   as 2 doubles on ss
"Haitian Fight Song"   as 1 doubles on ss

"Moanin'"   tuba as third low brass (opt. tbn 3 to replace it)
"Nostalgia in Times Square"   no doubles

Smaller Bands

"Big Jim Blues"   4, 3, 2, 4
"Proving Ground"   5, 4, 4, 4 can be played with 3, 2, 1, 3

Larger Bands (more than 5–4–4–4)

"Four Brothers"   cl, 5, 5, 3, 3 (guit opt)
"I've Got You Under My Skin"   5, 5, 5, 3 (original recording has guit, in addition to pno)
"Intermission Riff"   5, 5, 4, 4
"King Porter '94"   5, 5, 4, 5 (bari on b.cl throughout. Rhythm section: vibraphone, synth 1 and 2, bass, drums)
"Temple Street"   5, 5, 5, 4 (as 1 on ss throughout, tpts double on flugs)
"Three and One"   5, 5, 4, 4 (5th tpt player plays solo flug throughout)
"What's New?"   5, 5, 5, 4
"Young Blood"   5, 5, 5, 3

Feature

Saxes

as	"No Looking Back"
as	"Star-Crossed Lovers, The"
as	"Black, Brown, & Beautiful"
ts	"Good Bye Pork Pie Hat"
ts	"Full Nelson"
ts	"Cottontail"
tenor saxes	"Ecclusiastics"
tenor saxes 1-2-3, bari	"Four Brothers"

Brass

Tpt	"Lil' Darlin'"

Mixed Instrumentation

bari flug bass	"Three and One"

Solos

any	"Turn Around"
any	"Miles Mood"
any, as, ts, tpt, tbn	"Moanin'"
any, dms	"Blues and the Abstract Truth"
any, pno	"Just Friends"
any, tpt, tbn, pno	"Tribute"
any, ts, tpt	"Nostalgia in Times Square"
any, ts, tpt	"Savannah in Havana"
any, ss tpt pno dms	"Haitian Fight Song"
as	"Black, Brown, & Beautiful"
as	"No Looking Back"
as	"Star-Crossed Lovers, The"
as, tpt	"Stolen Moments"
as, tpt (ts, tbn opt)	"Fables of Faubus"
as, tpt, dms	"Tiptoe"
as, tpt, dms, bass	"Tennessee Waltz"
as, tpt, pno/bass duet	"In a Mellow Tone"
as, tpt, pno/bass duet	"Ko-Ko"
as, ts	"Body & Soul"
as, ts, pno, bass	"Intermission Riff"
as, ts, tpt, tbn	"What's New?"
as, ts/tpt duet	"In the 80's"
as, cl, ts, tpts 2-3	"Main Stem"
as, ts, tpt	"Young Blood"
bari, flug, bass	"Three and One"
bari, tpt, ts, as, tpt	"I've Got You Under My Skin"
bass	"Duke Ellington's Sound of Love"
cl, bari, tpt, tbn	"Caravan"
cl feature	"Ballad for Benny"
cl, tpt, tbn	"Across the Track Blues"
cl, tpt, tbn, pno	"Harlem Airshaft"
cl, ts, tpt, vln, tbn, pno	"C Jam Blues"
dms (soloistic fills)	"King Porter '94"

guit, tbn, ts	"Big Jim Blues"
pno	"All of Me"
pno, tpt (opt.flug)	"Child Is Born, A"
pno, ts, as	"Airegin"
pno, ts, dms	"Wind Machine"
pno, tbn, ts	"Zweet Zurzday"
pno, tbns 1-2-3	"Back Bone"
ss, tpt, tbn, guit, pno	"Groove Merchant"
tbn, tpt, pno	"View from the Side, A"
tpt	"Miss Fine"
tpt	"Proving Ground"
tpt	"Lil' Darlin'"
tpt, pno (obligato)	"Katy"
tpt, tbn	"Such Sweet Thunder"
ts	"Good Bye Pork Pie Hat"
ts	"Full Nelson"
ts	"Oclupaca"
ts 1-2-3, bari	"Four Brothers"
ts, bari, tpt, pno, reeds, brass	"Cottontail"
ts, flug, pno	"Cherry Juice"
ts, pno	"Minor Excursion, A"
ts, tbn	"Basically Blues"
ts, tbn, guit	"Wyrgly"
ts, tpt	"Daahoud"
ts, tpt, dms	"Happy Song, The"
ts, tpt, pno	"Big Dipper"
ts, tpt, pno	"Moten Swing"
ts, tpt, tbn	"Elvin's Mambo"
ts, tpts 2-3-4	"Don't Git Sassy"
ts 1-2, tpt	"Ecclusiastics"

Soli

Saxes (AATTB unless indicated)
"Body & Soul"
"Cherry Juice"   SSTTB
"Cottontail"
"Don't Git Sassy"   SATTB
"Duke Ellington's Sound of Love"
"Four Brothers"   TTTB
"Groove Merchant"   SATTB
"Miles Mood"
"No Looking Back"
"Proving Ground"
"Stolen Moments"
"Such Sweet Thunder"
"Three and One"

Reeds
"Across the Track Blues"

Saxes and Brass
"Groove Merchant"
"Moten Swing"
"Cottontail"

Brass
"Cottontail"
"Groove Merchant"

Saxes and Trombones
"Harlem Airshaft"

Saxes and Rhythm
"Basically Blues"

Trombones with Bass
"Tiptoe"

Piano and Bass
"Savannah in Havana"

Mixed Trio
"Three and One"   bari, flug, bass
"Zweet Zurzday"   ts, tbns 2-3

Style

Ballad
"Black, Brown, & Beautiful"
"Child Is Born, A"
"Duke Ellington's Sound of Love"
"Good Bye Pork Pie Hat"
"Katy"
"Star-Crossed Lovers, The"

Ballad/Swing
"Ballad for Benny"
"No Looking Back"

Bebop
"Daahoud"
"Just Friends"

Blues
"Across the Track Blues"   blues slow
"Back Bone"
"Basically Blues"   Basie style
"Big Dipper"   ostinato groove
"Big Jim Blues"   blues med slow
"Ko-Ko"   blues/jungle
"Nostalgia in Times Square"   blues swing

Bounce
"Intermission Riff"

Contemporary
"King Porter '94"
"Temple Street"

Eclectic
"Ecclusiastics"   gospel/swing
"Fables of Faubus"

Jazz Waltz
"Tennessee Waltz"

Latin
"Caravan"   Latin/swing
"Elvin's Mambo"   Latin jazz
"Happy Song, The"   samba
"In the 80's"   mambo
"Oclupaca"   Latin/swing/shuffle
"Savannah in Havana"
"Turn Around"   samba
"View from the Side, A"   Latin/swing/march
"Zweet Zurzday"   Latin/swing

Shuffle
"Don't Git Sassy"
"Groove Merchant"
"Harlem Airshaft"
"Minor Excursion, A"

Swing-easy
"Lil' Darlin'"   slow
"Moten Swing"
"Such Sweet Thunder"   swing with tango beat

Swing-medium (120+)
"All of Me"
"Body & Soul"
"C Jam Blues"
"Cottontail"   medium up
"Full Nelson"
"Haitian Fight Song"
"In a Mellow Tone"
"Miles Mood"   medium up
"Miss Fine"
"Proving Ground"
"Stolen Moments"   swing/bolero
"Three and One"
"Tiptoe"
Tribute   Basie style/march
"What's New?"

Swing-fast (200+)
"Airegin"
"Blues and the Abstract Truth"

"Cherry Juice"
"Four Brothers"
"I've Got You Under My Skin"
"Main Stem"
"Moanin'"
"Wind Machine"
"Wyrgly"
"Young Blood"

swing/shuffle

Tempo

Quarter note unless marked

48	"Good Bye Pork Pie Hat"
52	"Star-Crossed Lovers, The"
60–64	"Ecclusiastics"
63 dotted half	"Tennessee Waltz"
64	"Duke Ellington's Sound of Love"
68	"Child Is Born, A"
69	"No Looking Back"
72	"Big Jim Blues"
76	"Katy"
76	"Black, Brown, & Beautiful"
80–88	"Lil' Darlin'"
88	"Ballad for Benny"
88 half	"Caravan"
90	"Across the Track Blues"
92 half	"King Porter '94"
99	"Such Sweet Thunder"
100–112	"Basically Blues"
moderato	"Back Bone"
110	"Zweet Zurzday"
112	"Moten Swing"
112–116 half	"Turn Around"
116 half	"Just Friends"
116 quarter and half	"View from the Side, A"
120	"Body & Soul"
120	"Full Nelson"
120	"Tribute"
120	"Miss Fine"
120 half	"Elvin's Mambo"
120 half	"Happy Song, The"
120 half	"Wyrgly"
125–136	"In the 80's"

Form

The general categories listed here refer to the basic form of the tune rather than the large form created by the whole arrangement. For discussion of large form see individual titles.

SONG FORM

AABA

"Ballad for Benny"
"Black, Brown, & Beautiful"
"Body & Soul"
"Cherry Juice"
"Four Brothers"
"Harlem Airshaft"
"Katy"
"Lil' Darlin'"
"Miles Mood"
"Moanin'"
"Moten Swing"
"Savannah in Havana"
"Zweet Zurzday"

Ternary ABA

"Duke Ellington's Sound of Love"
"The Star-Crossed Lovers"

Modified AABA	
"Daahoud"	additional sections
"Fables of Faubus"	non-standard section lengths
"No Looking Back"	within ABA form
"Proving Ground"	additional sections
"Tribute"	additional sections
"What's New?"	additional sections
"Young Blood"	variable section lengths

Rhythm Changes	
"Cottontail"	in B♭
"Tiptoe"	in A♭

Two-part AB

"Caravan"
"Just Friends"
"Three and One"
"Wind Machine"

ABAC	
"Airegin"	
"All of Me"	
"A Child Is Born"	strophic melody
"In a Mellow Tone"	

Forms with Three or More Parts

"Don't Git Sassy"	ABCA1
"Ecclusiastics"	ABCD
"Elvin's Mambo"	AB with C
"I've Got You Under My Skin"	AABC
"In the 80's"	multisectional
"Temple Street"	ABCAABDA
"Turn Around"	ABC with additional sections
"A View from the Side"	ternary

Riff Variations

"Intermission Riff"

BLUES

Major

"Across the Track Blues"
"Back Bone"
"Basically Blues"
"Nostalgia in Times Square"

With Modified Number of Measures

"Big Dipper"	4-bar extensions and interludes
"Big Jim Blues"	18 bars
"C Jam Blues"	additional 4-bar breaks on solo choruses
"Main Stem"	12+18

As Part of ABA Form

"Full Nelson"

Major and Minor

"Oclupaca"
"Such Sweet Thunder"

Strophic

"A Child Is Born"	ABAC harmony
"Groove Merchant"	
"Miss Fine"	
"Tennessee Waltz"	

With Much Through Composed Material

"Don't Git Sassy"
"Duke Ellington's Sound of Love"
"The Happy Song"
"King Porter '94"
"A View from the Side"
"Wyrgly"

Minor

"Good Bye Pork Pie Hat"
"Haitian Fight Song"   with ostinato
"Ko-Ko"
"A Minor Excursion"

With Modified Number of Measures

"Blues and the Abstract Truth"

As Part of ABA Form

"Blues and the Abstract Truth"
"Stolen Moments"

Key

Major

C

"All of Me"

"Back Bone"

"C Jam Blues"

"The Happy Song"

"Tennessee Waltz"

"What's New?"

"Wind Machine"

D♭

"Body & Soul"

"Don't Git Sassy"

"Duke Ellington's Sound of Love"

"Intermission Riff"

"Star-Crossed Lovers, The"

F

"Ecclusiastics"

"Elvin's Mambo"

"Full Nelson"

"Lil' Darlin'"

"Tribute"

G

"Basically Blues"

"Big Dipper"

D

"Across the Track Blues"

"Big Jim Blues"

"Main Stem"

E♭

"Black, Brown, & Beautiful"

"Daahoud"

"I've Got You under My Skin"

"Katy"

"Nostalgia in Times Square"

"Proving Ground"

"Savannah in Havana"

"Three and One"

"Zweet Zurzday"

B♭

"Ballad for Benny"

"Child Is Born, A"

"Cottontail"

"Miss Fine"

"No Looking Back"

"Turn Around"

"Wyrgly"

"Young Blood"

A♭
"Airegin"
"Four Brothers"
"Groove Merchant"
"Harlem Airshaft"
"In a Mellow Tone"
"Moten Swing"
"Tiptoe"

Minor
C
"Stolen Moments"
D
"In the 80's"

E♭
"Airegin"
"Four Brothers"
"Groove Merchant"
"Harlem Airshaft"
"Ko-Ko"
F
"Caravan"
"Fables of Faubus"
"Good Bye Pork Pie Hat"
"Moanin'"
"Oclupaca"

G
"Black, Brown, & Beautiful"
"Cherry Juice"
"Haitian Fight Song"
"A Minor Excursion"
B
"Temple Street"   partially modal

Modal
"Miles Mood"   C dorian
Other
"Blues and The Abstract Truth"   C Ma center
"King Porter '94"   A♭ center
"Such Sweet Thunder"   G mi/Ma
"View from the Side"   A G center

Modulations

Intended as a modulation of the *whole piece* **to a different key or mode and return to the original.**

	Modulates to:
"Basically Blues"	A♭ Ma
"Blues and the Abstract Truth"	D dorian
"Body & Soul"	FMa (on second bridge)
"Four Brothers"	E♭ Ma, B♭ Ma
"In the 80's"	C mi
"Main Stem"	G Ma
"Oclupaca"	A♭ Ma
"Stolen Moments"	D mi
"Tennessee Waltz"	E♭ Ma
"What's New?"	F Ma, Gma

Progressive Tonality Piece ends in a different key or mode than the initial one.

	Modulates to and ends in
"Black, Brown, & Beautiful"	F Ma
"Happy Song, The"	modulates to E♭ Ma and ends in D Ma
"Katy"	A♭ Ma
"King Porter '94"	progresses from A♭ to A tonal center
"Miles Mood"	B♭ Ma
"No Looking Back"	C Ma
"Turn Around"	G♭ Ma
"Wind Machine"	modulates to E♭ Ma and ends in F Ma
"Wyrgly"	progresses from B♭ to F♯ tonal center
"Young Blood"	E♭ Ma

Meter

All titles in 4/4 except:

"Child is Born, A"	3/4
"Ecclusiastics"	12/8
"Good Bye Pork Pie Hat"	12/8
"Tennessee Waltz"	3/4

INDEXES

Index by Title

Index by Composer

Index by Arranger

Index by Grade

Index by Date

APPENDIXES

Appendix A

Chart Selections by Contributor

Kevin Blancq

	Composer/Arranger
"All of Me"	Simons, Seymour, and Gerald Marks/arr: Billy Byers
"Almost Cried"	Ellington, Duke
"Big Dipper"	Jones, Thad
"Black, Brown, & Beautiful"	Nelson, Oliver
"Cute"	Hefti, Neal
"Harlem Nocturne"	Hagen, Earl
"Mambo No. 5"	Prado, Perez
"Moten Swing"	Wilkins, Ernie
"Red Bank Boogie"	Basie, Count/arr: Buck Clayton
"Shiny Stockings"	Foster, Frank

Brian Coyle

"ABC Blues"	Brookmeyer, Bob
"Child Is Born, A"	Jones, Thad
"First Circle"	Metheny, Pat/arr: Bob Curnow
"Funguiado"	Fischer, Clare/arr: Fischer, Dick
"Love Walked In"	Gershwin, George/arr: Richmond, Kim
"Moanin'"	Mingus, Charles/arr: Sy Johnson
"Moten Swing"	Wilkins, Ernie
"Transblucency"	Ellington, Duke
"View from the Side, A"	Holman, Bill
"Wyrgly"	Schneider, Maria

Thomas Everett

"Basically Blues"	Wilson, Phil
"Better Get Hit in Your Soul"	Mingus, Charles/arr: Sy Johnson
"Blues and the Abstract Truth"	Nelson, Oliver
"Cute"	Hefti, Neal
"Far East Suite"	Ellington, Duke, and Billy Strayhorn
"Hit and Run"	Brown, Ray/arr: Denis Di Blasio

"Ko-Ko"   Ellington, Duke
"Maids of Cadiz"   Delibes, Leo/arr: Gil Evans
"Pussy Cat Blues"   Mingus, Charles/arr: Sy Johnson
"Skylark"   Carmichael, Hoagy /arr: Bob Brookmeyer

Lou Fischer
"All Things Considered"   Fischer, Lou
"Be Bop Charlie"   Florence, Bob
"Blues for Stephanie"   Clayton, John
"Greasy Sack Blues"   Rader, Don
"Happy Song, The"   Mintzer, Bob
"Hay Burner"   Nestico, Sammy
"Katy"   Nestico, Sammy
"Sweet Georgia Upside Down"   Kelly, Phil
"Tennessee Waltz"   unknown/arr: Holman, Bill
"Where or When"   Rodgers, Richard, and Lorenz Hart/arr: Gordon Goodwin

Victor Goines
"Big Jim Blues"   Williams, Mary Lou
"Cherry Juice"   Jones, Thad
"Cool Breeze"   Eckstine, Billy, Tadd Dameron, and Dizzy Gillespie
"Harlem Airshaft"   Ellington, Duke
"Isfahan"   Strayhorn, Billy
"Manteca Suite"   O'Farrill, Chico
"Moten Swing"   Moten, Buster and Bennie/arr: Ernie Wilkins
"Swingin on C"   Durham, C.
"Tone Parallel to Harlem, A"   Ellington, Duke/arr: Wynton Marsalis
"When Lights Are Low"   Carter, Benny/arr: J. Cooper

Fred Harris
"All of Me"   Simons, Seymour, and Gerald Marks/arr: Thad Jones
"Bastien"   Souriau, Magali
"Duke Ellington's Sound of Love"   Mingus, Charles/arr: Jack Walrath
"Ecclusiastics"   Mingus, Charles/arr: Sy Johnson
"El Espejo"   Klein, Guillermo
"Moonday"   Souriau, Magali
"Oclupaca"   Ellington, Duke
"Remember Mingus"   La Porta, John
"Rockin' in Rhythm"   Ellington, Duke
"Skylark"   Carmichael, Hoagy /arr: Bob Brookmeyer
"Star-Crossed Lovers, The"   Strayhorn, Billy

Keith Javors
"Fables of Faubus"   Mingus, Charles/arr: Steve Slagle
"Little Minor Blues, A"   Maiden, Willie
"Little Pixie II"   Jones, Thad
"Stolen Moments"   Nelson, Oliver

"Temple Street" — Wilson, Dale
"Things to Come" — Gillespie, Dizzy
"To You" — Jones, Thad
"West Side Story Medley" — Bernstein, Leonard/arr: Bill Reddie

John La Porta
"4468 Road" — La Porta, John
"Child Is Born, A" — Jones, Thad
"Cute" — Hefti, Neal
"Four Brothers" — Giuffre, Jimmy
"Moten Swing" — Wilkins, Ernie
"Mother's Invention" — LaPorta, John
"Ray's Idea" — Brown, Ray/arr: Gil Fuller
"Savannah Is Havana" — Lopez, Vincent
"Spanish Rhapsody" — LaPorta, John
"Yesterday's Blues" — LaPorta, John

Richard Lawn
"All About Rosie" — Russell, George
"Basie Straight Ahead" — Nestico, Sammy
"Corner Pocket" — Frank Foster
"Daybreak Express" — Ellington, Duke
"Ding, Dong, Ding" — Brookmeyer, Bob
"Incredible Journey" — Mintzer, Bob
"Miss Fine" — Nelson , Oliver
"Just Friends" — Davies, Raymond, John Klenner, and Sam Lewis/arr: Bill Holman
"Readymix" — Holman, Bill
"Three and One" — Jones, Thad
"Tribute" — Mintzer, Bob
"Warning, Success Can Be Hazardous to Your Health" — Akyoshi, Toshiko
"Wyrgly" — Schneider, Maria

Jeff Leonard
"C.B. Express" — Nestico, Sammy
"Cottontail" — Ellington, Duke
"Groove Merchant" — Richardson, Jerome/arr: Thad Jones
"Harlem Airshaft" — Ellington, Duke
"Isfahan" — Strayhorn, Billy
"Lil'Darlin'" — Hefti, Neal
"Minor Excursion, A" — Caffey, David
"Moanin'" — Mingus, Charles/arr: Sy Johnson
"Stolen Moments" — Nelson, Oliver/arr: Dave Barduhn
"Tribute" — Mintzer, Bob

Bart Marantz
"Agin Cajun, The" — Mantooth, Frank
"Budini" — Montgomery, Buddy/arr: Don Sickler
"Cute" — Hefti, Neal

"Daahoud" — Brown, Clifford/arr: Mark Taylor
"In a Mellow Tone" — Ellington, Duke
"Miles Mood" — Berg, Shelton
"No Looking Back" — Niehaus, Lennie
"Proving Ground" — Niehaus, Lennie
"Toss and Turn" — Niehaus, Lennie
"Turn Around" — Harris, Matt

Bob Morgan
"All Blues" — Davis, Miles/arr: Vince Mendoza
"Back Bone" — Jones, Thad
"Body & Soul" — Green, Johnny/arr: George Stone
"In the 80's" — Mintzer, Bob
"Lil'Darlin'" — Hefti, Neal
"Miss Fine" — Nelson, Oliver
"Shiny Stockings" — Foster, Frank
"Smoke Gets in Your Eyes" — Kern, Jerome/arr: McConnell, Rob
"Stompin' at the Savoy" — Goodman, Benny/arr: Bill Holman
"Three and One" — Jones, Thad
"Waltz You Swang for Me, The" — Jones, Thad

Ted Pease
"Cherry Juice" — Jones, Thad
"Don't Git Sassy" — Jones, Thad
"Hello and Goodbye" — Brookmeyer, Bob
"I've Got You Under My Skin" — Porter, Cole/arr: Bill Holman
"Moten Swing" — Wilkins, Ernie
"Shiny Stockings" — Foster, Frank
"Stompin' at the Savoy" — Goodman, Benny/arr: Bill Holman
"Three and One" — Jones, Thad
"What's New?" — Haggart, Bob, and Johnny Burke/arr: Bill Holman
"Young Blood" — Mulligan, Gerry

Dave Rivello
"Absolution" — McNeely, Jim
"Celebration: Jig" — Brookmeyer, Bob
"Celebration: Remembering" — Brookmeyer, Bob
"Celebration: Slow Dance" — Brookmeyer, Bob
"Celebration: Two and" — Brookmeyer, Bob
"Extra Credit" — McNeely, Jim
"Green Piece" — Schneider, Maria
"Hang Gliding" — Schneider, Maria
"More about Thirds" — Holman, Bill
"Rain Codes" — Mendoza, Vince

Gunther Schuller
"Across the Track Blues" — Ellington, Duke
"Ballad for Benny" — Nelson, Oliver
"Blues in Hoss' Flat"

" (Blues in Frankie's Flat)"	Foster, Frank
"C Jam Blues"	Ellington, Duke
"Cottontail"	Ellington, Duke
"Duke, The"	Brubeck, Dave/arr: Clare Fischer
"Early Autumn"	Burns, Ralph/arr: Woody Herman
"Fables of Faubus"	Mingus, Charles/arr: Steve Slagle
"Four Brothers"	Giuffre, Jimmy
"Full Nelson"	Nelson, Oliver
"Good Bye Pork Pie Hat"	Mingus, Charles/arr: Sy Johnson
"Impressionism"	Kenton, Stan/arr: Pete Rugolo
"In a Mellow Tone"	Ellington, Duke
"Intermission Riff"	Wetzel, Ray
"King Porter '94"	Morton, Jelly Roll/arr: Bob Brookmeyer
"Ko-Ko"	Ellington, Duke
"Main Stem"	Ellington, Duke
"Nostalgia in Times Square"	Mingus, Charles/arr: Cuber, Ronnie
"Shiny Stockings"	Foster, Frank
"Short Stop"	Rogers, Shorty
"Skylark"	Carmichael, Hoagy/arr: Bob Brookmeyer
"Tiptoe"	Jones, Thad

Haig Shahverdian

"Airegin"	Rollins, Sonny/arr: Michael Abene
"Don't Git Sassy"	Jones, Thad
"Elvin's Mambo"	Mintzer, Bob
"Lush Life"	Strayhorn, Billy/arr: Eric Richards
"Melt away a Time for Love"	Mandel, Johnny/arr: John Clayton
"Mooche, The"	Ellington, Duke
"Night Flight"	Nestico, Sammy
"Rockabye River"	Ellington, Duke
"West Side Story Medley"	Bernstein, Leonard/arr: Bill Reddie
"Wind Machine"	Nestico, Sammy

Dee Spencer

"All of You"	Porter, Cole/arr: Frank Mantooth
"Caravan"	Ellington, Duke, and Juan Tizol
"Haitian Fight Song"	Mingus, Charles/arr: Sy Johnson
"It Don't Mean a Thing (If It Ain't Got That Swing)"	Ellington, Duke
"Ko-Ko"	Ellington, Duke
"Moanin'"	Mingus, Charles/arr: Sy Johnson
"Such Sweet Thunder"	Ellington, Duke
"Things Ain't What They Used to Be"	Ellington, Duke
"Zweet Zurzday"	Ellington, Duke

Janis Stockhouse

"Bye Bye Blackbird"	Dixon, Mort, and Ray Henderson/arr: Dominic Spera
"Harlem Airshaft"	Ellington, Duke
"Lil'Darlin'"	Hefti, Neal
"Miss Fine"	Nelson , Oliver

"Rockin' in Rhythm"   Ellington, Duke
"Shiny Stockings"   Foster, Frank
"Sho' Nuff"   Vollmers, Pete/arr: Dilkey, J.
"Tall Cotton"   Nestico, Sammy
"Tiptoe"   Jones, Thad
"Told You So"   Holman, Bill
"Walt's Barbershop"   Baker, David

Appendix B

Charts Selected by Multiple Contributors

Number of Selections	Title	Composer	Arranger
5	"Moten Swing"	Wilkins, Ernie	Wilkins, Ernie
5	"Shiny Stockings"	Foster, Frank	Foster, Frank
4	"Cute"	Hefti, Neal	Hefti, Neal
3	"Lil' Darlin'"	Hefti, Neal	Hefti, Neal
3	"Harlem Airshaft"	Ellington, Duke	Ellington, Duke
3	"Ko-Ko"	Ellington, Duke	Ellington, Duke
3	"Miss Fine"	Nelson, Oliver	Nelson, Oliver
3	"Moanin'"	Mingus, Charles	Johnson, Sy
3	"Skylark"	Carmichael, Hoagy	Brookmeyer, Bob
3	"Three and One"	Jones, Thad	Jones, Thad
2	"Tribute"	Mintzer, Bob	Mintzer, Bob
2	"Big Dipper"	Jones, Thad	Jones, Thad
2	"Cherry Juice"	Jones, Thad	Jones, Thad
2	"Cottontail"	Ellington, Duke	Ellington, Duke
2	"West Side Story Medley"	Bernstein, Leonard	Reddie, Bill
2	"Don't Git Sassy"	Jones, Thad	Jones, Thad
2	"Fables of Faubus"	Mingus, Charles	Slagle, Steve
2	"Isfahan"	Strayhorn, Billy	Billy Strayhorn
2	"Four Brothers"	Giuffre, Jimmy	Giuffre, Jimmy
2	"Rockin' in Rhythm"	Ellington, Duke	Ellington, Duke
2	"In a Mellow Tone"	Ellington, Duke	Ellington, Duke
2	"Child Is Born, A"	Jones, Thad	Jones, Thad
2	"Tiptoe"	Jones, Thad	Jones, Thad
2	"Wyrgly"	Schneider, Maria	Schneider, Maria
2	"Stompin' at the Savoy"	Goodman, Benny	Holman, Bill
2	"Far East Suite"	Ellington & Strayhorn	Ellington & Strayhorn

Appendix C

List of Most Represented Composers

Number of individual charts, without counting duplicates:

Duke Ellington and Billy Strayhorn	17
Thad Jones	9
Charles Mingus	8
Oliver Nelson	7
Bill Holman	7
Sammy Nestico	7
Basie Band (Neal Hefti/Frank Foster)	6
Bob Mintzer	5
Bob Brookmeyer	3

Appendix D

Jazz Ensemble Publishers and Distributors

Advance Music
Maierackerstrasse 18
D-72108
Rottenburg/Neckar, Germany

www.advancemusic.com

Hal Leonard Publishing Corporation
7777 W. Bluemound Road
P.O. Box 13819
Milwakee, WI 53213

www.halleonard.com

Jazz at LincolnCenter
33 W 60th St.
New York, NY 10023-7999

www.jazzatlincolncenter.org

Kendor Music, Inc
P.O. Box 278
Delavan, NY 14042

www.kendormusic.com

Kjos Music Publishers
4382 Jutland Dr.
San Diego, CA 92117

www.kjos.com

Margun Music
(distributed by Schirmer)
G. Schirmer
257 Park Ave South, 20th floor
New York, NY 10010

www.schirmer.com/margun

Second Floor Music
(distributed by Hal Leonard)
130 W 28th St. 2nd Floor
New York, NY 10001-6108

www.secondfloormusic.com

Sierra Music Publications
P.O. Box 928
Port Townsend, WA 98368

www.sierramusic.com

UNC Jazz Press
School of Music
University of Northern Colorado
Greely, CO 80639

www.arts.unco.edu/UNCJazz

Walrus Music/Otter Music Distributors
P.O. Box 1910
Pismo Beach, CA 93448-19109

www.walrusmusic.com

Warner Bros. Publications
15800 NW 48th Ave
Miami, FL 33014

www.warnerbrospublications.com

Caris Music Services
2206 Brislin Rd.
Stroudsburg, PA 18360

www.carismusicservices.com

JW Pepper & Son
2480 Industrial Blvd.
Paoli, PA 19301

www.jwpepper.com

Marina Music Service
P.O. Box 16471
Seattle, WA 98116-0471

www.marinamusic.com

Appendix E

Answers to Self-Tests

1. d	11. c	21. a	31. d	41. b	51. b	61. d
2. d	12. d	22. b	32. a	42. a	52. c	62. b
3. d	13. c	23. c	33. c	43. b	53. b	63. c
4. d	14. a	24. a	34. d	44. c	54. d	64. a
5. a	15. d	25. b	35. b	45. b	55. c	65. d
6. b	16. d	26. b	36. a	46. a	56. c	66. b
7. d	17. c	27. b	37. c	47. a	57. d	67. a
8. b	18. d	28. b	38. d	48. c	58. b	
9. c	19. b	29. d	39. b	49. b	59. a	
10. b	20. b	30. c	40. c	50. d	60. d	

Glossary

Jazz has developed, whether in parlance or in print, its own terminology. I favor using it unless clearer terms for the same concept already exist in classical theory. Multiple definitions are listed when applicable to the same term. English language terminology is favored, though universally understood Italian terms such as *tutti* or French as *ensemble* are retained.

Bitonality—the simultaneous use of two different tonalities or keys.

Cascade Effect—the movement of a line from unison to harmony, generally through progressive splitting of parts. Also called *Fan* in choral music. See also *Reverse Cascade Effect*.

Closed voicing—voicing spanning an octave or less.

Codetta—a brief coda-like passage concluding an inner section of a piece as opposed to a coda at the very end of the work.

Coda—passage occurring after the structural conclusion of the piece. The purpose of a coda is to balance the form by extending or repeating some conclusive material after the recapitulation of the main material has taken place. A coda can range from an additional bar with a final chord to a passage of considerable length. Though it is valuable and practical to "go to the coda sign," coda signs in jazz ensemble charts might or might not coincide with the beginning of the actual coda. In addition, sometimes the coda is not marked by a coda sign.

Concerted—harmonized passage in rhythmic unison.

Exposition, Development, Recapitulation—because these terms have a strong association with sonata form, I tend to use them sparingly, mainly where a link to that tradition might be detected. They are used in a more general way, without the connotations they have in sonata form. Hence, when used, "recapitulation" means "return of the head or other material" rather than "return of material previously presented in contrasting keys that set up a long-range key polarity that needs to be resolved."

Feature—one or more instruments carry the main tune, generally in a mixture of written and ad libitum parts, often followed by a full-fledged solo.

Head—the main tune and its harmonies.

Head out—the concluding head, played after the solos.

Inversions—first and second inversion of triads, and first, second, and third inversions of sixth and seventh chords, indicated in chord symbols with a slash between the triad, sixth or seventh chord, and the bass note. See *Slash chords*.

Octatonic—collection of eight notes alternating half steps and whole steps. In jazz it is also called symmetric diminished, diminished, half/whole scale, or superlocrian. Here the following abbreviations will be used for its three transpositions: oct 0 (C–D–Eb–F–F#–G#–A–B), oct 1 (C#–D#–E–F#–G–A–Bb–C), oct 2 (D–E–F–G–Ab–Bb–B–C#).

Open Form—a section that can be repeated ad libitum, generally ending with a new "on cue" section.

Open voicing—voicing spanning more than one octave.

Ostinato—The word means "obstinate" and indicates a short pattern (melodic, harmonic, or rhythmic), that repeats persistently.

Pad—sustained background harmony.

Polychords—two different, complete, simultaneous harmonies (such as A-7 over C7sus, or G7 over an Ab triad).

Punctuation—short, concerted chords (generally in the brass and spaced apart one or two measures) that accompany a melody or solo and generate rhythmic excitement.

Reverse Cascade Effect—the movement of various lines converging from harmony to unison. Less frequent than *Cascade Effect*.

Rhythm Changes—chord progression of the song "I Got Rhythm" by George Gershwin. Used as the progression for many jazz tunes. Usually in the key of B♭.

Roman Numerals—I, II, III, IV, V, VI, VII denoting major chords; i, ii, iii, iv, v, vi, vii denoting minor chords. Flats, sharps, and naturals and sevenths are added. In jazz only upper case is used (ex: II-7, V7). Lower case is used here for certain analyses because of their great immediacy and clarity.

"Shout" or *"Shout Chorus"*—the arranger's improvisation on the material. Rather than involving mostly harmonization and embellishment of the original tune, it is frequently an actual composition where materials are developed or composed anew, and constitutes a sort of "development section." It generally occurs in the second half of the arrangement, is climactic, and involves the whole ensemble. It often features extensive cross rhythms, counterpoint, active rhythmic figurations, and solo breaks or fills by the drummer. Frequently followed by a full or partial restatement of the tune, it is often a good testing ground for the band's maximum dynamic range. When a shout is not present, solos, soli, modulations, or pedals might carry out some of its dramatic function.

Slash chords—seventh chords over a bass note not part of the chord (such as 9, 11, 13, and their alterations). See *Inversions*.

Solo—portion of the arrangement that provides a formal framework for selected players to improvise on, often in a combo format. Generally features the chord progression of the tune, though at times alternate or free changes are used. Frequently there are optional or mandatory backgrounds by the ensemble and the number of choruses can be expanded or "opened up" for various repetitions. The choice of which soloist(s) improvise(s) in these sections is often flexible.

Soli—rhythmically concerted passage for two or more instruments but less than full (tutti) ensemble. Generally features a section, combination of sections, or instruments drawn from different sections creating a "band within a band" small group feel. The material played can be the primary tune or a "written-out improvisation." The definition of soli as a *harmonized* passage is followed here. Similar *unison* passages are listed as "unison" though they are called "soli unison" in some scores.

Stab—this might be a term still in use, however, every time I hear it, it seems to elicit a sharp pain in my back, so *punctuation* is used instead.

Triads over bass note—triads (generally major or minor) over a bass note not part of the triad. See also *Upper Structure Triads*

Tutti—a passage where the whole ensemble is playing.

Tutti Concerted—a passage where the whole ensemble is playing in rhythmic unison.

Upper Structure Triads—triads (generally major or minor) over a chord sound. The most common are on dominant chords and are related to the mode or chord scale of derivation: IIMa (from Lydian b7), bVIMa (from altered scale), VIMa (from octatonic scale). On major chords IIMa (from Lydian) is common. In jazz ensemble they are generally found in the trumpets. See also *Triads over bass note*.

Vamp—a simple chord progression, often one or two chords, played ad libitum until a soloist enters or the melody begins. Vamps are also found at the end of a piece, where they allow for a fade out.

Wedge—passage where two main lines converge or diverge in contrary motion.

Bibliography

Jazz Ensemble Development and Directing

Dunscomb, J. Richard, and Willie L. Hill, Jr. *Jazz Pedagogy: The Jazz Educator's Handbook and Resource Guide*. Miami, FL: Warner Bros., 2002.

Garofalo, Robert. *Improving Intonation in Band and Orchestra Performance*. Fort Lauderdale, FL: Meredith Music, 1996.

Henry, Robert E. *The Jazz Ensemble: A Guide to Technique*. Englewood Cliffs, NJ: Prentice Hall, 1981.

Hunsberger, Donald, and Roy E. Ernst. *The Art of Conducting*. 2nd ed. New York: McGraw Hill, 1992.

Jarvis, Jeff, and Doug Beach: *The Jazz Educator's Handbook*. Delevan, NY: Kendor Music, 2002.

Lawn, Richard. *The Jazz Ensemble Director's Manual*. Rev. ed. Oskaloosa, IA: Barnhouse, 1995.

Maltester, John F. "Why "Wing It"?" In *Conductors Anthology*. 2nd ed. Vol. 2, *Conducting and Musicianship*. Anthology Series, vol. 6. Northfield, IL: Instrumentalist, 1993.

Mintzer, Bob. "Thoughts on Directing a Jazz Ensemble." In *Conductors Anthology*. 2nd ed. Vol. 2, *Conducting and Musicianship*. Anthology Series, vol. 6. Northfield, IL: Instrumentalist, 1993.

Score Study

Battisti, Frank, and Robert Garofalo. *A Guide to Score Study for the Wind Band Conductor*. Fort Lauderdale, FL: Meredith Music, 1990.

Jazz Arranging and Composition

Dobbins, Bill. *Jazz Arranging and Composing*. Rottenburg, West Germany: Advance Music, 1986.

Lajoie, Stephen. *Gil Evans and Miles Davis Historic Collaborations: An Analysis of Selected Gil Evans Works 1957 to 1962*. Rottenburg, Germany: Advance Music, 2003.

Lowell, Dick, and Ken Pullig. *Arranging for Large Jazz Ensemble*. Edited by Michael Gold. Boston, MA: Berklee Press, 2003.

Mancini, Henry. *Sounds and Scores: A Practical Guide to Professional Orchestration*. Northridge Music, 1973, and Miami, FL: CPP-Belwin, 1986.

Mauleon, Rebeca. *Salsa Guidebook for Piano and Ensemble*. Petaluma, CA: Sher Music, 1993.

Muccioli, Joe ed. *The Gil Evans Collection, 15 Study and Sketch Scores from Gil's Manuscripts*. Milwaukee, WI: Hal Leonard, 1996.

Nestico, Sammy. *The Complete Arranger*. Delevan, NY: Fenwood Music Co. Distributed by Kendor Music, 1993. Musical score, CD audio.

Pease, Ted. *Jazz Composition: Theory and Practice*. Edited by Rick Mattingly. Boston, MA: Berklee Press, 2003.

———, and Ken Pullig. *Modern Jazz Voicings: Arranging for Small and Medium Ensembles*. Edited by Michael Gold. Boston, MA: Berklee Press, 2001.

Riddle, Nelson. *Arranged by Nelson Riddle*. Miami, FL: Warner Bros., 1985.
Sebesky, Don. *The Contemporary Arranger*. Van Nuys, CA: Alfred, 1994.
Sturm, Fred. *Changes over Time: The Evolution of Jazz Arranging*. Rottenburg, Germany: Advance Music, 1995.
Wright, Rayburn. *Inside the Score*. Delevan, NY: Kendor Music, 1982.

Jazz Theory and Harmony

Levine, Mark. *The Jazz Theory Book*. Petaluma, CA: Sher Music, 1995.
———. *The Jazz Piano Book*. Petaluma, CA: Sher Music, 1989.
McGrain, Mark. *Notation*. Boston, MA: Berklee Press, distributed by Hal Leonard, 1986.
Nettles, Barrie. *The Chord Scale Theory & Jazz Harmony*. Rottenburg, Germany: Advance Music, 1997.

Improvisation

Crook, Hal. *How to Improvise: An Approach to Practicing Improvisation*. Rottenburg, Germany: Advance Music, 1991.
Reeves, Scott. *Creative Jazz Improvisation*. 3rd ed. Upper Saddle River, NJ: Prentice Hall, 2003.
———. *Creative Beginnings*. Upper Saddle River, NJ: Prentice Hall, 1997.
Terry, Clark, and Phil Rizzo. *The Interpretation of the Jazz Language*. Bedford, OH: M.A.S., 1977.

Reference—Dictionaries and Encyclopedias

Kernfeld, Barry, ed. *The New Grove Dictionary of Jazz*. 3 vols. 2nd ed. New York: Oxford University Press, 2001.
Sadie, Stanley, ed. *The New Grove Dictionary of Music and Musicians*. 29 vols. 2nd ed. New York: Oxford University Press, 2001.
Feather, Leonard. *The Encyclopedia of Jazz in the Sixties*. New York: Horizon, 1967.
———. *The New Edition of the Encyclopedia of Jazz*. New York: Horizon, 1962. Reprinted, 1984.
Feather, Leonard, and Ira Gitler. *The Encyclopedia of Jazz in the Seventies*. New York: Da Capo, 1992.
Carr, Ian, Digby Fairweather, and Brian Preistley. *Jazz, the Essential Companion*.Englewood Cliffs, NJ: Prentice Hall, 1988.

History and Appreciation

Gridley, Mark. *Jazz Styles*. 9th ed. Upper Saddle River, NJ: Prentice Hall, 2006.
Hasse, John Edward, ed. *Jazz: The First Century*. New York: HarperCollins, 2000.
Carr, Roy. *A Century of Jazz*. New York: Da Capo, 1997.
Feather, Leonard. *The Passion for Jazz*. New York: Da Capo, 1990.
Gottlieb, Robert, ed. *Reading Jazz*. New York: Pantheon, 1996.
Harrison, Max. *A Jazz Retrospect*. Boston, MA: Crescendo, 1976.
Kernfeld, Barry. *What to Listen For in Jazz*. Hartford, CT: Yale University Press, 1995.
Kirchner, Bill ed. *The Oxford Companion to Jazz*. New York: Oxford University Press, 2000.
Lees, Gene. *Arranging the Score*. Cassell, 2000.
Schuller, Gunther. *The Swing Era: The Development of Jazz, 1930–1945*. New York: Oxford University Press, 1989.
Tanner, Paul, David Megill, and Maurice Gerow. *Jazz*. Madison, WI: Brown & Benchmark, 1997.

General Index

a cappella: ensemble, 66–67
accent: on fourth beat, 74
altered scale, *5*
alternate fingerings: saxophone, 126
alternation of Latin and swing feel. *See* time feel
altissimo register: tenor sax, 54
anticipations, 29, 43, 85; eighth and quarter note, 142; of fourth beat, 124; on the upbeat of "four," 92
approaches: chromatic, *19*; diatonic, 81; double chromatic, 39, 58; double, from above and below, *130*; passing chromatic, 58; upper and lower neighbor, 58
arco: bass, 60, 65
"arranger's" chorus, 29, 98, 125
articulations, 19, *143*
augmentation, 63; rhythmic, 65, 79

ballad: reworked as swing, 29
"band within a band" writing, 43, 95, 128
baritone sax: and bass trombone functions in "Tribute," *133*; lead, 14; not on root function, 69; on tonic pedal, 87
Basie: four-part voicings (*see* voicings); piano signature of, 9
bass line cliché, 63, *114*
battle of tenor saxes, 50, 51
be bop scales. *See* scales
bend pitch up and down, 45
binary form, 53, 128
block voicings, 87, 102, 114, *142. See also* voicings
blue notes, 4, *19*, 21, 31, 49, 105, 125
blues: aab phrasing in, 4, 10; aab phrasing not in, 76; eighteen-bar, *21*; lick, *21*; minor and major contrast in, 120–21; reharmonized progression in, 60; scale, 10; tonic chord in, *12*; twenty-four bar, 26. *See also* form

cadence: deceptive, v–vi, 24
cadential patterns, 49, 61, 104

cadenza, 49, 50, 65, 104; improvised introduction, 60
call and response, 54, 57, 63, 91, 98, 107; between second tenor and baritone sax/trombones, 70; brass-saxes, 57; climactic, 76; in Ko-Ko, 87
canon: four entrances, in pairs, 125; half note lag, 26, 87; one beat lag, 65, 126; two bar lag, 146
cascade. *See* cascade effect
cascade effect, 147; unison to four part, 29; unison to two and three part, 40; two- to five-part, 146
cha cha patterns, 112
chain: dominant, 133; descending fourth, 26; technique linking motives, 108
chorale: Bach, 96; four part brass, 27
chords borrowed from the parallel minor key, 11, 14, 83, 104. *See also* modal interchange
clarinet: lead, over brass, 39; lead, over saxes, 3, 149; and tenor in octaves, 148
clave, 74–75, 112–13
claves, 112–13
clusters, 27, 59, 71, 98, 123–24, 148; five part, 59; five and seven part, 6, 119; intervallic constant structures with, 6–7; complete seven or eight note mode, 23; seven-note "complete major scale," 45–46; six-part, 32; whole tone, 87
coda: climactic, 46, 52
collective improvisation. *See* improvisation
color coupling: clarinet, 149
comping, 33, 102, 130; Freddie Green style, 9; trombone section, 19
compound rhythm, 36
concerted ensemble: tutti, 5, 29, 96, 98; tutti, without bass and bass trombone, 144; unaccompanied, 73–74; without drums, 66
constant structures, 65; alternating two chords in, 118; chromatic, 85; clusters with, 6–7; five part, 32; major